RVing Across America

RVing Across America

A Quest to Visit All 50 States

Alyssa Padgett

Created in an RV in the United States of America

Disclaimer:

Some of the names in this book have been changed because that's the respectful thing to do when you're talking about people behind their backs. Okay FINE, there are some people whose names I just can't remember. How creepy would it be if you found out that the girl you met eight years ago in the hot tub at an RV park not only remembered your name but published it for the world to see? That's level ten stalker crazy. I'm hoping to come off as fairly normal in this book.

Some names in this book are accurate though because I have video footage of those people telling me their names.

Dang. That probably didn't help my case.

Legal Notice:

Cover Designer: Lee Taylor

Graphics: chokkicx

Print ISBN: 9798439286010

Contents

Dedication

To Heath—

Your lack of hesitation when I said "What if we went to all 50 states?" is just one of the many reasons I'm glad I married you.

The fact that you drove most of the 20,000 miles of this adventure is another.

I love you.

Chapter 1

"Yeah, when it rolls off, smashes into a minivan, and kills everyone, you're going to have one hell of a bad day," the trucker offered before walking back across the gas station parking lot.

I looked at my newlywed husband and saw his eyes widen as big as saucers. Here we were on day five of marriage contemplating the likelihood of us killing a family in a minivan. This is not exactly the picturesque honeymoon I imagined when I suggested going to all fifty states. I thought I'd spend most of my time on beaches or getting lost in new cities. Heath and I would wander through mountain trails and return to our campsite at night to read a good book by a crackling campfire that miraculously never soaked your clothes with smoke. Nightly s'mores were a given.

Instead, I've been sweating under the sun in the parking lot of the only gas station in Junction, Texas—where I believe there are only three buildings in the whole town and one of them is abandoned—trying to calculate the odds that the car we are towing behind our 29-foot RV will indeed roll off its dolly while we cruise down the interstate and inevitably collide with another vehicle.

I put the odds at 100% because it's evident now that we have no clue what we're doing.

I knew we'd have to figure out this whole "full-time RVing"

thing on the fly as we traveled, but I didn't anticipate that on our first full day of traveling we would be stranded in a desert looking at my car dangling ever so slightly off the front of our dolly.

Heath decided to wait until the day before we left Austin to even attempt to hook up the tow dolly. We wanted to have a car while we traveled so we didn't have to drive our home on wheels everywhere. Heath's grandpa offered to let us borrow his tow dolly for the year to easily roll the car behind the RV, but Heath didn't even ask his grandpa how to hook it up. He picked it up, drove away, let it sit for a few weeks, and then waited until we had 24 hours left on the clock to open YouTube and search for "how tow dollies work."

Guess what isn't on YouTube?

How the mostly-rusted tow dolly your grandpa has had sitting on his property for the past decade is supposed to work.

Before we left Austin yesterday, our helplessness finally attracted one of our neighbors in the RV park. He kindly spent his afternoon teaching Heath how to set up the tow dolly while I filmed the instructions on my phone so we wouldn't forget. Fancy straps that required yet another trip to Camping World were involved. We left feeling confident that we knew how to operate the tow dolly after our tutorial. We even knew how to prevent the car from rolling backward off the dolly.

But no one taught us how to prevent the car from rolling *forward* off the dolly.

And when we exited to fill up the gas tank, the car was rolling forward off the dolly and getting dangerously close to creating a major issue, like dramatically entering my RV bedroom.

We tried calling Heath's grandparents as soon as we pulled over. Heath's grandpa had already given us tons of advice on RVs, and he probably knew everything about this old tow dolly of his. If anyone could help us out of this pickle, it would be him. But guess where Verizon and their "largest LTE coverage" doesn't have signal? West Texas. Our phones didn't even bother to show the little signal bars and just shined a bright *No Service* message instead.

We climbed back into the RV and Heath booted up our hotspot to hopefully give us an internet signal. If we can't make a call, maybe Google can save us.

We already tried the other building in town too—a tire shop—and they brought out a giant electrical drill. I'm not sure what they expected to happen, but it didn't fix whatever was wrong with our tow dolly. When they looked at the dolly, they said they didn't know what was causing our car to roll off the front either, so we didn't have high hopes.

We were determined to exhaust all of our options to fix the dolly, but the trucker solidified what Heath and I already feared: If we wanted to make it out of Texas and actually visit all fifty states on this honeymoon, we had to leave the car and the dolly behind. In the middle of nowhere. Which would leave us to drive this 29-foot home across 20,000 miles and every major city in the US.

The other option involved Heath driving the RV and me driving the car separately behind him. Not really an option if I want to spend any time with my new husband on our honeymoon.

Or we could just go back home, sell the RV, and resign to the fact that we don't even have the mettle to cross into one new state.

"The jetpack says it's connected on both things. And it still won't work or load anything!" Heath said, his voice growing frantic.

"I'll figure it out, Heath. Just give me a second," I said, fiddling with our Verizon jetpack and starting to sweat in our increasingly hot RV. In retrospect, we should've tested the connection before we hit the road so we knew how this whole hotspot thing worked. But we also should've figured out how the tow dolly worked before leaving Austin, so let's just add it to the list of reasons why Heath and Alyssa are ill-equipped to travel.

"So we're in Junction, Texas," Heath said to the giant video camera he set up on our table. He had pointed it toward our couch where I balanced my laptop on my knees, carefully inputting the given Wi-Fi password that looked something like hm38&7jPE4$Qi*Ld0f and took twenty minutes to type correctly.

"It's basically the last town until El Paso which is a long way away from here," he continued, "And we're getting gas and notice that the whole car is falling off the trailer. And yeah, it's basically breaking. So we pull over to a tire shop. They can't fix it. They got out their big heavy..." He paused and furrowed his eyebrow. "Things...out here and they can't do anything about it...And we're also in, I guess, the middle of nowhere because I can't get service on our brand new Wi-Fi hotspot. Largest LTE my ass."

"Heath, we can't use cursing in the documentary," I interrupted his tirade.

"Sorry. I'm annoyed. This is our only way to get internet on the road and it doesn't work."

"I'm pretty sure you're doing it wrong. Oh," a window appeared on my laptop. "Welcome to your jetpack. See you have to *set up* the device first."

"Oh. Okay," he turned back to the camera. "I apologize, Verizon. How did you do that?"

"I just put in the password," I said with a hint of frustration in my voice.

"Even if we can find someone to fix it," Heath began, turning off the camera and addressing me, "do we want to keep the car?"

"Do I want to keep my car? Um, yes. We can't just leave it in the middle of nowhere."

"No, I mean do we want to keep it for the trip?"

I thought about it for a second. I'd had that trusty little SUV since high school and when we decided to go to all fifty states for our honeymoon, Heath sold his car so we could take the Honda. We never thought about traveling without a car, not when we needed to travel so many miles. "How are we going to go to New York City without a car? Drive the RV in?"

"We rent a car or grab a taxi. There's no way I am driving an RV into New York City," he said emphatically. "Listen, all I'm saying is that we're only a few hours away from Austin, and towing the car is already stressing me out. I'm not sure the engine can handle it. I mean I know according to the manual that it can, but the engine is definitely straining from the weight. You can feel it. We've tried re-setting up the tow dolly a hundred times in the past two hours and I can't stop picturing the Honda careening toward a screaming family now."

"So, what do you suggest we do?"

Neither of us said anything for a few minutes. I may have gotten our jetpack set up and connected to my computer, but the circle was still spinning as it tried in vain to load a webpage. We were on our own facing the first big challenge of our marriage: have the convenience of a car or watch the rearview mirror in horror as our car collided with the traffic behind us. The choice was obvious, but that didn't make it any easier.

And to think a few months earlier, my biggest concern centered around staples...

Staring down at the 10,000 mangled staples taunting me from their pile in my office trash can, I wondered how on earth this was considered success after college. My new boss said the best thing I could do during our slow season was digitize all of our records. I didn't foresee that meaning removing staples from decade-old paperwork for eight hours a day, five days a week.

Can 22-year-olds get carpal tunnel?

My pulse throbbed *yes* in my red, swollen right thumb.

After weeks of digitizing, I had finished one filing cabinet. Only nine more to go. At this rate, I'd be scanning coffee-stained paperwork until Christmas.

Life unfolded every day in its own slow, unsatisfying way. That's the place where you need to be stuck—sometimes for years or, in my case, a full seven months in the "real world"—before you recognize that the only way to get unstuck is to do something dramatic. And not cut your bangs dramatic.

I made that mistake in college and they had finally grown out. I'm talking really dramatic. Like quitting your job, buying a sketchy RV off of Craigslist, and visiting all fifty states for your honeymoon.

But to get to that dramatic exit from normal life, you first have to drop the staple remover and Google carpal tunnel symptoms.

I definitely had it.

Spending my days sitting in silence alone in my office was not how I pictured my first year as a professional adult. I did have my own office, which seemed like a major milestone based on what I knew about office life from TV. But I always kept my door open to the main office where my co-workers worked, although I rarely saw them. They were always at off-site meetings or running around the property with power tools or working from home because they had 30 years of experience and had benefits like that.

Back in college, I spent my summers volunteering with this nonprofit. We volunteered at food banks and built houses after Hurricane Katrina. The work was exhausting but fulfilling. Each day we connected with families who shared their gratitude for us working to restore their community. It was the foundation for why I took this job. I loved the energy of life in New Orleans, the mission of the nonprofit, the food (of course), and that feeling like I was working at a place that made a difference to people.

At least, that's what I repeated to myself as I stood up from my desk with a fresh stack of paperwork, ran it through the scanner, and emailed it to my computer. Because instead of volunteering and working in the city, my main task was to digitize paperwork and answer the phones and it did not at all feel like I was making a difference. The only interesting part of my day was when I missed pulling a staple—loudly jamming a wad of papers into our industrial-sized copier—and then had to fix it myself. It didn't take long for me to know the machine backward and forward.

My mind flashed to that episode of *The Office* when Pam realizes she knows the copier backward and forward...only to immediately quit her job because she wanted more out of life than copier expertise. Might as well have been the story of my life.

But no one was in the office to witness me dramatically announce that I was quitting, plus I had to pay rent. So I continued pulling staples, walking four feet to the copier, feeding in the paper, emailing the digital copies to myself, organizing the digital files, and rewarding myself for each finished folder with a piece of dark chocolate from my desk drawer.

I groaned aloud in frustration, not that anyone heard me.

I didn't *hate* my job though. When I wasn't filing paperwork, I was managing content for our social media accounts and creating a content strategy for the website. I loved that part of the job. I worked on our company blog and wrote stories about the people who were rebuilding and transforming their communities, like Mack who took the garage where he used to restore antique cars and turned it into a community center in the Lower Ninth Ward. *He* was doing something meaningful.

Isn't that what we all want out of our work? To do something that pays the bills, lights us up, *and* makes a difference?

The problem was, all of that work that I loved took about

four hours a week. So I spent the other 36 hours getting cozy with my staple remover.

When I was offered the job, it sounded bold to pack up my car and move to New Orleans. After growing up in a suburb of Dallas and only moving a whopping three hours south to Austin for college, living out of state thrilled me. This would be the perfect post-college adventure, I told myself when I accepted the job.

It wasn't.

Unless your idea of adventure is going home after work every day to an empty apartment and bingeing *Gossip Girl* and *How I Met Your Mother* on Netflix. They were my only friends in the city and we hung out together for hours each afternoon while I Googled "how to bake a potato" and "how did I kill this orchid already?" Because those are the things you have to figure out once you've flown from the nest for the first time. I lived in one of the most raucous, social, delicious cities in the country...and I sat at home eating alone on my couch watching reruns every day.

On a particularly boring day, I remember leaning back in my questionably brown office chair removing staples while trying to think of something interesting or adventurous about myself. Nada. If we had hung out around that time, I could have shared what was on my Netflix queue and which bottle of $5 wine I enjoyed that week. That is as titillating as our conversation would get.

Oh! I did try to go camping once in college in an effort to be adventurous and outdoorsy. I woke up with the flu. *That's* how bad I was at adventures. Who catches the flu from fresh air?

Maybe those extreme outdoor adventures aren't for me, I

thought. (Is sleeping in a tent considered extreme? I hope so. You're on the *ground.* In the *elements.*)

I shook my head at the thought and picked up a stack of freshly digitized files. The statute of limitations didn't even require keeping records for longer than seven years in Louisiana (another exciting thing I Googled as part of adulthood), but we decided to digitize them all anyway. I casually dropped the files into a half-full cardboard box marked for shredding.

Thud.

One more folder down, three hundred and seventy-two more to go.

What am I doing with my life?

If I had a nickel for every time that question flashed across my mind I would never need to work again.

I did everything right.

Graduated from college.

Got a job with a salary and benefits.

Lived on my own.

In fact, I was pretty sure I was killing it on the adult checklist. I hadn't hit the whole get married and buy a house level yet, but I was following the clear-cut American dream.

I thought that was what I wanted. That once I had it, I'd feel fulfilled. Happy. Like everything I had done culminated into this one perfect life. Instead, I felt empty. Hollow. Waiting for something to rouse me out of the monotony of the life I created for myself.

As my mind drifted, I thought about a quote I'd seen online from Mary Oliver that read: "What is it you plan to do with your one wild and precious life?"

I honestly don't know, Mary.

There's no clear-cut checklist for abandoning the American dream in search of something more, not that I even knew what I was searching for.

For all I knew, the entire "real world" was as soul-crushingly dull as staple removal.

I sighed while I ran my fingers over all the folders hanging in the open filing cabinet next to my desk, settling on a skinny one with only three sheets of paper inside. And no staples, I noticed picking up the pages. Yes! My favorite folder of the day, I thought, smiling to myself.

Oh for the love! I reacted to my own thoughts. If I start having favorite folders of to-be-scanned-and-shredded paperwork, I am seriously going nowhere in life.

I pulled out my phone to call my boyfriend as a distraction from my own monotony.

Heath and I started dating right before I moved to New Orleans. On our first date, I questioned why I even said yes when we both knew I was moving away soon. But he was so handsome and he liked me and even though it didn't seem like the smart thing to do, I couldn't say no. After exactly six days of dating, I bought a plane ticket four hours before takeoff and flew to Colorado to join his family's annual ski vacation. "It would be a good story," he reasoned with me, calling from the ski slopes. "And an awesome third date, by the way."

Heath was like that. He made everyone around him, myself included, want to do big things. Even if they were scary or impractical or, in the case of the plane ticket, expensive. So I bought the ticket and hopped on a plane. It was the most spontaneous and impetuous thing I'd ever done. Oh, does that count as something interesting about me? Bought a day-of plane ticket once?!

Landing in Denver, my heart pounded with excitement—and not just because Heath picked me up in a white-out blizzard and we very nearly went off the road more than once.

The impromptu third date made me feel alive. Heath and I felt our connection deepen and we had a blast on the slopes. I think that week was the perfect example of why it was so easy to fall in love with him—he made life exciting. With him, I was the kind of person who would spur of the moment travel halfway across the country to ski.

As I daydreamed over the memory back in my office, I felt the spirit of that trip was the essence of what I was missing. I couldn't just buy another plane ticket to recreate that moment, but I craved the feeling of chasing adventures just outside of my comfort zone.

The question was, how do you chase that feeling while still being a responsible adult?

"Hey, babe. How's it going?" Heath answered my phone call with his mouth full.

"My desk is covered with crumpled up papers covered in old coffee stains while I'm eating lukewarm leftovers I brought from home. How are you?"

"I just got some Domino's delivered to my cubicle. It's delicious."

I sighed internally. For Heath, that was as good as it got. He found a software sales job right out of college and found his work just as soul-crushing as I did. He ran a small t-shirt company in college, closing it so he could focus on school and graduate on time, but the entrepreneurial bug had bitten him and he wanted to work on his own. Software sales were just a way to pay off his student loans in the meantime.

"When we get married, where do you want to live?" I asked him out of nowhere.

Heath laughed. Hopefully in response to my random question and not at the not-too-subtle *when* we get married comment. "Where do *you* want to live?"

Inwardly, I worried that we would get married, buy a house, have kids, and still be stuck at jobs that bored us instead of challenging us. I didn't see a picket fence, but I feared that we would get swept up into life and wake up ten years later wondering where our youth disappeared to. We didn't want marriage to instantly mean settling down. That phrase scared Heath—settling down. He had things to do in life. I had dreams to chase in life too.

We were a little stuck at the moment, but we vowed that getting married would be the starting line for us doing big things together. Well, we didn't really *vow* yet. He needed to propose, then came vows, then came a beautiful life together.

"I don't know," I replied. "The beach. Or the mountains. Somewhere that isn't 100° with 100% humidity every day."

"Same, babe. I rode my bike to the office this morning and my shirt was drenched. I'm going to have to start driving again, even though it takes longer with Austin traffic. What makes you bring this up?"

"I just want something new. A new place to live. A new job. Something. *Anything.* I want to feel like I'm living my life instead of life just happening. Every day is the same."

The hardest part about not knowing what you want to do with your life is that you're already doing life. Every day.

There's no "take a break while I figure out my life" pause button. You just keep living, aimlessly. In my experience, these are days when the only highlight is a happy hour or bingeing Netflix without getting the guilt-inducing "are you still watching?" notification.

"I feel the same way," he said, dropping his voice to a whisper in his cubicle. "I've been working here for months, but every day just blends together. I can't think of a single memory that sticks out. I found this guy on Instagram who is a National Geographic photographer and lives and travels in a truck camper. He posts all these epic pictures of camping out in the middle of nowhere. And then I look around my cubicle and wonder what I'm doing with my life."

That was the first time I heard of anyone full-time traveling who wasn't a grandparent. My grandparents traveled in an RV for my entire childhood, pumping the brakes every few years to visit for the holidays before they were on the road again. I thought full-time travel was only for retirees or people selling dip mixes at craft shows like my grandpa.

But based on Heath's description, this guy had figured a way around the whole wait-till-you're-retired-to-travel thing. He gets to wake up somewhere new every day. He can go anywhere he wants. And taking pictures every day? Easiest job ever. You are living my dream, random guy my boyfriend found on Instagram.

I would love to travel like that. Growing up, I remember watching the Travel Channel and ogling the beautiful places I'd never heard of. I remember my dad once pointing at the TV to the woman walking down a pier in some coastal town and saying "Alyssa, you should do that when you grow up." Get paid to travel? Yes, please.

But I'm not 10 anymore and "travel the world" wasn't a major offered at my liberal arts college.

"You're preaching to the choir. I just needed to vent. I've got to get back to work. This paperwork won't scan and shred itself!" I said, my voice trying to sound chipper but failing miserably.

"Hey, I promise once we get married, we will do something awesome and you won't have to scan paperwork anymore."

I smiled into the phone feeling the slightest ray of hope peek into my day. "I would love that. See you in a few weeks?"

"See you then. Love you."

"Love you."

I hung up the phone and slid open my desk drawer to grab a piece of chocolate. One day soon, my (unofficial) husband and I would chase a more exciting life together. For now, file folders and chocolate were as good as it was going to get.

With daylight hours diminishing in middle-of-nowhere Texas, Heath interrupted our tense silence by recommending we leave the dolly and car at his Granny's house. "It's about an hour from here. I saw the exit sign for Leakey a little ways back. We can stay the night, regroup and drive tomorrow. And just not have a car for the next seven months."

Mulling it over, he was right. "That's our only good option, isn't it?" I asked. Losing the car would complicate our travels. We couldn't just run to the grocery store (how many parking spots would this giant motorhome take up?) and with only one vehicle, we would *always* be together. But the risk of keeping the car was too high.

"It's the best option. We'll figure it out," Heath squeezed my hand. "You wanna drive the RV and I'll drive the car?"

"Ha, nice try."

"You have to drive it sometime!" I knew I would drive the RV eventually, but the sheer size of the machinery intimidated me. Besides, Heath often pointed out that he drove moving trucks in college and could handle anything the roads threw at him.

"Tomorrow sounds good."

"I'm holding you to that."

I sighed, changing the subject. "Which way to Granny's?"

"Follow me."

Heath climbed into the RV and I hopped into my car, following him left out of the gas station and under the interstate. We started climbing a west Texas hill when Heath pulled off on the side of the road suddenly.

What now?

He didn't climb out of the RV so I pulled over and jogged to his window.

"What's wrong now?"

"I don't actually know where I'm going. I mean I know where her house is when we get to town. I just don't know the address. Or how to get to town."

I laughed and rolled my eyes. "I have a GPS in my car. How do you spell Leakey? You can follow me."

Chapter 2

The idea to buy a 20-year-old RV off of Craigslist and drive it across the country for our honeymoon came in stages.

Before Heath proposed, the focus was not on the shiny diamond ring I was waiting for. I'd already subtly left my laptop open months ago displaying pictures of rings I liked and I was pretty sure he took the bait.

No, the focus was on our marriage. The white dress and walking down the aisle would happen, sure. But Heath and I spent every spare moment dreaming up what our lives would be like once we were finally together. Where would we live? What would we do? Since I knew I would be moving away from New Orleans so Heath and I could finally live in the same state, we had an idea. In order to thrust ourselves out of monotony, we would start our marriage with action. We would move somewhere new. Marriage was a blank slate for us to write our own future—who said we needed to stay in the south? We started dreaming of where we would live if we could move anywhere.

"California is your number one. I love the idea of Oregon or Colorado," I said, zooming out on the map of the country on my laptop screen. We were sitting on Heath's bed in his microscopic studio apartment in downtown Austin. There wasn't enough floor space for a couch. Or a desk. Or a dishwasher for that matter. So we were cuddled up on his bed daydreaming about where we could start our lives together.

"I've always heard great things about North Carolina," Heath added.

"Hm," I studied the map on my screen. "Mountains *and* beaches. Very good call."

"I thought you'd like that," Heath laughed. "Add it to the list. And Nashville!"

"Yes! So many writers and creative entrepreneurs live in Nashville. I think we would fit in there. Where else?" Heath leaned his head against my shoulder to better see the map.

"No other states stick out to me. Unless we hit the lottery and can move to Hawaii. Five states is a good start." Heath laid back on his bed staring at the ceiling. "How do we choose which one to move to? They don't make five-sided coins to flip."

I leaned back on the pillows and thought about it. "We haven't spent much time in these places. I've never been to Oregon or North Carolina or Nashville. And we would need to narrow down specific cities or areas to live in. I'm not sure how we would do that without actually visiting. We could do month-long Airbnb stays? But that might get expensive. Definitely couldn't do hotels. Plus a month isn't really enough time to find a job in each place and we will need to make money..." I sighed.

"What if we make it our honeymoon?" Heath suggested. "We quit our jobs, spend a few weeks in each place, and then after a couple of months, we move to our favorite one."

"I like that idea. Certainly would make it more pragmatic and acceptable to explain to our families. Okay," I started typing destinations into Google Maps. "If we get married in Austin, it's a 21-hour drive to LA."

"It's a straight shot on the interstate. I've made it in under 24 hours before," Heath said with a weird sense of pride.

"Okay, good job," I quipped. "15 hours to Portland—"

"We should take the Pacific Coast Highway the whole way up!"

"Well, this is our honeymoon now. It does need plenty of time on the coast," I continued typing. "Then 19 hours to Colorado...sheesh 17 more hours to Nashville. And then 12 hours to the Outer Banks. We basically drive across the entire country."

"Sounds good to me," Heath shrugged. "You know I used to drive moving trucks in college. I always liked cross-country moves."

I stared at the blue lines on the screen in front of me. 84 hours of driving time—and that didn't even include returning to Texas to pick up all of our possessions that we would put in storage while we traveled.

Heath and I had taken plenty of road trips together since we'd met. Before we even dated, we drove from Austin to Wisconsin with friends to attend a conference. After I spontaneously flew up to Colorado for our third date, we road-tripped all the way from the Rockies back to Texas.

Beach trips, visiting family, back and forth visiting each other across state lines—the hours together in the car passed easily between talking and singing along to Spotify. We liked life on the road to our next destination, laughing at ridiculous billboards and staring at the landscapes sprawling out our windows. In many ways, our relationship started on the road.

The best memories I could cherry-pick from our time together were being spontaneous and visiting somewhere new. The more we talked, the more I felt like this could be the perfect start to our marriage.

"If we returned to Texas after…" I trailed off furrowing my brow as I added one last stop to my mapped route. We would basically make a huge circle around the country. "Wait a second…"

"What?" Heath asked.

"Shh," I said, running out of fingers and counting in my head.

21.

Interesting.

I dragged the blue line between Colorado and Tennessee up to include driving past Mount Rushmore and through Chicago. That adds five… We could easily drive north of Portland into Washington. That's 27…

I sat up straight.

"What if we did them all?" I countered.

"I thought we already said we wanted to do all five," Heath replied.

"No. What if we did them *all* all? Like all 50. Look at this map. We are literally driving coast-to-coast and honestly, it sounds like a waste to just drive straight across the country in our car. What if, instead, we just hit every single state along the way? Not just pass through, but really stop and visit each state. It wouldn't even add that much driving," I started talking faster as the idea gained momentum. "And I know it's on your bucket list to visit all fifty states and mine too. What if instead of just moving somewhere new, we started our marriage by visiting all fifty states?

"I know it's out there," I continued, "but when else would we *ever* visit North Dakota?" I reasoned. "This is something we said is a dream we want to accomplish someday. Why not now? Let's start our marriage by accomplishing this dream together. What do you think?"

In the pause while I waited for Heath's response, all you could hear was my rapid breathing. As soon as the idea formed in my brain, something clicked. I'd spent months alone in a quiet office imagining what life could be like if I chased after something meaningful and took action toward dreams instead of letting them fade quietly in the background. I wasn't sure how visiting all 50 states would help us break free of feeling stuck, but at least it would give us direction. A clear objective to work toward while we figured out what we wanted out of life.

Plus it would make for an epic honeymoon and plenty of stories. This was exactly the challenge I was searching for.

"Alyssa," Heath said with a slow smile spreading across his face until it reached his blue eyes. "Let's do it."

I lit up at his instant agreement to jump into the unknown of long-term traveling. This wasn't a big surprise since this was the kind of idea that Heath would pitch. In college, before we dated, I was attracted to this guy who didn't seem to have any fear. He ran his business and had a website making money for him while he was sitting next to me in class. He was always talking about the book he was going to write, the blog he just started, the big things he would accomplish in life. I jealously wondered how he could just *do* these things. We were just kids in college, but he was unafraid and ready to take on the world.

Early in our relationship, I suspected that our life together would be spent chasing after his whims, but maybe his bravery and fervor rubbed off on me. Without him in my life, I would sit in my swivel chair in New Orleans removing staples and quietly dreaming about doing bigger things, but only dreaming. I was terrified of what I was proposing and how we could even make it happen, but I knew I had a partner in Heath. Someone who would grab my hand and jump into this adventure headfirst.

"A fifty-state honeymoon?" I asked cautiously, just in case he misunderstood the tremendous scope of what I just suggested. Hours of driving. Thousands of dollars in gas. Tons of planning and preparation.

"A fifty-state honeymoon road trip. This sounds way better than a cruise in the Caribbean," Heath said.

"And more expensive," I sighed, remembering that we were two college graduates about to quit our jobs. But I've had this dream for approximately 42 seconds and I was not giving it up yet. If Heath was in, I was in. I made a mental note to Google "how to tell your boss you're quitting to marry a redhead and travel the world together."

"We'll take your car and sell mine," Heath said resolutely.

"Where are we going to sleep?" I asked, the logistics and costs of this adventure pinging in my mind. There were a thousand reasons why this wouldn't work. No jobs and no money being the two glaring hurdles.

"Hey," Heath said, reading the stress overtaking the adrenaline of our idea and slipping his arm over my shoulder. "We have a few months. We'll figure it out," he said with confidence.

What is it about travel that makes it seem to be the solution to all of life's problems?

Is it the romance of watching the sun sink over the Pacific Ocean?

The intrigue of running across bears on a hike in Montana?

I wasn't exactly sure, but I could feel it. Traveling to all fifty states would solve everything.

First, I had to go back to New Orleans and quit my job.

It seemed wise not to dump my fifty-state road trip idea on any actual mature adults until we had more concrete plans, so I kept that to myself. My boss had a hard enough time understanding why I was quitting at all.

"I didn't realize your boyfriend proposed!" He exclaimed. "Congratulations!"

"Well, he hasn't yet. *Technically.* But we are going to get married," I replied confidently. "So when my lease is up in two months, I'm going to move back to Texas and get married." And then move all over the country trying to visit all fifty states in our first year of marriage.

"I see," he replied with thinly concealed skepticism. "Well, I appreciate the heads up. Why don't you type up a job description and you'll be in charge of hiring your replacement?"

The problem with making big, bold plans is that most people are supportive with their words and their faces say "Wow! You're an idiot." Or, in this instance, "Aw honey you have so much to learn about the real world. No ring means there's no way you're getting married."

If anyone ever replies to your life goals with "good for you!"

that is code for "I won't say *I told you so* when you inevitably fail, but I will be thinking it."

My coworkers expressed their skepticism over the next two months, solidifying my decision to wait to tell anyone about our secret 50-state honeymoon plan. For now, that idea lived in a secret Pinterest board where I saved travel tips and lists like "small towns in America you must visit."

Working on our travel plans in the background let me indulge in our crazy dream without actually confronting the realities of it. I kept getting stuck on how we could actually make enough money to travel. With actively traveling, there was no way we could find jobs in each place we visited. Heath mentioned finding a work-from-home job, but all of the work-from-home options seemed like customer support. Nothing like driving up the coast of Oregon while helping people a thousand miles away reset their Wi-Fi password. Not to mention we had no idea how we could even have internet or cell service to work from the front seat while we explored.

The list of things to figure out grew every day, but the thrill of travel had me too enchanted to stress over tiny details. I couldn't be sure that it would work out. All signs pointed to us running out of money before making it to all fifty states.

But I couldn't shake the feeling that if we could do this—if we could travel to all fifty states in our first year of marriage—we could do anything together. I thought about other things on my bucket list. Write a book. Hike to the top of a mountain. Eat a potato in Ireland. Ride every ride at Disney World. (Is it obvious that I was 15 when I wrote this list?)

If we could do this, we could inch a little closer to making all of those things a reality.

Writing and summiting mountains were two things I could do this year if we took this trip.

And if we failed...

Well if we failed, we could come back and find real jobs again. We were young. We could ease back into our careers with a few memories under our belt.

I didn't want to fail at my one chance at life. That's what it felt like when I was sitting in my office. Like I was messing up my one shot to do something meaningful. I was tired of feeling like I was fading into the background. Like I spent most of my time consuming instead of creating. Like even though I spent my days accomplishing everything on my to-do list, I still felt empty.

I was waiting for something to happen to lift me out of the rut I'd created for myself, but Heath and I quickly realized no one was coming to save us from our outwardly successful office jobs. If we wanted something bigger out of life, we had to climb out of our rut and chase after it.

And failing at this sounded a million times better than staying in my safe job doing nothing.

On my last day of work in New Orleans, my car was packed with everything I owned. I shifted the car into reverse and backed out of my parking spot at work for the last time with an eight-hour drive to Texas ahead of me.

Next time I hit the road, it would be for our honeymoon—we just had to iron out a few details first.

Chapter 3

"It fits perfectly in the back seat!" Heath shouted excitedly showing me the Amazon listing. With only a couple of months left until our wedding, we were focused on figuring out the logistics of our honeymoon.

I looked up from my computer screen where I was working on a blog post and admired the sparkle shining from my newly adorned ring finger. When I posted our engagement announcement on Facebook a couple weeks back, I was tempted to tag my old coworkers in the post just so I could rub their faces in our finally formalized commitment. But Heath said that was petty so I just refreshed the likes until I made sure they liked my post and knew they were wrong about us. It's undetectable pettiness that way. The diamond marked the beginning of our lives together and sparked honeymoon planning in earnest.

"It looks like a pool floatie!" I protested instantly, looking at the listing on Heath's phone.

"It's an air mattress. We can camp in the back of the car and save a ton of money."

"You. Want me..." I said slowly. "To spend our whole first year of marriage. Sleeping. In the back seat. Of my *car*?!"

"Ye-es?" Heath questioned. "No?"

I don't know a lot about men, but I know that all it takes is one conversation for a man to derail your entire life plans, like my life plan to always have access to an actual mattress. Heath took our lack of finances to mean "I'm open to the idea of living in my car." We may be taking a big risk here, but that was a little extreme.

Since driving back to Texas, I had a lot of time on my hands to research and figure out how this road trip would work. After spending hours studying maps and researching places to visit in each state, I calculated that it would take seven months to drive through the lower 48 at a minimum. We would head west from Texas and blaze through the desert's summer heat as fast as possible to hit the California coast. Then we would go east to watch the leaves change in the fall and head south for winter. If we married before the end of May and hit the road immediately, we could knock out the contiguous US and be home for Christmas.

"Heath," I started, looking at the picture again. "I love you. I do not love you enough to spend a year sleeping on an air mattress smaller than a twin-sized bed with you every night."

"Fine. You come up with a solution," Heath grumbled under his breath, opening Instagram on his phone.

I opened the tab on my computer to Airbnb. Those are cheaper than hotels, right? Plus then we can cook all our meals and have a more homey feel than a hotel room anyway. I typed in Los Angeles first. There wasn't anything under $100 a night, unless I wanted to sleep in someone's spare bedroom. And perhaps be murdered.

Next.

Hotels were more expensive, plus the cost of eating out.

Heath already tossed out the idea of camping in a tent for part of our adventure, but I had a feeling there were bears in Yellowstone that would be eager to eat me. And while our route included tons of national parks and small towns, camping—as we've established—isn't exactly my forte.

"Hey, remember that guy I told you about?" Heath asked.

"The YouTube guy?"

"No."

"The guy from the elevator at your office?'

"No."

"Just tell me which guy, Heath!"

"The guy on Instagram who is a photographer and lives in a truck camper."

"What's a truck camper again?"

"It's like this," he said, angling his phone toward me. A large awkwardly shaped box sat in the bed of the truck hanging over both the cab and the back bumper. "It actually has a bed, kitchen, bathroom, and even a shower."

"Really?" My interest piqued at the word shower.

"It's kind of like a tiny home on wheels. I bet we could get a small RV on Craigslist for pretty cheap and fix it up. You can park it anywhere too so we can camp for free and save money on hotels."

"Oh yeah! I remember my grandparents telling me about camping in their RV in Walmart parking lots. It's a thing apparently."

"Is that a yes?" Heath pulled up his phone and started searching for used campers on Craigslist. I had calculated that if we spent $75 a night on average between hotels, Airbnb stays, and tent camping—which was starting to sound impossibly low based on my quick research—we would pay at least $15,000 in lodging costs during our trip. Not to mention the high costs of eating out when we didn't have a kitchen. This would be a $25,000 honeymoon and we didn't have that kind of money lying around. But if we could camp for free every night and have our own bed and shower, it was a no-brainer.

"That's a let's see if we can find a camper," I answered. "Where do you shop for RVs?"

A few weeks into scrolling page after page on Craigslist, researching RVs, and after a couple of disappointing close calls, Heath showed me a listing.

"He relisted it at $12,000," Heath said, showing me a listing we'd come across twice but ruled out due to the price. This lower price was much closer to our price range, but still more than we wanted to spend. Heath called the owner, Brian, who was at work but said his wife was home and could give us the tour. We hopped in the car and followed directions to his address. We easily spotted the 1994 RV among the newly built brick houses. It wouldn't win any awards for being the nicest first home, but sitting among a row of identical houses it represented taking the road less taken. Pure adventure on wheels.

It's one thing to dream about doing big things with your life. It's another to drop thousands of dollars on a tiny camper and decide to live without a home address with your newlywed spouse while wondering ever so quietly in the back of your mind if any marriage could actually survive 20,000 miles in less than 100-square feet.

Growing up you daydream about what your life will look like after marriage. What kind of job will you have? Where is the house? Dog or no dog? At one point, my life plans entailed finding the most secure job I could and steadily putting away savings. This is what I thought success would look like.

Instead, I found myself driving to a stranger's home to buy what looked like an RV off of *Breaking Bad*. Yet, at the same time, I couldn't help but shake a feeling that we were on the right path, that somehow this was what we were meant to be doing. If I had told someone this at the moment, they'd have thought I was crazy. In what world is buying an old RV off Craigslist to travel the US considered "the right path"? Yet, it felt right.

When Heath and I daydreamed about what our lives would look like, it ultimately came down to living a good story together. Somehow, while driving up to Brian from Craigslist's house, I felt that our life was about to be catapulted into our first big chapter.

The cream exterior of the RV looked faded and the maroon swirls on the side were chipping. It looked every bit of twenty years old. Brian's wife, Cindy, opened the door and let us climb inside. She didn't bother to give a tour of the rooms since you could instantly see every part of the RV from the doorway.

Walking in, the first thing I noticed was the color. The cabinets were a hideous shade of brown and the furniture and wallpaper were a weird blue-pink pattern that looked like the designer was trying to decorate a nursery without asking what the baby's gender was first. There was a small corner kitchen with enough counter space to fit a tiny cutting board between the sink and the stovetop. There was an oven—a luxury we hadn't seen in many campers—and a microwave. The fridge was original to the RV and extremely dated, with faux wood paneling that only added more brown to the room.

There were cabinets everywhere. Above and below the fridge. Above the pink and blue couch. Above the dining table and oversized blue chairs. The loft bed above the cab even had hidden storage bins under the windows. Plus the entire outside of the RV was door after door of storage. Who needed this much storage space? I wondered.

Past the kitchen, a small hallway with a door on either side opened to the bedroom. There was enough room on each side of the bed to walk around and access the tiny closets. I laughed when I noticed the dark magenta floral-patterned mattress wasn't even a rectangle. The corners of the mattress were custom cut off to make it possible to walk around the bed.

As terrible as the interiors of the RV looked, it offered everything. We had a bed, a shower, a toilet, a full kitchen, a table where we could eat and work, even a loft bed where we could host guests if anyone wanted to visit us on the road. Plus, there were windows and skylights everywhere letting in natural light and giving us panoramic views of suburbia.

"You can crank these up," Cindy demonstrated reaching up to the skylight in the bathroom and turning the small handle. "And then this little button turns on the fan." She pushed the button and the fan whirred overhead. "There's a fan in the shower too to help air it out. And you probably saw the big A/C in the ceiling in the living room."

Most impressively, as Cindy answered our questions and showed us how different features worked, the RV didn't feel crowded. It didn't take us long to find out that buying a truck and a truck camper cost roughly the same as a small motorhome with less square footage. We toured a couple of truck campers, but we could barely both fit inside with the sellers. In the motorhome we had 29 feet to walk around and move. Plus we could tow our car! (Or so we thought.)

"Do you want to check out the outside?" Cindy asked.

Popping the hood, everything looked about as foreign as every engine looks to me. The storage bays contained a similarly baffling number of hoses and pipes and switches. We should've asked someone to come with us to test the mechanical aspects of the RV—the engine, the generator, the water pump.

But I didn't know what half of those things were yet and I certainly didn't think about hooking up the rig to electricity or water to see if those things even worked. Instead, we opened cabinets and looked around windows for signs of leaks—the only thing we knew to look for because water damage is "cancer for an RV" according to Heath's grandpa.

Cindy offered a test drive and we excitedly accepted. What if this could be the first time to drive our new home? We left our car keys with Cindy and took the old motorhome for a spin. The engine cranked on smoothly so that seemed to signal that all the foreign parts under the hood worked. I cranked on the heat and Heath hit the windshield wipers as the clouds in the sky started to darken. Was this a bad omen?

Heath shifted into reverse, swiveling his head from mirror to mirror to the rearview camera screen—a big selling point on this old rig. The owners had actually installed a rearview camera and mounted the screen on the rearview mirror. I silently wondered why the motorhome had a rearview mirror built-in at all, considering the mirror showed off a view of the living room and kitchen and not the actual road. Maybe one day if we had kids then we could make sure they weren't getting into mischief by checking the rearview mirror. No, don't get ahead of yourself. First, buy a house on wheels. Second, make it to all 50 states. Third...well, I don't know what's third but it's not kids yet.

As Heath inched backward down the driveway, a school bus turned onto the street and a neighbor began backing out of their driveway. Rain began to pour and they both sat in the road waiting on us while Heath backed out at a snail's pace. There's nothing like people waiting on you to make you ten times more nervous about driving your potential home. Something banged and rattled as the back tires made it to the asphalt.

"What's that noise?" Heath asked, whipping his head back and forth between the mirrors and the backup camera screen.

"The kitchen blinds," I said looking over my shoulder. "That can be the first thing we replace."

The banging sound continued as Heath narrowly avoided backing into a neighbor's trash cans and had to reverse, straighten out a bit to avoid hitting a car parked on the street, reverse again, and then finally start driving straight down the narrow suburban street, waving to the (hopefully) patient bus driver as we slowly motored away.

In reality, it probably only took 30 seconds, but it was painfully embarrassing. We knew nothing about RVs and nothing about driving RVs. This was a terrible idea.

Heath turned out of the neighborhood onto a country road and floored it. My stomach dropped like I was flying down a roller coaster track.

"Geez babe, slow down!"

"This is a test drive! I need to see how well it can handle

going 65 since we'll be driving on mostly the interstate and highways. If this old engine can't handle high speeds, then we don't want to buy it. How does it feel to you?"

A gust of wind rocked the RV from side to side and the kitchen blinds banged and rattled in the background.

"A little terrifying." I gulped, gripping the door handle.

I turned my head over my shoulder looking at the house behind me. Other than the hanging blinds, everything else was still. Locked into place despite flying down the highway at—I glanced at the speedometer—50 miles an hour. Fifty miles per hour never felt so fast.

This was the first RV I'd been in since I was a kid. Once my grandparents took me and my sister and my mom all the way from Texas to Georgia. They drove through the night and I remember sleeping in the bed while my grandpa drove thinking it was the coolest thing I'd ever experienced. A bed on wheels?!

Heath played with the blinkers and the washer fluid and shifting gears while I stared out the windshield quietly starting to picture it all.

Soon we were in the middle of nowhere Texas and the rain began to let up. All around there was nothing but green fields and cows. The road was smooth and wide open ahead of us. Blue skies fought their way through gaps in the clouds. Maybe *this* was an omen. Blue skies ahead?

"Should I turn around?"

"Sure," I agreed, lost in thought until Heath slammed on the brakes coming to an abrupt stop in the middle of the country road. I screamed as the seatbelt caught me.

"Heath!"

"I have to check that the brakes work!" he chuckled to himself, clearly amused. "You'll be glad I did when someone cuts us off in traffic and I have to slam on my brakes to avoid a wreck. They work well."

I shook my head, relieved the seatbelt had also worked well, while Heath made an eight-point U-turn on the empty two-lane country road before heading back toward Brian's house.

"I can picture us really doing this. I mean, I know we've been talking about it for months, but being in here with you now, I can see it. Us living in this RV. We're really doing this, aren't we? We are RVing to all fifty states for our honeymoon," I said dreamily.

Heath reached over and squeezed my hand.

"Both hands on the wheel!" I squealed.

Chapter 4

"I'm sorry, what?" My mom asked.

"We're buying an RV and going to all fifty states for our honeymoon," I repeated.

I knew I would have to tell my parents about our honeymoon plan sometime. The wedding was three months away and my mom was feeling the pressure of such a short engagement. I was waiting until the wedding stress dissipated before dropping our honeymoon adventure plans on her. Turns out, wedding stress never really relents, so the weeks stretched on and I kept putting off the conversation.

I was dragging my feet on sending out wedding invitations since they would include our gift registry and the website we set up so people could donate to our honeymoon fund. What I hadn't anticipated was that my mom would find my secret wedding registry on Amazon and ask me why I let Heath pick out a bunch of camping supplies. You can't keep secrets from your mother for long.

"Well, actually," I stammered. I need camping stuff? I chose those things? We are going to buy a camper? None of the words coming to mind made any sense. "I've been meaning to tell you and Dad about our honeymoon plans."

"Oh, you decided where you want to go? If it's a Disney Cruise, we are coming with you!" My mom said excitedly before calling my dad in from his study.

This was already going poorly.

"Well," I began again as my parents both stared at me. They suddenly seemed very tall. *That's weird.* Usually, I'm slightly taller than my mom. Not today. She grew at least six inches in the past two minutes.

"We came up with this idea to go to all fifty states," I gushed, eager to get this awkward moment over with. "And we figured out that the most responsible way financially to do it would be to buy a camper and drive around the country. So, we found one on Craigslist and toured it and Heath is going to pick it up on Friday and we leave the day after the wedding." The shaky words poured out of me in a single breath.

The two-second beat that followed my monologue lasted seventeen years. Telling them I was pregnant with Zac Efron's baby would've shocked them less.

My mom's mouth hung open, moving ever so slightly like she was trying to form words but nothing came out. My dad must've noticed because he quickly said "sounds fun" before ducking out of the room. The man knows when to cut and run.

"I'm sorry, what? What possessed you to think *that* was a good idea?" my mom began. My mom isn't a harsh or domineering woman. She's always supported me, although the whole quitting my job thing was met with a raised eyebrow. "I mean," she scoffed, looking for the words. "You're doing *what* exactly? And how are you going to pay for this? You said you were looking for jobs in Austin!"

Okay, I would need to apologize for that lie later. Why look for jobs when you were driving off into the sunset in two short months?

"We want to travel together and start our marriage with an adventure," I reasoned. "And I'm going to write a book!" I wasn't actually sure if I would write a book, but it was on my bucket list and if I was ever going to do it, this time without a job was kind of perfect. Plus, with parents it's best to present new things with confidence and gloss over the 100 things you have to figure out to turn a dream into a reality. Saying I was writing a book made it at least sound like I had one thing figured out.

"And you're a wonderful writer, but how are you going to pay for this?" she repeated.

"Savings…mostly…" I whispered. No need to mention most of my savings was going toward the RV.

"Wait, is Heath quitting his job too?"

"Yes."

My mom did that thing all moms do where they pause and look at the ceiling shaking their heads as if willing God to come down and talk sense into their daughter because they've lost the energy to deal with the insanity.

"Well, if that's what you want to do," she started, pausing to think of the right words. "Then enjoy it."

I was 87% sure that was her way of saying good luck. But in that intense scary way that the bad guy in *Taken* says good luck.

After telling my parents about our plans, I had to tell every aunt, cousin, and friend at my bridal shower the very next day about my wild honeymoon idea. The look in my mom's eyes as she asked me to explain the idea to my cousin Amy told me that she was both not on board and praying I changed my mind. I think she hoped that everyone in the room would disapprove of our plan and convince me to take the path well-traveled instead. But this was my bridal shower, and it's an unwritten rule that you're nice to the bride at her own shower.

Sharing the news publicly went from terrifying to exhilarating. I had something unexpected and interesting to share with people. They could give me ideas of places to visit and ooh and ahh over the pictures I took of our new home.

People were quasi-supportive.

What a cool idea!

How fun! Smart to travel now—you can't travel once you have kids.

Although we quickly noticed that no matter how supportive people sounded, they all had a tendency to project their own fears onto our plans.

Sounds fun, but I could never do that. Don't you want a house?

Where are you going to get your mail if you're always traveling?

Oh, I would never be able to quit my job and not know how I was going to earn my next paycheck. Too stressful!

They peppered us with questions too. Some exciting like, "Where are you going to go in Washington?" And some stressful like, "What are you going to do when you finish all 50 states?" Well, I don't know yet! I'm just trying to buy this RV and get married first, but thank you for the toaster and the existential crisis!

I'll give them credit, though. No one ever asked, "Do you think you will actually make it to all fifty?" That was the question bouncing around my head on a loop. I didn't know the answer.

Looking at the spreadsheets I'd created, we did not have the money. Sure, we were hoping that our slightly tacky attempt to ask friends and family for money through our wedding registry would help us along the way. But unless someone gives us $10,000—or maybe more…I really have no clue how much full-time travel costs—we *will* run out of money at some point.

I wondered what we would do when that happened. Would we be in New York? Or California? Would we raise money or come home or sell the RV? Would we actually make it to all fifty? I tried to push the thoughts from my head before they consumed me.

We'll figure it all out.

Eventually.

Maybe.

Hopefully.

Chapter 5

After buying the RV, Heath came to me with a plan for making this trip more realistic financially. While I had been sitting down with Google Maps and spreadsheets, Heath was doing what he did best: scheming.

"Do you remember my old boss Steve? Well, he connected me with this YouTuber," Heath said, calling me from Houston, "...and I grabbed a coffee with him at Barnes & Noble on my way out of town."

"That's nice," I said absentmindedly. After buying the RV, Heath drove it to his parent's house to give it a little facelift and a fresh coat of paint. It desperately needed to be brought into the 21st century and he was priming and painting the cabinets white while he talked to me on speakerphone.

"He just did this thing called rejection therapy where you try to intentionally get rejected so that you no longer fear it. He just finished 30 days and posted a video each day on YouTube. One of his videos at Krispy Kreme got like millions of hits and he was on the news and everything."

"Oh yeah, I think I remember watching part of that," I recalled, still wondering why my fiancé was meeting with a guy who made videos about donuts.

"Well, I told this guy all about our fifty-state honeymoon and how you want to be a writer and I want to run my own business but I don't know exactly what I'm doing with my life right now. I mean, obviously, neither of us do, we just bought an RV so we are clearly a little crazy. So, he suggested that I have a project to work on while we travel," Heath jabbered on. "He just casually threw out the idea of working a job in all fifty states so I could figure out what I want to do as a business. And I loved it.

"I can learn about business, get my hands dirty, try new things. I already researched and sent an InMail to this company called Snagajob if you've heard of it. They are the largest hourly job board. I met their HR rep at a conference last fall and she was really nice and put me in contact with their marketing director and I sent him a message—" Heath paused. There was so much excitement in his rambling that I think he forgot to breathe. "And I kinda just laid it all out for this guy. Told him I'm 23 and visiting all 50 states with my soon-to-be wife and trying to figure out what we want our life together to look like. And I asked if they would be able to help me find jobs in all 50 states.

"Which would be really helpful because I think that would be the hardest part of the project. So, what do you think?"

I stood in the dining room of my apartment quietly listening to Heath's ideas.

"Let me get this straight," I started. "We quit our jobs so we can travel and explore the world together. And you. Want to work. For our entire honeymoon?!"

"Well, no." He paused. "Yes. Kind of? I don't know, I just had the idea. You don't like it?"

"I just pictured this being more like a honeymoon. You're talking about finding *fifty* jobs. That's insane."

These next few months of adventure were like our own adult

gap year. We would pursue our dream of traveling. I had impulsively told my mom I was going to write a book, so that was on my to-do list now. Heath would...well I hadn't really thought about what Heath would do yet. Now that he came to me with his own idea, it hit me again that this was also the beginning of our marriage. This is our first foray into the world together and our first chance to work together.

I was desperate for travel, but Heath had dreams too, and I hadn't put much thought into what he might want out of this trip. This wasn't the "Alyssa gets to live her dream of visiting all 50 states" trip. This was our first chance to pursue something bigger together.

A few months back, Heath had posted his bucket list on Facebook. That's how I knew he also wanted to visit all 50 states. But I hadn't stopped to consider that he might have other dreams he wanted to pursue once we were married, too. Dreams that were even bigger than that one.

"Yeah, but it's a *year*," Heath argued, exaggerating the fact that the lower 48 would only take us seven months with the route I outlined. We hadn't figured out Hawaii and Alaska yet. "Are we really just not going to work at all for a whole year? And then what, come back and get real jobs again because we are broke and living in an old RV somewhere?"

"How long is it going to take you to find and work 50 jobs?" I countered, frustrated with our conversation. It hurt my brain to think about life after our honeymoon. I couldn't think that far ahead and when the adults in our lives asked if we would come back to Texas and get real jobs, my stomach churned in protest. I didn't know the solution to finding a way to make money or how we would spend our days. I just knew I wanted to travel, and this plan seemed at odds with that. "This is crazy," I said, shaking my head.

"You are going to spend this year writing. I want to use this year to figure out what kind of business I want to run. I think this will help me do that," Heath said, pointedly not answering my question about how long it would take to job hunt and work in every state across the country. "So, what do you think?"

Being the loving soon-to-be wife, I knew I should be supportive of his dream the same way he jumped on board as soon as I mentioned visiting all fifty states. He supported me instantly and he deserved a partner who would do the same for his dreams.

"I think that we couldn't even find one remote job that we could do while we travel, so finding 50 jobs will be impossible. I definitely don't want to work 50 jobs with you, and I don't know what I'll do on days when you're working. Just sit in the RV in the parking lot of the office wherever you're working that day?"

Okay, maybe not exactly supportive or loving but I didn't say aloud what I was thinking. It took months for Heath to find his first job—the one he was quitting so we could travel together. If he had to find a job in each state, it would take us twelve YEARS for him to complete this goal. (Yes, I whipped out my calculator and figured that out.) Not to mention, this is my honeymoon! No one wants to hear that their husband wants to actively job hunt and work 50 different jobs on their honeymoon. That's easily the least sexy honeymoon activity of all time.

But like any true dreamer, Heath continued pushing forward with his new venture despite my respectful skepticism. Okay fine, my outright this-is-a-stupid-idea-and-I-don't-want-to-hear-about-it attitude. Heath is a fearless go-getter and I think my initial disapproval only made him dig his heels in deeper to prove that this could work.

Where I saw it as distracting from the joy of travel, Heath saw it as a platform for his future entrepreneurial endeavors. I was focused on making the most of the year ahead, but he wanted to set us up to continue chasing our dreams after the honeymoon. He wanted to run his own company and working across a few dozen different industries would give him a crash course in business. He was still excited to travel the country together, but couldn't resist the chance to think bigger. This was the dream he was most passionate to spend our first year together chasing. I was doing my best to wrap my head around it.

And then, a week later, Heath dropped a bombshell on me.

The marketing director Heath reached out to on LinkedIn had forwarded Heath's message to someone else in the company who picked up the phone and called Heath.

"Hey Heath, this is Jon. I work in public relations at Snagajob and we love your idea to work a job in each state. Can we fly you out to our HQ in Virginia and make this happen?"

I wasn't on the call, but according to Heath, that's precisely what was said. This company loved his idea and wanted to help make it happen after one conversation. While I was busy getting my wedding dress altered, Heath immediately flew to Virginia and met the Snagajob team.

"Hourly America," Heath said to me on the phone from Virginia, giving a name to his crazy idea that I still thought was

100% the dumbest idea ever. "And they want us to make it into a documentary."

"That's on your bucket list," I replied, surprised. I remembered seeing it written beneath "visit all fifty states." The best man at our wedding, Jim, ran his own production company. A year earlier, he released a feature-length documentary on the destruction from the wildfires in Texas. We attended two different premieres for his film and the experience stuck with Heath. He saw families come up to Jim after the film with tears in their eyes giving him a hug and thanking him for sharing their stories when no one else cared. Heath wanted to be able to do that for someone, despite the fact that he'd never picked up a camera before.

"I know! They said they would send us all the equipment and even pay us a little bit."

My ears perked up instantly. "Wait, what? They want to pay us? To travel to all fifty states?"

Pay me to travel? You have my attention.

I could hear Heath smiling on the other end of the phone a thousand miles away. "Yep. And we decided that I should only work each job for one day. Makes it easier for everyone that way. So Snagajob will find me a job since they run a job board, I show up for one day to film the experience, and then I write a blog post on it. And businesses don't have to pay me for the jobs, we decided. Otherwise, I would literally have 50 W2s for all of 2014 which sounds horrible. Makes it an easier sell for the business too."

And that folks, is how you get your wife to agree to a seemingly ridiculous plan.

I did the quick math in my head. If we traveled for 200 days,

Heath would work one out of every four days. That wasn't that bad. Plus, this suddenly went from being a crazy idea to an idea that:

A) Actually put money in our bank account, and

B) Accomplished something on Heath's bucket list.

We decided to be the kind of couple that pushed each other to chase our biggest dreams. It was a platitude of sorts that we said to each other ever since we started dating and I asked Heath why he never asked me to stay in Texas. He said that I always dreamed of living in New Orleans and he wasn't going to stand in the way of that, even though he'd miss me. The idea of championing our partner's dreams stuck, even though supporting each other through the crazy dreams was clearly new to me. His dream wasn't what I expected, but it's what he wanted. This new idea to work a job in all 50 states was his goal. I wanted to travel and spend time in national parks. With his new plan, it seemed like a solid middle ground. We could work enough to cover some of our bills and still leave free time to explore.

And I really can't stress enough the peace of mind that came with knowing we wouldn't be making $0/month for the next year. Snagajob threw out paying us $25 per blog post which, if we made it to all fifty states, equated to a couple of hundred dollars a month during our travels. It was pennies compared to what our expenses would be, but when you're Heath and my mom is asking you how on earth you'll provide for her daughter, pennies sound pretty dang good.

We had a few thousand in savings after buying the RV, but we knew it would not be enough to make it to all fifty states. We didn't know how much gas or campsites would cost, but we knew it would add up fast. Our goal was to stretch our savings for as long as possible and cross our fingers that people gave us money for our honeymoon instead of gifts. Not exactly a solid plan, but it was all we had come up with.

To make it work we'd have to be scrappy. But coming home early because we ran out of money was not an option (or at least I didn't want it to be). This was one small step toward actually finishing what we set out to do.

"Heath," I said with a deep breath. "Let's do it."

"Seriously?!" Heath asked incredulously. "I thought I would have to sell you more. Or find a way to convince them to pay us more."

"Well, feel free to do that. But I think you're more excited about pursuing this project than you are about actually traveling. And I'm not going to be the person who tells you no when it comes to your dreams."

"You said no when I said it was my dream to move to North Carolina and become cotton farmers," Heath debated.

"That was a terrible dream and I will forever stand by that. I will support your good idea dreams if they also will make us some money and allow us to travel," I rebutted.

Heath laughed. "That's very specific. What about the documentary? I've been thinking about it and you would basically have to film everything."

"I hadn't thought about that." I mulled it over for two seconds. "But I can do that. I mean, I don't know how and it'll probably suck at first, but I can learn," I said, trying to make up for my previous lack of support. You just point and shoot, right?

"So I can tell Jon that we're in? And also I'm going to see if

I can get them to at least cover our gas. Maybe like $1000 per month?" Heath estimated.

"That would be amazing." I didn't know how much gas would cost or even what our total mileage around the country would end up being, but $1000 a month to travel the country and let Heath make his documentary? That was a steal.

"And you're really sure you want to commit to this? Because if you say no, we'll figure something else out."

I thought for a moment, picturing our life together. Sure, I didn't know anything about production. Or RVs. Or writing blogs for an hourly job board. Or Montana.

2014 was about to throw everything at me at once. On top of figuring out how to travel in an RV, I would need to learn new skills fast and not be afraid to try new things. When I started daydreaming about an adventure, wasn't that part of what I wanted? Something to propel me out of the monotony and into something greater?

The more I thought about the documentary, the more I realized what we were signing up for. This wasn't just making a fun movie of a wild adventure. This was two newlyweds committing to working together on a project. I wondered how working together would play out. Growing up, my parents ran their own business together. I saw them divide responsibilities and volley relevant client information to each other across our kitchen island. They made it look easy. I quietly hoped I'd somehow absorbed this trait of being able to work with my spouse from my parents.

Heath was committed to fifty jobs and I was committed to working right alongside him. I wouldn't be frothing milk and icing cupcakes like Heath, but I would be collaborating with him on this bigger project. I might read fewer books and drink fewer piña coladas this way, but let's be real…I don't actually know how to make a piña colada anyway. And it wasn't like we could fit a library of books into our tiny home.

I was hesitant to admit, even to myself, that I needed this project too.

I fought Heath instantly on his plan to work across the country, but when he asked how I pictured us spending our days, I realized I had never actually pictured it. At least not realistically. I saw palm trees and snow-capped mountains and apple cider donuts. I didn't think about the day-to-day. Would we just constantly drive and explore and be tourists? Our bank account would never be able to sustain that vacation lifestyle.

Heath was right. We needed something to propel us forward as we traveled. I was already unemployed, moving into an RV, and heading off into the unknown wilderness. Why not add a video camera?

"I'm in," I finally said. "Especially if you can get them to pay us more for also filming a documentary."

"I love you," Heath said. I swear I heard him exhale over the phone in relief. "I'm so lucky to be marrying you."

I smiled. "I love you too."

I sighed in relief, despite adding one more element to our travels. This felt like adding a missing piece. But, with the unknown of travel drawing closer every day, fear blossomed in my chest. We had proclaimed to everyone we loved that we were going on this grand adventure. If we failed, how much harder would it be to return home knowing we had all of these people rooting for us?

But now we had a goal and a purpose. *Hourly America*, as

we named it. My idea was to spend my days hiking, ambling through scenic small towns, reading books, and writing stories about our adventures. The reality was traveling to all 50 states in a year wasn't going to be all sunshine and selfies. Things would get hard. Abandoning my car in the desert that first week would look easy in comparison to some of the other challenges we would face.

Creating this secondary goal to not only travel but to film a documentary along the way locked us into a whole new level of adventure. Literally, because we signed a contract with Snagajob committing to visit all fifty states in a year's time. We were all in, for better or for worse.

We didn't know anything about RVing. And we really didn't know anything about filming a documentary. But we were diving in headfirst.

How hard could it be?

Chapter 6

Dropping off the car and the malfunctioning tow dolly at Heath's granny's house, we were back on the road a few thousand pounds lighter.

The engine was no longer whining as it chugged along the highway, leading us to believe it wouldn't have handled towing a car across the country very well, so we no longer stressed over leaving the car behind. We drove easily down the interstate toward New Mexico. We didn't have any more time for unexpected stops if we wanted to stay on schedule.

"Your turn," Heath said, walking through the kitchen/living room and grabbing a bag of tortilla chips.

"My turn for what?" I asked innocently from the comfort of the passenger seat.

"You know what." He pointed to the driver's seat and sat a small bowl of salsa in the cupholder.

I groaned internally. And probably aloud.

But Heath was right. I couldn't leave him to handle 20,000 miles of driving himself. I needed to learn how to drive all 29 feet of our motorhome. Probably should've done that before leaving Austin.

Add it to the list.

It's not like I didn't believe I could physically drive my house, I thought as I climbed down into the driver's seat for the first time. There just wasn't an antiperspirant strong enough to battle the sweat that would pour out of me as I tried to navigate this beast.

"It's just driving straight on the interstate, babe," Heath said, reading my mind. "Let's go. Oh wait," he turned over his shoulder to reach into the camera bag we stored behind the passenger seat. "Let me set up the GoPro to commemorate this moment." Snagajob had sent us a GoPro to mount on our dash to record scenery as we drove, or in this case, notable driving moments.

I buckled up and shifted the RV into drive to pull forward out of the rest stop. I slowly let my foot off the brake but the RV didn't budge.

"It's a heavy machine. You gotta give it a little gas to move," Heath instructed.

"Right, right, I knew that." I pressed on the gas and the rig lurched forward. I tried not to be insulted seeing Heath's hands gripping his armrest a little more firmly. You never know how sensitive a vehicle's accelerator and brakes will be when you drive it for the first time, I caught myself wanting to explain. But I bit my tongue and focused on pressing firmly on the pedal. Heath was right, I thought, now paying closer attention to the RV. The engine had a certain "I'm struggling" feeling to it when we pulled the car, but now that I was on the open road, I could feel it speeding up with ease.

"You've got some semi-trucks coming up," Heath said as I began to merge with the interstate traffic.

"I see 'em," I muttered, slowing down slightly as the machines flew past.

But these were not semis. These were homes on wheels. And not like our tiny home on wheels. These were four semis carrying double wides on their beds, with half a dozen "wide load" trucks escorting them down the lonely stretch of interstate at a breezy 55 miles per hour…in a 75 MPH speed limit zone. Not that my house could handle anything above 70. But 55 was *crawling* and we were running out of daylight. I shot Heath a look, as if he purposefully manifested a caravan of mobile homes just to challenge me.

I merged onto the highway and picked up speed, quickly coming up behind my first oversized load. I had been so worried about handling the length of the RV, I never thought about the width being a problem.

"You can do it," I heard Heath say for about twenty minutes while I mustered up the courage and the speed to make it around the houses. In between encouragement, he said *I'm sorry babe* about a hundred times while he lounged in the passenger seat munching on chips and salsa. Neither of us could have anticipated that the deserted stretch of highway we'd driven for the past couple of hours would suddenly become a suburban neighborhood.

If the highway had a small shoulder on the left, I might've passed easily. But the small lanes offered only an inch or two of asphalt over the yellow line. So I sped up and slowed down over hill after hill behind the semis who definitely took up a lane and a half. Every time I tried to pass, I accelerated too slowly to overtake the semi before a dozen cars were piled up behind me.

"We should name him," Heath suggested.

"What?"

"Just trying to make conversation while you're waiting to pass this semi. We should name the RV."

"Well he's slow as a turtle," I said as cars zoomed past me on the left mocking me. At this rate, we would get to New Mexico sometime next week. "Oh, what was that kid's cartoon with the turtle?"

"Franklin?"

"Yes! Franklin. This 29-foot hunk of metal is definitely a Franklin."

"I like it," Heath agreed with a smile. "Franklin the RV."

A few more minutes passed until there were no cars in my rearview mirror. I needed as much road as possible to pass these houses.

"You got this," Heath said as I merged over into the left lane to attempt passing again. The semi driver in front of me inched to the right, a small act of mercy after seeing me attempt this maneuver 20 times only to give up. I hit the gas on a downhill stretch, easily over-taking the first house this time. I continued alongside the second house, hitting those loud bumps on the yellow line and hearing every dish I owned rattle like crazy.

"You got this. You got this," Heath continued to say as I white-knuckled my way past house number two. A few cars piled up behind me, so I slid in between the houses to let the tiny cars flit past with ease. Finally, after years of struggle (or about thirty minutes), I passed all of the houses and cruised at an easy 65 miles per hour. Heath cheered; I took my first deep breath.

"Okay now that you're used to driving and past the stressful part, we need to take a picture to commemorate your first time driving."

"Fine," I exhaled, "but there's no way I'm looking at the camera. Gotta focus."

Heath chuckled. He turned on the GoPro and connected it to the app on his phone.

"Smile!" he said, snapping a couple of photos. "Okay, now act like you just had to pass a bunch of oversized loads." I glared at Heath with my best side-eye before snapping my attention back to the road.

"That's perfect," he laughed. "Your first day driving the RV and you nailed it."

"You know what would be funnier? Snap one where I'll just drive and you should pretend to be scared."

"Good one," Heath said, making a scared face while I smiled at the open road. Heath laughed looking at the final product on his phone.

Later, I would look at that photo and tell Heath that it made me look like a bad driver or like I didn't know how to drive the RV. "No one will think that," Heath assured me. "And besides, no one will see it other than us. Any driver would've been stressed passing those monstrosities. You nailed it today."

I couldn't help but feel this was my first of many tests over the next seven months. The first stretch of the comfortable little bubble I'd built up around myself while watching Netflix in a plush chair in my cozy office. In my heart, I could sense that the coming months would stretch the person I was into a version of myself I may not recognize in a year. What kind of person would I be?

Apparently not someone afraid of driving a 29-foot RV around a caravan of double wides.

Bring it on, America.

After Heath fell asleep in the passenger seat while I cruised down the interstate, we made our final stop in Texas. I found a small campground in Fort Stockton for only $13 with our Passport America card, an RV membership Heath found online that saved us 50% at certain campgrounds. We considered camping for free at the Walmart a mile away, but with oppressive west Texas heat, we could use some A/C. Free was great, but $13 would still be a steal.

Yes, not only can I drive the RV, but I can keep this road trip within our budget too. I glowed with pride over my cheap find. We pulled in at sunset, paid for our site, and got everything hooked up. Heath handled the hoses outside while I handled the inside. Which basically consisted of picking the coffee pot up out of the sink and setting it back into its spot on the counter.

"All done," Heath called out stepping inside. "I cannot wait until we hit California. It's over 100° out there and the sun is almost set!"

"Yikes. I'm going to boil some water for spaghetti for dinner. Sound good?"

"Sure," Heath said, collapsing on the couch after a long day's drive.

I turned on the knob on the sink and it bobbed up and down from the water pressure. We used a water pressure regulator—per Heath's grandpa's recommendation—but that didn't mean the surge of pressure didn't attack the faucet any time we hooked our water at a new campsite.

Brown sludge spewed from the faucet.

"Ahhhh," I screeched, trying to turn the water down and avoid getting sprayed.

"What's that?" Heath asked.

"Water, supposedly. Maybe it will run clear eventually?" Heath and I exchanged a look as the water continued to run brown and then orange. A minute passed but the water still didn't clear up.

"This is why I said we should always have water bottles on hand. I know you hate using plastic, but look at that! We cannot drink that. We can use the water onboard our tank tonight and I'll go disconnect the water hose. I'll have to flush it out of the hose and our pipes at our next campground."

"Wait, what are you talking about?" I asked Heath.

"The water tank on board that you can use if you turn on the water pump. It's what we've been using when we're driving and stuff. So we don't always have to hook up to water at RV parks if we have water in our tank," he explained like a professional RVer.

I had washed my hands on the trip and it never occurred to me to ask where the water came from. You turn on the faucet, water comes out. That's how all sinks had worked in my lifetime. Of course, there was a tank and a pump somewhere storing water. Heath must have watched a few more YouTube videos than he let on.

"Do we have enough water in our tank?" I asked.

"Well when we bought the RV, she said these old level readers aren't really accurate anymore. But I think so. I put some in before we left Austin a few days ago. We just won't shower so we don't run out."

Our first RV park had clear water. I took it for granted. It also had a hot tub, giving me unrealistic expectations for every other RV park where we would camp. Without a car, we were stuck in the RV at the RV park for the night. Not that there was a ton to do in the town of Fort Stockton. Is this what RVing would be like? I wondered. I pictured a lot more natural beauty and exploring, not watching the sunset over the roofs of other RVs parked in this block of gravel.

"Yeah I'd rather not shower, than shower in that brown sludge." I paused. "So, is this what RV parks are like?"

The look on Heath's face told me he really didn't know.

Chapter 7

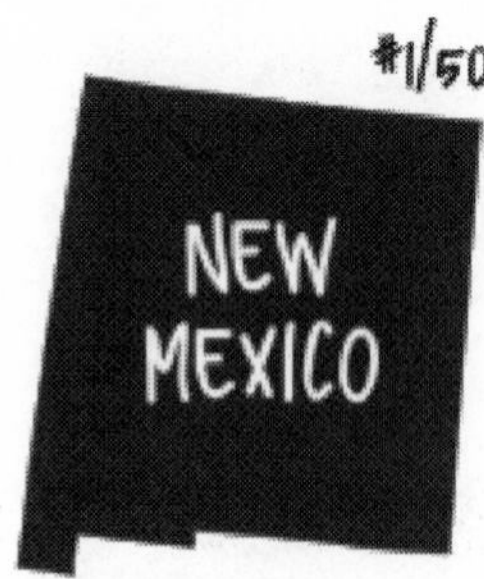

I woke up before my alarm with a tangle of nerves in my stomach. Like the first day of school meets a first date meets the top of a roller coaster with a really steep drop coming up in 2.3 seconds.

We made our way from the brown-water campground in west Texas to Albuquerque, New Mexico with no further incident. Snagajob lined up Heath's first job at a taekwondo studio in the city. I burst out laughing when I heard Heath on the phone with Jon. How on earth was my husband—who had never taken any martial arts—supposed to teach kids taekwondo? I was anxious to see exactly what Heath working all these jobs would look like.

When we arrived in Albuquerque, we shifted into tourist mode. We visited Petroglyph National Monument where we bought a National Parks pass for the year. And, after a short debate on if it would be worth $2, a map of all the national parks in the country so we could visit as many as possible throughout the year. I had an initial list of places I wanted to visit—Portland, the coast of Maine, the mountains of Vermont, Charleston—but Pinterest had opened my eyes to national parks I'd never heard of. Grand Teton? Tie-ton? Tea-ton? Tee-ten? I didn't know how to say it, but the pictures online had me adding it and a dozen other natural wonders to our route. It's funny, a lot of people talk about how there are so many great places to visit in our backyard of America, but until you start looking you really don't appreciate that cliché. Once I started researching beautiful places to visit, there seemed to be a never-ending catalog of places we had to see.

Maybe it was like this with a lot of life. Your world seems small until you turn around and really start looking at it, yet it's always there, just waiting for you to lift your head up and look around.

Since we had our home wherever we traveled, the far-reaching wilderness of the west was now completely open to us.

We hiked a short trail to an overlook that boasted distant mountain views—and views of a bunch of people's backyards—and then drove downtown to walk around "old town" with its adobe buildings. With our tight budget, we decided not to shop or eat out, so we walked aimlessly around the quaint square hand-in-hand taking pictures and chatting about our future.

But this wasn't just another lovely honeymoon day. It was Heath's first job and I wanted to call in sick.

When I agreed to film this documentary with Heath, I'm not going to lie, I was mostly thinking about what an awesome wife I was for helping my husband reach one of his dreams.

The reality of lugging around a camera all day somehow didn't come to mind.

The morning of my wedding, a giant box had arrived on my doorstep. I tore into it excitedly thinking it was an epic wedding gift, but it was full of clunky camera equipment.

It's normal for people to be nervous on their wedding day. However, most people are nervous because they're trying to decide if the person they are marrying is the one. I wasn't unsure about that. Heath was the right guy. He brought me fresh, hot coffee in bed every morning and that is a man to never, ever let go.

I was nervous for a slew of other reasons. I was nervous about us loading what few possessions we had into a crickety, old RV and not even making it out of Texas before the thing broke down. I was afraid of running out of money before we finished the west coast. I was afraid that I'd agreed to film a documentary and had no idea what that even consisted of. I was afraid people would think I'm a fraud.

And somewhere in my heart, there was a fear I couldn't quite put words to, but I could feel. A fear that this was just the whim of a young girl who knew nothing of the world and thought a honeymoon road trip would solve everything. The fear niggled in the back of my mind that of course a road trip wouldn't solve everything. It probably wouldn't solve anything.

What if we finished all fifty states and just came back to work boring jobs in cubicles again? Or worse, what if we didn't finish and still ended up living boring lives, scared to try anything bold again because this adventure had already knocked us down?

That terrified me more than the unknown of operating a professional video camera.

I know that not all fears are rational. I saw a story once about a snake who slithered through toilet pipes in Thailand and bit a guy while he was going to the bathroom. Now I'm terrified that I will find a snake in our RV toilet. Probably not rational, but you can bet I'm still going to check that toilet for snakes before I go to the bathroom.

But fear has a tendency to permeate everything it touches and when I opened that giant box just hours before getting married, I was jittery with nerves.

Why had I agreed to this?

Oh right, fifty states. My idea.

I wasn't even sure what I wanted or what I thought I would get out of our trip.

In New Orleans, I was bored with my own life and disenchanted with the pattern of commute, work, sleep, repeat. I wanted to mix things up and find a way to challenge myself to become the person I wished I was. Someone adventurous and well-traveled who wasn't scared to chase after dreams instead of letting them sit unrealized in a journal somewhere.

This documentary was the vehicle that would push me out of my comfort zone and get me unstuck. Well, technically the RV was the vehicle, but this learning how to film a documentary nonsense was like the gasoline. Or the gas pedal. This analogy is really falling apart.

Anyway, I practiced with the camera a couple times, like when Heath set it up to record us in the gas station parking lot back in Junction, Texas. I barely knew the basic necessary functions. Why do all the buttons have tiny pictures on them instead of words explaining what the buttons do? What in the Sam Hill does * mean? Does it add little stars to the video? And zebra stripes? How is that helpful?

I was only beginning to grasp how much work filming a documentary actually required. Filming. Saving and storing footage. Editing. Producing.

While I was thinking about my inexperience—and how holding this bulky camera was likely equivalent to doing bicep curls for 12 hours a day—Heath wasn't faring much better than me under the stress of this new challenge.

"I don't have shoes!!!" he yelled dramatically to start the day. A few hours after we left Austin, Heath realized he had piled his tennis shoes, swimsuit, and towel all on the back tire of the RV. And then we drove away with everything still on the tire. It was all likely smashed and covered in grease a thousand miles away now. "I need to go shoe shopping. Now!"

"Can I finish my cup of coffee at least?" I asked while he tornadoed around the RV getting it ready to embark. I wasn't sure I'd actually ever seen Heath nervous before. My first impression of Heath back in college was that he oozed confidence. He had that macho, jock, I'm-super-good-looking-despite-the-fact-that-I'm-a-redhead swagger. He was the kind of guy who rolled into class late, forgot he was supposed to present a project, so he made something up on the spot and no one was the wiser. Nothing rattled him.

But now he was pacing the RV, securing our coffee pot in the sink and tidying it up to hit the road. The one perk of no car was that we at least didn't have to pack up gear and snacks and water for the day. Our whole house would be right outside. On the other hand, we needed to unhook and secure everything for driving and in all our packing genius, a coffee cup with a lid didn't make the list.

Keeping up their end of the deal to help Heath find half of his jobs, Snagajob called a small nonprofit called Project Dojo and the owner, half-asleep at the time, agreed to let Heath become assistant sensei (assistant to the sensei?) as his first job. That was all we knew. I imagined he would be wiping down mats or practicing wax on, wax off on the sensei's car for the afternoon. It was hilarious to me that this was Heath's first job. I'm not sure what Heath envisioned when he committed to this goal, but I don't think either of us imagined he would be working barefoot in a dojo all day.

We quickly packed the RV and made it to Walmart. Heath ran in to buy a new pair of tennis shoes and $20 drained from the bank account. I added the unexpected expense to our budget spreadsheet.

"I can't find their address on Google Maps," I told Heath once he made it back to the RV. "Or their website. They've made no impression on the internet." We needed to be at the dojo in twenty minutes, but in all the excitement (re: anxiety) over the first job, we missed something vital—an address. "Did Jon email it over?"

Heath scrolled through his phone searching through his messages. "All he said is 'Project Dojo in Albuquerque'. You really can't find it?"

"Not yet. Let me see if I can find it on Facebook."

I opened the Facebook app ignoring my notifications—checking social media was reserved for when we had a Wi-Fi connection so we didn't zap all our data. Now it was a last resort for searching for Project Dojo. I scrolled through the list of results until finally finding what looked like a very old, un-updated page.

"Here's the address. It's on this same road actually." I typed in the address to Google Maps manually and glanced quickly at the map. One mile away toward the left. I closed the app to save data. We weren't that far away. "Alright let's go left out of here," I directed Heath, snapping my seatbelt.

"Camera first?"

"Oh. Right." I leaned forward to turn on the GoPro mounted on our dash and hit record. "Rolling!" I said.

"Good morning," Heath began.

We hadn't really decided what the documentary would be about yet. We'd discussed it, but all we'd come up with was that I would film Heath while he worked each job. We weren't going into it with some kind of predetermined story or hypothesis about work across the country or the people we would interact with (though we'd already been asked about it).

I think in a lot of ways our goal was more internal than external. We weren't trying to make some big impactful documentary to wow the world. Inwardly, we just wanted to prove to ourselves that we were capable of breaking out of our bubble and doing something different. What would different mean for us? I still had no clue. The documentary and RV were a start.

But I wasn't un-stapling papers anymore. I wasn't sitting behind a computer in an empty office binging on dark chocolate. I was moving. We were moving. Somewhere. As a team.

Heath started the engine and drove toward the parking lot

exit while telling the camera all about his upcoming job and how nervous he was.

"No left turn," Heath muttered, stopping at a one-way service road. The highway we needed was above us. A minor inconvenience my Google Maps app should've alerted me to, but I did only look briefly. He turned right out of Walmart and drove half a mile down the road to an intersection so he could pull a wide U-turn and take the ramp up to the highway.

Making U-turns in a 29-foot vehicle isn't easy. Actually, impossible is a better word. You're better off not even trying. Turn as he tried, we ended up in the far right lane, missed the ramp, and found ourselves stuck on the service road. At least we were heading in the right direction now.

"Maybe there will be another ramp," I offered, maintaining optimism and quietly accepting the undeniable fact that we would be late to our first job. But quickly the service road ended at the interstate, forced us to head north, and in seconds we were out of the city altogether. Heath grew quieter, and the camera rolled on.

After two long miles, we finally hit an exit. Heath slowed, stopped at the red light, turned left, stopped at the next red light, turned left, and entered the interstate again. By the time we finally made it to the same road we started on—this time up the ramp and driving the right direction—ten minutes had passed.

"So where is this place?" Heath asked, surveying large parking lots and strip malls.

"Oh! Right," I opened Google Maps again. Because I smartly closed the app to save data, I had to open Facebook again and re-type in the address while Heath sputtered down the road.

"Huh. That's weird," I thought out loud.

"What?"

"It's telling me to make a U-turn."

"You have got to be kidding me."

"I'm just following the GPS!"

Heath grunted in annoyance, pulled into a left turn lane, and attempted another U-turn. He couldn't quite swing into the right lane of traffic and ended up in a gas station parking lot.

"Wait," I said as Heath began to merge with traffic and my phone began recalculating directions. This was it. We'd been married for what…eight days? But this was where our marriage was going to end. Heath would kill me. "Um okay, so now it's telling me to U-turn again."

"THAT'S IT. GIVE ME THE PHONE." Heath shouted.

"Don't get mad at me! It's not my fault the GPS doesn't know where it's going! I'm just reading out what it says!"

Heath snatched my phone from my hands, pinching the screen and moving it around. I suddenly remembered the GoPro capturing every beautiful moment of our drive and made eye contact with the lens. I can read a map. This is not my fault, I wanted to tell the camera. So far if there was a theme for our documentary, it would be "newlywed couple fights over GPS while driving 29-foot RV down the highway." Not sure this would make for quality cinema.

"Okay, I have to go left out of here." A concrete barrier blocked him from turning left out of the gas station so he pulled out to the right, took the next left turn lane, and U-turned again with a little help from an empty parking lot. Three completely silent minutes later, he pulled into the left turn lane just past a new strip mall and made one final U-turn since there wasn't a left turn lane into the parking lot.

For those of you keeping track at home, that was four U-turns in under 20 minutes. Five if you count the very long round trip detour down the interstate.

Heath pulled into the parking lot and took up four spots in the back away from the storefronts. He threw the RV in park and sighed with relief. We were fifteen minutes late, but we made it.

"Let's have a good day?" Heath asked in an attempt to wipe away our GPS squabbles and move forward together.

"Let's have a good day." I unbuckled and kissed the top of Heath's head as I stood up and stepped into our house from the cab. Hoisting the camera bag on my shoulder, I took a deep breath. The bag was loaded with extra batteries and a chest mount for the GoPro, which I looked over to see Heath removing from the dash mount.

I had one strategy for my first day of filming: get everything. My theory was that if I had 12 hours of footage, all of it couldn't be bad, right? Most of it, definitely. But not all. I spent a couple of hours earlier in our week practicing with the camera. I could zoom in and out and make sure audio was recording. From what I could gather, that was all you really needed to know how to do. Well, that and pressing the record button. That was easy. How obvious would it be to everyone we were about to meet that I'd never filmed anything in my entire life? Not too obvious, I hoped.

I lifted the heavy camera out of the bag. No turning back now. (Wait, were all five of those U-turns missed chances to turn back?)

"Okay, let's start with me walking out the door and locking up the RV, and then you can follow me into the dojo," Heath directed.

"And after you close the door, maybe tell me what we're doing today. Since you got cut off earlier while we were driving." And busy making consistent U-turns.

We handled each other with the quiet professionalism of two people frustrated at how the day started but forced to jump right into filming since we were already late.

"Got it."

We climbed out of the RV and I got into position. The morning sun blinded me as I squinted into the camera's eyepiece. I shuffled my feet from side to side trying to frame up the perfect shot of Heath and our RV.

Heath closed the door, locked it, and turned to the camera with his mouth open. He paused.

"Sorry, let me try that again," he murmured, nervously shaking his head. He fiddled with the keys, opened the door, and closed it again. This time he turned with a smile on his face. "I'm Heath Padgett and I'm about to work my first job as part of *Hourly America*. Let's go!" The words sounded confident and cheesy, but his body language was all nerves. I was grateful to be behind the camera lens where my nerves remained hidden and not permanently committed to film.

I followed Heath down the sidewalk past glass windows and doors advertising daycare centers and music lessons. Heath glanced over his shoulder, smiled at me, and took an audible deep breath. Opening the door, he stepped in confidently and then stopped short. I bumped the camera square into his back.

"Oh. My bad. Sorry!" Heath called out to a yoga class.

"Wrong business," he laughed, turning to address the camera. Two doors down, a gleaming glass door said "Project Dojo" and three adults in martial arts gis stood waiting.

Nothing like starting the day by apologizing to three black belts.

Heath opened the glass door and extended his hand in greeting. With my eyes glued to the camera screen, I failed to notice that Heath was no longer holding the door open and it closed on my face. I startled, using my foot to eek the door open enough to squeeze in while keeping the camera trained on Heath.

Note to self: research how camera people make it through doors without getting smacked in the face.

"Travis? Good morning. I'm so sorry we are late guys. We got a little lost," Heath was saying during the first physical fight of the day—me and the door. I saw Travis, his wife, and his real assistant sensei all nervously make eye contact with the camera in my hands. Should I tell them not to look at the lens? With my eye pressed to the viewfinder, I watched them stare down the camera straight into my soul.

"No worries, it happens to the best of us," Travis said, regaining my attention and reminding me to keep the camera steady on this interaction.

Travis, his wife, and his assistant sensei wore all black, reminding me that they were extremely skilled in taekwondo. But they were all smiles and seemed excited for us to spend the day with them. The quiet dojo was one large open room covered mostly with blue mats with a line of plastic chairs up against the wall where I assumed parents could watch the class, or where I could sit out of the way to film.

"So what I'm thinking for today is we have a few classes for kids this afternoon and then an adult class tonight that I would love for you to join. I'll just take you through basically what any of our days look like with cleaning the dojo and getting it ready and then you can help me teach the classes this afternoon," Travis said.

"Sounds great. I've actually never done taekwondo before though, so I don't know if I can really teach anything."

Travis clasped his hand on Heath's shoulder. "Hey, the first class is a bunch of four and five-year-olds. You'll pick it up fast. Now let's get you into a gi."

Chapter 8

The good kind of tired.

That's how Heath described his first day once we drove our RV back to the campground and the A/C cooled us off. We left the RV park 14 hours earlier and finally could crash after a long day. Or in Heath's case, ice everything on his body after being kicked for the past four hours. Those kids were small but mighty.

We never stopped moving all day long. Heath cleaned the dojo, interviewed the employees, and helped stuff envelopes for an upcoming mailer. Before classes started, Travis took us around to all the other local studios in town to meet their owners—including a 70-year-old sensei who was equally frail and intimidating. The man commanded reverence and also commanded that I turn the camera off. I nearly dropped it; I was so startled by his firm demand.

The day ended with Heath holding up a body shield mat and letting kids kick him over and over. At one point, Travis demonstrated a kick for the kids and Heath fell backward on his butt from the force. The kids burst out laughing. Watching Heath work was infinitely more entertaining than I thought. I was a little unsure of how filming this unexpected documentary would go and if it would distract from the adventure of traveling. But so far it seemed like the best way for us to meet interesting people and try new things. I had experienced more interesting and new things in one day than I had in the seven months I lived in New Orleans. We both ended the day sore and sweating.

"I think I'm going to shower in here tonight," I told Heath. It was nearly ten o'clock and I'd only showered in RV park showers so far, but never so late at night.

"Ooh your first RV shower. I'm so proud of you," Heath teased, turning on the hot water heater.

Should I have tried the RV shower before we left Texas? Maybe. Heath did, so we knew the hot water worked. You just needed to give it a few minutes to warm up. Heath also learned during his first shower in the RV that the grey tank offers a finite amount of space. He forgot the tank was closed and flooded the whole RV...the day after we installed new flooring. Water was bubbling up from the shower drain and spilling over onto the shiny new floors while Heath tried to pull on clothes so he didn't have to run outside naked to hook up our sewer hose.

The shower itself was a little dingy, but not terrible. The walls were yellow plastic, but a shade of yellow where you knew it used to be white a couple decades ago. I wasn't avoiding our shower, I just...okay I was avoiding it a little.

I waited a few minutes before hopping in and turning on the

water, but I shrieked and quickly dove out of the steady stream of ice water and onto our bed.

"It's freezing," I screeched at Heath, who couldn't stop laughing.

"Turn the water off and wait a few more minutes. It just takes time."

I shivered in a towel and waited ten more minutes for the water to warm up.

My back ached and my feet throbbed from running around with the heavy camera all day. I didn't need a FitBit to tell me I hit my 10K steps following Heath around the dojo. When was the last time I worked this hard? My brain hadn't stopped running since I woke up. I learned five new settings on the camera and filmed our first-ever interviews for the documentary. Of course, I had completely forgotten that Snagajob shipped us a tripod, so I sat on the ground and balanced the camera on my knees for the whole interview. This is how professional documentarians do it, right?

When *was* the last time I worked this hard? I couldn't even pick out a week in college that challenged me as much physically and mentally as one day as a documentarian. (Or is it filmmaker? Producer? Can I oust Heath and claim the title of director?)

Heath was right about the good tired thing. My body screamed in protest, but I still felt proud. Up until this point, the most physical activity I'd accomplished was a tough mudder. A couple of girls I'd met in New Orleans signed me up before I could realize what I'd committed to—running a 5K through mud and obstacles. Who comes up with this stuff? It was the first and last time I ever ran anywhere and I didn't move the rest of the day. But I still felt accomplished after doing something so completely out of my comfort zone.

I think that's how our days are meant to be spent. Not running, for goodness sake. That's legalized torture. Our days are meant to push us and mold us into a better version of ourselves.

And the new version of Alyssa really needed a shower.

This time I tested the shower water before hopping in. Admittedly, jumping in without testing the water first was a rookie mistake. The water had warmed up significantly and I stepped happily into the steam hoping the hot water would relieve my aching muscles. It was scalding hot, actually. Good Lord, I'd been in there for 15 seconds and I looked like a lobster. I hid in the corner of the shower—if you can even call it a corner because the water was still attacking me as I tried to save my body from the liquid fire and figure out which 20-year-old, faded nozzle controlled the hot water.

The A/C unit, unwisely located directly next to the shower, blew on full blast, freezing whatever exposed skin wasn't under attack by the boiling water pummeling me from the showerhead. It's not often you shiver and feel like your skin is on fire at the same time. The only thing protecting me from the onslaught of icy air was a formerly white shower curtain that...oh my gosh...is the shower curtain touching my leg right now 20 years old? I shivered.

Finally, I turned the heat down enough to step into the water and get my hair wet. I struggled to wash my hair in the small space. No wonder so many people asked me if I was going to cut my long hair before we moved into the RV. All of my hair could barely fit under the stream of water. I was showering in a Tic Tac carton. I added and rinsed shampoo, failing to get all the bubbles out before Heath started complaining.

"You're taking too long!" He whined.

"It's been three minutes!"

"I need to shower, too. You're running us out of hot water!"

"I'm putting in conditioner!" Sheesh. "One more minute!"

I lathered my hair in conditioner, adding it to the remaining shampoo I hadn't had the chance to fully rinse out of my hair. I felt the water slowly drop in temperature and tried to hurry up and get all the soap out. I hopped out just in time for the hot water to run out—which took all of about five minutes total.

Where was that rejuvenated and relaxed feeling I used to have getting out of the shower after a long day? Instead, the A/C was still on full blast, so my still bright red skin froze as soon I stepped out. It didn't help that in order to get out of the shower, I had to climb over our laundry basket, which could only fit right outside the shower door, and then had to squeeze past Heath who was inconveniently standing by the bed waiting for his turn to shower.

"Turn off the air! I'm an icicle!" I begged Heath, diving onto the bed as my only way to vacate the tiny hallway. "Never again," I declared. "It's too small to clean yourself," I whined.

"I can fit in there just fine," Heath countered.

"Are you calling me fat?" I've found that when I ask this question, Heath always rolls his eyes and laughs awkwardly because men don't really know how to recover from that question and any potential argument dissipates. It's really come in handy.

I dried off my skin while Heath undressed and turned on the

showerhead to see if I left him any warm water. I did not. Ten minutes to warm up, five minutes to run out.

And that's when it happened.

The biggest, most terrifying spider of all time stood directly between me and my clothes.

Okay, in reality, the spider was maybe the size of a nickel and it was on the window shade *next* to my underwear drawer, but by the way I screamed and pointed, I'm sure Heath thought I spotted a tarantula in our bed.

To fully set the scene, we were at a quaint RV park on the outskirts of Albuquerque and we almost didn't get a campsite because the park was so full. We hadn't yet learned the need for advanced reservations. It was a beautiful night after the sunset and the air cooled. People were outside laughing and roasting s'mores over campfires and enjoying summer camping trips with their families.

Inside our RV, however, I'm shrieking, "Kill it! Kill it!" and Heath has a panic-stricken look on his face as he searches around for something, anything to annihilate the spider with. But he was already halfway in the shower, completely naked with the water already running. I tossed him my towel to smack the spider to death but it had no effect on the ferocious beast.

"Get me a shoe!"

I opened the closet door next to me, picked up a flip-flop with two fingers, as if it were somehow contaminated by the spider, and tossed it to Heath.

Heath, with years of baseball under his belt, swings that flip flop with all his might, presumably killing the spider instantly. But, at that moment, the spider was the least of our worries.

He hit the window shade where the spider was residing with so much force that it immediately retracted. It just rolled right on up to the top of the window. Which is what it's supposed to do, but our bedroom windows started at knee height and went all the way to the ceiling. Trust me when I say they were not tinted. They were not tinted AT ALL.

So when the shade rolled up, there we were.

Completely naked.

For all our neighbors to see.

Standing in shock in front of a very open window.

It was completely dark outside. Every light in the bedroom was turned on. It's not like a normal house where there's furniture to hide behind in this sort of situation. And RVs are all squished together in RV parks. There's no way people can't see us and there is no conceivable way of reaching over to close the window without climbing over the bed and giving everyone a *really* good show.

It was like an uncensored episode of *Naked and Afraid*. Except our fear wasn't dying in the wilderness, just dying of embarrassment.

I shrieked and hit the ground. Heath army crawled over to the window and reached his fingertips up to pull down the shade while the lukewarm water ran out in the still-running shower.

And that was the first and last time I showered in our RV.

Chapter 9

Heath's second job and my second day of filming were much less eventful (and less painful) than the first. He worked an easy four-hour lunch shift at a Buffalo Wild Wings in Prescott, Arizona, a small town with big trees that somehow didn't give off that expected Arizona-desert vibe. It was a weekday, so the work was slow and we spent most of the day making friends with the wait staff.

When Heath agreed to do 50 jobs across the country, there wasn't a real rhyme or reason to what jobs he would do. He just thought it would be a fun, push your comfort zone kind of project. When Snagajob came along, they decided that Heath would work only hourly jobs, since that's what their job board consisted of. Minimum wage jobs come to mind when you say hourly, but there are a ton of other hourly jobs that fit the bill like lawyers and electricians. We were only two days in, but Heath was already loving being behind the scenes at different businesses.

We had also quickly established a little routine for each job:

- Introduce ourselves.
- Share what we're working on and fumble over words trying to describe our brand new project while skipping over the part where we share that we have a grand total of two days of filming experience...ever.
- Film Heath working.
- Make all the employees slightly uncomfortable because I'm following them around with a camera.
- Interview Heath's co-workers.
- Get everyone to sign film waivers saying we could include their faces and stories in our film.

My film skills were subpar, but after our second job, I was beginning to feel more confident about our documentary. Heath and I worked together better than I thought we might, and we moved in sync through the restaurant as I followed him with the camera.

As soon as Heath's lunch shift was over, we drove the RV straight to Walmart for the oil change we forgot to do after buying the rig. We shopped for groceries while the mechanics worked, a brilliant way to take advantage of being kicked out of your house for an hour. In no time, the RV was packed and ready to hit the road for our first national park—the Grand Canyon. You can't go on an RV trip out west without stopping at the Grand Canyon. It's a rite of passage. Plus, it's one of the seven wonders of the world and one of the most popular national parks in the country. Skipping it would cause a national uproar.

I bounced in my seat, giddy with excitement. Heath and I both had visited New Mexico multiple times growing up, but Arizona was a total mystery to me. I gazed out the windows soaking up the endless red views. I'd never been much of a desert person. Blame it on the dry air that's given me three nose bleeds already. But the constant views of jagged red rocks and distant mountains had me captivated.

With our late afternoon departure, we hoped to hit the Canyon right at sunset, camp overnight, and drive the rim north toward Utah in the morning. Arizona was different than I pictured it. In my mind, I saw endless flat dirt punctuated by Saguaro cacti. Instead, Heath drove us over mountains and past red rocks as we cruised down exit 163 to head north into the national park.

I snapped my gaze away from the window when Heath stopped suddenly.

"Dude. It's green. Why did you just stop in the middle of the intersection? You're blocking traffic." I looked at him confused.

"The pedal is on the floor right now... I think we just died." Heath's eyes were wide and I hoped he was joking. But the engine was eerily silent.

He turned off the engine and restarted the RV. Pedal to the metal, we jostled about ten feet forward and barely turned right into a parking lot before the car's engine dwindled down to its imminent death.

Heath turned over the engine again when I pointed at the meter on the dash with the picture of an oilcan sitting far past low. Not that I had any idea what it meant, but being in the red looked bad.

"Seriously? Walmart changed our oil and checked our fluids not even an hour ago," Heath lamented.

Curse you Walmart! And I was just praising your convenience.

I hopped out of the RV to follow Heath to the engine and met eyes with a girl standing next to her car with her arms crossed in frustration. A man was bent over messing with her back tire. Just beyond them, I noticed a familiar sign.

By the grace of God, we died in a mechanic's parking lot…at 4:45 PM on a Friday night. A friendly mechanic saw us and walked over to see if we needed help. He climbed into our RV, cranked the engine, pressed the pedal, and instantly knew the problem.

"It's your fuel pump."

Now I don't know much about cars, but I know they need fuel. So this pump kind of sounded essential. Sitting on the couch behind the driver's seat, I watched the mechanic turn over the engine seven times to make it from where we broke down to the service bay doors. Apparently, the initial jolt of starting the engine could push you forward 20 feet before dying and repeating the process.

"I'll have to see what type of pump this thing takes. In the newer ones, you have to replace the whole thing, but on old ones like this, sometimes you can just replace the one piece that isn't working," the young mechanic explained. "It's much cheaper that way. We'll work on it tomorrow morning."

The fact that there was a "much cheaper" option told me that no matter what, we were spending a few hundred bucks in the next 24 hours—if not more.

"Tomorrow morning?" Heath asked, glancing over his shoulder at me. "We need a place to stay tonight." And we can't drive anywhere.

"Just stay here," the mechanic suggested gesturing toward the parking lot which doubled as a fill-up station. Heath and I looked at each other and shrugged. This was definitely going to be the most expensive campsite outside the Grand Canyon once we got the mechanic's bill, but it beat being homeless for the night. The mechanic checked a few things on the engine to confirm it was the fuel pump while Heath and I paced in the shade of the building fanning ourselves with our hands in futility.

"At least we broke down at a mechanic? That's lucky." I suggested to Heath, saying the words but not really feeling them. Sure, breaking down in the desert without cell signal and trying to get a tow would've been worse. Do you need a special tow truck to pick up an RV of this size? Probably, I thought. At this rate, I wasn't confident that the RV could actually make it across the country, so I should probably look that up.

"Can you imagine? This is the first town we've seen in over an hour and cell service was spotty at best," Heath pointed out. "We could be on the side of the interstate right now, so that's something."

"That's something," I agreed, fanning my face in the shade. I inhaled deeply and closed my eyes. I have a place to sleep tonight. The RV is an easy fix. Two states down, 48 to go. We can still totally make it without going broke and ending up parking in my parents' driveway casually asking what they are making for dinner as a strategy to save on buying our own food. I feebly tried to reassure myself.

Done with his assessment and confident he had the parts for the job, the mechanic walked over and offered to move the RV into the shade for us. "You can't block the bay doors overnight," he explained. He hopped into the driver's seat and cranked on the engine, slowly backing up, then re-cranking on the engine to pull forward, and finally after five attempts pulled the RV 100 feet away.

Heath and I opened all the windows to let in some air, but at 5:00 PM in the Arizona desert, it was triple digits inside the RV. Heath sank into one of our chairs and I laid down on the couch.

"It's a little setback, and we knew it was going to happen. Well, we didn't know *this* would happen. But we knew this RV would probably break down on us at least once," Heath said.

I nodded in agreement, too exhausted from the stress and the heat to make conversation.

The atomic clock that came with the RV let us know it was 106° inside. We spent every night on the road at an RV park with electrical hookups and our A/C unit on high. This was our first night without any of that. While Instagram showed us that you could theoretically camp from anywhere, we didn't grasp the particulars of how this worked yet. Would our food stay cold in the refrigerator? How do you run your air conditioning if it's this hot and you don't have electrical hookups? I at least knew about the onboard water tank now.

"I'm going to lay down for a sec," Heath said, getting up and collapsing on the bed. "I need to clear my head and cool off."

"Go for it," I replied, although internally I wondered how laying in bed would cool him off. Until the sun sank over the horizon, we were living in a sauna. "I'll start a quick dinner." I grabbed a pot from under our oven to boil water and felt the *chug, chug, chug* of our water pump. The water from our tank was practically bathtub temperature so dinner would cook fast. A small perk of desert life, I noted. I placed the pot on the back left burner and grabbed our lighter, flicking it on before pressing and turning the knob to HI.

I pulled out a skillet to brown some ground turkey meat for spaghetti when Heath grumbled from the bed.

"It is not going to get any cooler in here if we have fires blazing. Can we *please* eat out?"

I looked at my husband's pleading eyes and sweating brow. I knew every moment of this trip wasn't going to be fun. We weren't going on a seven-month vacation, despite what responsible adults may have thought. This was a radical lifestyle change. One that had already pushed us out of our comfort zone in 74 different ways and would change the way we approach problems.

The answer to Heath's question was no.

No way we can afford that.

We can't even afford whatever this fuel pump is going to cost us, and I have a feeling it's going to be a lot.

But ten days into RV life and two weeks into marriage, there was something about my husband's plea (or maybe the impending heatstroke) that led me to turn off the stove, toss our groceries back in the fridge, linger slightly in the refreshing cool air of the refrigerator, and gladly accept Heath's invitation to go out for the night. Sometimes you just need to cut your losses and get some fresh air.

The tiny town of Williams, Arizona doesn't have much to offer, but its small size meant we walked easily from the mechanic's shop to the town center. We walked hand in hand past a green baseball field until we heard live music coming from a little cantina. We grabbed a table and ordered chips and queso—a comfort food we often enjoyed back in Austin—when the couple at the table next to us struck up a conversation.

This was the first of many times we would have to explain our fifty-state adventure to total strangers.

It went a little something like this:

"So we, uh, we were working office jobs and didn't really like it and didn't know what we wanted to do with our lives so we just decided to quit our jobs and visit all fifty states and make a documentary where I work a job in each state and Alyssa is filming it."

"And your first job was at a dojo? I run a dojo in town," our new friend Jimmy exclaimed after Heath spilled our whole story. "Y'all ought to come by! I'll let you break your first boards."

Of all the people to sit down next to in the small town of Williams, we happened to sit next to a couple who owned the local dojo. I'm not sure how or why, but in some ways, it felt like kismet. Ten minutes earlier, we were on the verge of a mental breakdown to accompany our actual breakdown. I was questioning whether this was all a mistake. Before we could accept their response, Jimmy and his wife Karen insisted on buying us a round of beers to celebrate our new union and our road trip.

There's something about the kindness of strangers in moments like this that gives me so much faith in humanity. This couple didn't know us. They didn't care where we came from or what we believed. They just sent their positive energy and good vibes to us when we really needed it. We left dinner feeling encouraged. We hadn't made the wrong decision. This was just a bump in the road. We'd figure this out.

Heath and I decided to say yes during this journey. The point of this trip wasn't to be comfortable but to be pushed. This meant that if strangers invited us to their dojo and a mechanic offered to let us sleep in his parking lot, the answer was yes. We got directions from Jimmy to his dojo—just two blocks away—and promised to come by in the morning. We would be in class with a bunch of kids, but we were used to that by now. Plus, breaking something by kicking it really hard sounded like the kind of stress reliever I needed.

We walked home from the restaurant—home is where you park it, as they say—and climbed into the RV with the sun low in the sky. Despite the temps dropping outside, it was still 106° inside. Too hot to even lay down on top of the bed without sweating. After a quick "What are we going to do? It's too hot to sleep in here! Also are we sure it's safe to sleep at this gas station on the side of the interstate? What are we doing with our lives?! This was a terrible idea!" downward spiral of a conversation, Heath interrupted my sweating.

"You know what? When I got our RV insurance, Good Sam said part of the full-time RV insurance policy was a $500 allowance for staying at a hotel if the RV ever broke down and we needed a place to stay. I think this counts," Heath remembered.

There are moments when you just know you married the right person. This was one of those moments.

"You call the insurance company; I'll call the Ramada down the street. And I'll see if they have laundry. We haven't washed clothes since Texas."

With my clothes in the washing machine, my house in the shop, and my hair wet from taking a gloriously long and temperature-consistent shower, Heath and I stepped into the Arizona sun ready to kick things.

I'm not sure the exact terminology you use to denote the beginning of a fight. You tip-off in basketball, kick-off in football, tee-off in golf. But kick things sounded pretty accurate for taekwondo, based on my one day of witnessing classes.

On our way to the dojo, we swung by the mechanic and confirmed that our RV would be ready to go soon. He promised we would be on our way by lunchtime so we continued a few more blocks until we spotted the open-air dojo.

Karen greeted us excitedly. Jimmy had already begun class, so she found us gloves and showed us where to leave our shoes. Heath fit in perfectly, matching all the kids in the gi he was gifted from his first job while I wore my one clean pair of athletic shorts and a tank top since my laundry tumbled in the washing machine back at the hotel.

We spent the next twenty minutes learning how to disarm someone if they grab your wrist or grab you from behind. We had fun even though we were two feet taller than everyone else learning with us. So far, our entire amateur martial arts experience involved fighting little kids. Easy stuff.

Finally, the moment arrived. Time to break stuff. Jimmy explained that we would break these boards with the step sidekick we just mastered (if you consider ten kicks into the air mastery, that is).

"To break the board, first you take your step, lift your leg and extend in a slow kick barely tapping your foot to the board," Jimmy demonstrated as he spoke. "Then you repeat the slow motion again, getting a feel for the movement. And third, use everything we learned today to kick the board and break it."

He made it sound easy, but he was holding a large, thick piece of wood. I had Heath take the lids off pasta sauce jars for me. How was Jimmy so confident that I could even break this board?

Heath went first. Slow movement, slow movement, kick. With all his force, he went a little high and knocked the corner of the board with his heel and almost kicked Jimmy's hand.

"Ah, try again," Jimmy encouraged.

Shaking it off, Heath tried again, this time with more focus in his eyes. Practice, practice, kick. Still a little high and to the left, but this time the board broke in two. Everyone cheered. Karen grabbed the two board pieces and wrote Heath's name and the date noting his feat.

Now it was my turn. I was nervous, but Heath took a bit of the pressure off of me by going first and missing his first attempt. I lifted my right leg and extended it, tapping the ball and heel of my foot to the wood. I could feel my heartbeat pulsing in my ears. *Would this give me splinters? And also why is doing this barefoot common practice? This makes no sense.*

But everyone in the class was watching me so instead of stalling and questioning my sensei, I stepped and cautiously lifted my foot repeating the motion.

The extent of my physical activity over the last year had mostly involved making the bold decision to walk to the mailboxes from my apartment instead of driving. Now, I was standing in a room full of strangers about to kick a board that

I was very positive would not break under the pressure of my size six foot. Is this a normal thing that happens when you start traveling? You end up being invited to break a board by complete strangers and hope to not embarrass yourself?

Before my final kick, a thought popped in my head.

During class, Jimmy talked about our breath and how we should exhale with each kick we practiced. Release your breath as you extend your leg, he coached. This would give us more strength in our kicks and conserve our energy.

I thought about our broken-down RV, the heat, the fact that we were already behind schedule, and how much every day we traveled was costing us. Not to mention how much I would need to pay a mechanic in a couple of hours. And that we were certainly going to run out of money before making it to all fifty states and had zero leads on how to make money on the road... I could feel the tension building in my shoulders as my list of worries grew.

I needed to release more than just my breath. Stress was going to hold me back from enjoying our travels if I let it. I felt like what Jimmy was nudging me toward when he said to release my breath was to release all the pressure I was putting on myself to make this trip happen without incident. That was impossible—travel came with unexpected mishaps. That's part of what makes life on the road interesting. But bottling up all that stress wasn't going to make life on the road any easier. I was ready to release all of that frustration into the exact center of that board and listen to the satisfying snap.

I took a deep breath, lifted my leg, and with all my strength kicked that board. With a loud crack, it busted in two and the crowd cheered. It felt good, cathartic even. Heath and I placed so much pressure on ourselves to make this trip a success to prove to everyone that we could do this. Confronting hiccups on the road was just part of what RV life was about, I was learning. On the road, you adapt. You enjoy the journey. You accept new opportunities as they come to you, like breaking a board in front of tiny strangers.

I felt good. Stronger, yet lighter. This journey would not be easy, but easy wasn't what I wanted anymore.

Heath wrapped his arm around me in a side hug while Karen handed me two nearly identical boards. *1st board stepping side kick 6/7/14,* it read.

We thanked Jimmy and Karen for the class and walked back to the hotel, boards in hand.

"That was so good," I told Heath.

"It was! And so random. There's no way it would've happened if we hadn't broken down, you know?" replied Heath with a smile, glistening with sweat in the sun. Maybe we weren't crazy. Maybe this was just another test for us as a couple to help us prove to ourselves what we are capable of.

"Right. That. But I was talking about breaking the boards. It's good to know that I'm a much better kicker than you."

Heath laughed. "I don't know about that!"

But there are pictures. I can prove it.

Chapter 10

$631.87 lighter, we started our engine, shifted into reverse, and backed out of the mechanic's parking lot. We only had to turn the engine on once this time as we pulled easily onto the highway en route to the Grand Canyon.

I flipped through the pages of the atlas we purchased at Walmart while Heath drove us north. Tracing the roads with my finger, it looked like we would enter at Mather Point. This was apparently the go-to spot for taking the best pictures of the canyon, even if we would be arriving at lunchtime instead of sunset as we planned. Jimmy gave us our first travel tip from a local letting us know the best way to see the Grand Canyon was to drive east along the rim and up to the north side. Much less crowded, he said. Jimmy was both a wise dojo leader and travel guide. A Swiss army knife of a human being really.

Endless desert stretched on either side of the RV as we drove north from the mechanic shop toward one of the most visited national parks in the world. Well, almost endless desert. We passed a ten-foot-tall Fred Flinstone and replica Bedrock that had us scratching our heads at the roadside attraction in the middle of nowhere. *Mental note: Google why this is here once we have cell data again.*

We had barely been on the road for over a week, but we were out of data on our hotspot already. Heath accidentally synced all of the GoPro footage from his first day of work from the camera to his phone over our data, effectively zapping all 10 gigs we had for the month. We had three weeks of no data until our data cap reset, plus exorbitant overage fees and a new $5 fee each month that would automatically turn off our data so Heath couldn't go over again.

No data, no car, hefty mechanic bill. So far our first 10 days of RV life were off to a pretty stellar start. At least we hadn't flashed everyone in the campground. Oh, wait...

Using the shiny new national parks pass we picked up in New Mexico, we showed our card and driver's license at the gate and pat ourselves on the back for avoiding the $30 entrance fee. At that rate, we only needed to visit two other national parks to pay off the $80 pass and start saving money.

Parking in the crowded RV section, we grabbed gelato sandwiches from our freezer to cool off—leftovers from our wedding a lifetime ago and a reminder that choosing gelato instead of a wedding cake was our first brilliant decision as a married couple. Then we began the hike from the parking lot to the rim.

Walking toward the rim of the canyon, I stood on my tiptoes anxious to glimpse the deep canyon I knew was ahead. This world wonder was only a thousand miles away my whole life and here I finally was. Crowds of people overtook the walking paths and stomped around or on plants. A cacophony of languages rang out all around. German, French, Spanish, Japanese—I think actual Americans visiting this wonder in their own backyard represented less than 10% of the crowd.

Squat green trees lined the sidewalk blocking the view until suddenly the canyon appeared.

Grand really isn't the best word.

Massive?

Majestic?

Inspiring?

Unreal?

Grand is too subtle.

For miles, layers of red rock stretched downward into the deep canyon. A few voices around me noted the river at the base of the canyon, but I could barely make it out in the distance. The canyon is too vast. Tourists with selfie sticks climbed down the stairs to the wide viewing platform and posed in front of the endless landscape. Just ahead, a long skinny bridge of rock tempted brave souls to cross under the safety rails and take pictures on the edge.

I stood at the top of the steps taking in the scene. There is a reason millions of people flock here year after year. Something about the color and the expanse of the canyon rooted me in place. I snapped a picture with my phone and shook my head at the image. It didn't capture half of the majesty in front of me. The colors were so much brighter. The rocks more imposing. It was a kind of beauty that couldn't be captured on screen. It needed to be experienced.

Heath grabbed my hand and led me away from the crowded Mather Point down the rim trail. After a few minutes, we found a quiet dirt trail through some trees that ended on flat white rock. I peered over the edge at the tumbling rocks and felt Heath wrap an arm around my waist.

"Not too close! I don't want you to fall."

I laughed. "You know, you're going to make one heck of a helicopter parent someday."

Heath shrugged and kept his arm wrapped tightly around my waist and his eyes on the horizon.

I knew I wanted to travel when I sat at my desk job back in New Orleans. I scrolled for hours through Pinterest oohing and ahhing over the beautiful places in the world that I could only see through pictures, pinning them to a dream board and wondering if I would ever make it to all of them…any of them. Travel always felt so unattainable. It required money and time—two things I didn't have.

Or at least I didn't think I had both of them.

One of the quotes Heath brought up on several occasions as we explained our trip to our friends and family was this idea that there is never a perfect time to travel. It went something like this: When you're young, you have the time and energy to travel, but often not the means. When you're middle-aged, you have the means and the energy, but not the time. When you're old, you have the time and the means, but not the energy. No matter when you decide to go, there will never be a perfect moment and always some sort of sacrifice.

I was beginning to recognize the truth in this. Heath and I had time and energy. We just didn't have all the money set aside that traveling required. Would it be better to wait until we had kids and ten years of work under our belt and try to squeeze it in then? Or perhaps after retiring from a long career? Maybe.

The risk now is that we look irresponsible, and the sacrifice is not being able to travel as comfortably as we'd like. But the risk in putting it off is that it might never happen—sacrificing the chance to chase our dreams.

Looking out over the beauty of the Grand Canyon, I began to feel that the risk of waiting was greater than most people realize.

I'm not sure how long we stood there listening to the wind whistle through the canyon before more hikers happened upon us. We asked them to take our picture and we took theirs, as I would learn is the custom at all national parks.

We walked the rim a little longer before making it back to the RV, deciding to take Jimmy's advice and find a way to see the canyon without the crowds.

"Basically, it's this road until it ends, then turn left," I instructed Heath as we turned onto highway 64 heading east. "Just two roads the whole way."

"Easy," Heath said from behind the wheel. I'd driven the RV a few times, but by default, he always climbed in the driver's seat and I played navigator. I'm not sure how he let me keep that title after the U-turn fiasco, but that was firmly in the past. I had paper maps, a GPS, and Google Maps as a backup. Between the three, I was confident I could at least get us across the country with our marriage intact while Heath cruised the roads.

Clearly not hearing my mental confidence in his driving, Heath slammed on the brakes in the middle of the road.

"Ah!" I screamed looking up from the atlas.

"Look look look!" Heath shouted as a large animal bounded across the road into the soaring pine trees.

"Dang it," I said, fumbling with the GoPro mounted on our dash. "I couldn't hit the record button in time. Were those deer or elk? They were huge!"

"I don't know, but I'm going to take this drive extra slow. Just in case there are more." I shook my head thinking about how Heath slammed on the brakes during our test drive of the RV. Turned out it was a good idea to make sure our brakes worked well.

We wove through a forest of tall pines, catching glimpses of red canyon every hundred yards, and parking at every scenic overlook to soak up a new angle of the canyon, each one just as awe-inspiring and humbling as the last. Soon the national park ended and gave way to Navajo land. The rocks changed color from bright red to whites and blacks, but the canyon didn't end. Instead, we saw a small entrance off to the left with only a few tourists wandering around the open-air shops selling jewelry. If you thought the Grand Canyon was only a national park, you'd be wrong. Part of it is. This stretch of canyon, seemingly bottomless but echoing with the sound of rushing water, was on Navajo land outside the park boundary.

We paid a nominal entrance fee, pulled the RV up to the split rail fence, and opened our windows to see the unsung beauty of this part of the canyon. The gravel lot around us was almost empty with a peacefulness that you expect from spending time in nature—but that you won't find at the top of the national park. The beauty of some of the places we were only beginning to visit on the road, was that they were relatively inexpensive (or "free" since we paid for a national park pass). In our old life—which seems like longer than two weeks ago—a night out for Heath and I would consist of going to a restaurant or a movie and spending $50. Now, we were seeing some of the most beautiful views of our life for practically nothing.

We sat at our kitchen table, popping open a jar of salsa and a bag of tortilla chips to snack on while we stared out the window. We would've stayed longer if we could, but the sun was sinking and we still had over a hundred miles to the north side of the canyon. In RV time, that was well over two hours of driving left. Longer if we kept stopping to soak up this natural wonder, and we planned to soak it up as much as we could.

Who knew if we would ever get to come back here? I hoped we would. Maybe one day with our kids? Or on another trip when passing through? Even though we were just dipping our toes into this world of national parks and new places, a part of me hoped it wouldn't be a one-and-done road trip, but forever etched into the narrative of our lives like the water had carved its way through thousands of miles of red canyon. Lofty dreaming considering we weren't sure we could even afford to finish this trip.

Heath turned left out of the gravel lot and continued north along the highway. We quickly pulled away from the canyon and into a dirt valley with cliffs and mountains surrounding us on every side. The sparsely populated roads featured precariously placed boulders the size of our home and rocks so red they couldn't be real.

"Vermillion Cliffs, I think," I explained to Heath pointing

ahead at red rocks bathed in sunlight. "We should drive through them soon. Looks like we'll drive through Marble Canyon first. And maybe over the Colorado River," I added, squinting at the map as Heath continued driving us down the highway.

I looked at Heath singing along to country music as he drove with a big goofy smile on his face. I shuddered at the thought of where I would be right now without him. It was a Saturday, so I probably would be sitting on the couch in my apartment in New Orleans eating popcorn alone and watching TV. I like Netflix as much as anyone, but it doesn't compare to the life I was living now.

I remember someone asking me once how I knew Heath was "the one" and the answer was easy. Being with him pushes me to be the person I want to be. He makes me better, gets me off the couch, and empowers me to take crazy risks like this wild honeymoon. While it was technically my idea to visit all 50 states, I think in part I said it out loud because I knew Heath would say yes. He would take my idea and push me to make it a reality. We were only in state #2, but I felt confident with him by my side that there was no way we wouldn't make it to all fifty...even if it took replacing a hundred fuel pumps.

Suddenly, after hours of flat open roads, we ascended quickly. The sun dipped over a hill as we climbed switchbacks.

"Are we driving up a mountain right now?" I asked Heath.

"I think so. I mean, we're definitely going up fast. I didn't think there were mountains like this out here. The engine does not like it," he replied as I noticed headlights piling up behind us. The engine whined as we ascended. I sent up a silent prayer that the new fuel pump could keep up. There were no mechanic shops nearby this time if the engine broke down. We hadn't passed any towns for hours. If the engine died going up this mountain... In that case, we'd probably just start rolling backward down the mountain. And we would have no cell signal to even call for help. I consciously rubbed the armrest as if that would comfort the RV and encourage it to keep pushing through the pain to the top of this mountain.

We slowly climbed higher and higher until we found ourselves nearly in complete darkness in a forest of tall pine trees. A brown sign appeared with an arrow pointing left: "Grand Canyon National Park North Rim." We slowed to move into the left turn lane.

"Hey, wait! I think I see RVs right there," Heath pointed, stopping in the left turn lane while the cars who were stuck behind us blazed by.

I peered through the pines where Heath was pointing. A campground! Hidden in the forest. We couldn't see any signs, but we definitely saw the outline of campers and campfires. Heath pulled back onto the road and slowly crept forward looking for a sign or a way to enter the campground. A half-mile down the road we saw a small brown National Forest sign with a tent symbol.

Jacob Lake Campground. I couldn't see a lake, but then again it was 8:15 at night and we had to grab a flashlight to read the instructions on how to pay for a campsite. Slowly, Heath idled through the campground, but every campsite was taken. Families sat outside around campfires. Groups of men, who looked like they'd been hiking all week, laughed over beers. Since driving this route wasn't in our initial plan, we had no idea where we were going to sleep tonight. Plus, since we didn't have any cell signal all day long to look up our options, we were just driving in the hope of finding a place to stay before the sky darkened. That hope was rapidly dwindling.

"There was a Chevron gas station back where we were going to turn left. We can always stay there instead of driving any more mountain roads in the dark," Heath offered. "Oh wait! Is that a site?"

An unlevel gravel road barely the length of our RV looped off between two towering pines to form a campsite. At least, that's what it looked like. So far we'd only camped at RV parks and in Heath's granny's driveway. I hadn't the faintest idea what a national forest campsite looked like. Well, to be completely honest, I didn't know America even *had* national forests until we saw approximately 50 signs reminding us that we spent the day driving in and out of Kaibab National Forest land. Were they just like national parks with more trees? Should this place have been on my bucket list, or did we just uncover a hidden gem?

Heath maneuvered between the trees and parked the RV, barely fitting in off the road. We opened the doors to get ourselves set up.

"Oh my gosh, it's *cold*!" I exclaimed. According to the compass app on my phone, we climbed to 7,920 feet. I grabbed our atomic clock off the wall and brought it outside to check the temperature. The temps had easily dropped 40 degrees from the heat we experienced at the south rim. My tank top and athletic shorts were in no way fit for this mountain cold. Goosebumps raised on my legs. Goosebumps! In June! In Arizona!

"There's no electricity or water."

"What?" Heath's words snapped me out of my internal happy dance that we found relief from the sweltering heat.

"It's called dry camping, I think. So we need to use the pump if we want water—I think we still have some in there. I put some in at the last RV park, but that was two days ago now."

"How will we make coffee?" I asked. Since the heat in our broken-down RV drove us to a hotel last night, we didn't get any experience actually living in the RV without electricity. The lights worked and our fridge ran off of propane while we drove, but none of our outlets did. We couldn't charge our phones, camera batteries, laptops, anything.

But most importantly, coffee.

I don't know why I never thought to buy a kettle and French press, but it never occurred to me. A Mr. Coffee machine plugged into the wall was our only method of creating the elixir of life each morning and without power that wouldn't be possible.

"I guess run the generator? If we can. We still haven't tried it yet." Another thing we probably should've tested when we toured the RV, or at least before hitting the road. "I think I saw generator hours posted on those signs when we first pulled in. I don't remember what they were. We probably can't make coffee right when we wake up though."

This is a point someone should've impressed upon me before I moved into this motorhome. Not knowing where I was going to sleep tonight? That I could handle. Not knowing if I could have coffee in the morning? This is now cruel and unusual punishment.

Not needing to hook anything up, we climbed back into our RV and opened all the windows to let the cool air in. We initially turned on all the lights, but the more lights we turned on, the dimmer all the bulbs appeared to be. Even the dimmed lights beckoned a thousand bugs inside. Reminder to self: Bugs are attracted to light. I knew this.

After a late dinner and a walk around the campground making new friends and touring each other's RVs, we lay in bed in complete silence. I found myself wondering what it is about campgrounds that make it acceptable to meet someone and welcome them into your home within 30 seconds, but it is definitely a thing.

Now it was quiet. It was a content quiet, with no noise other than the crackle of fires and distant laughter. Long gone were the memories of paying the mechanic this morning. Instead, I was still in awe that we had visited one of the most beautiful landscapes I'd ever seen. Drove through endlessly magical desert scenery. Oh yeah, we took a self-defense class too.

It was the kind of day that reminds you of all you can accomplish in a day. So many days of my life felt like an unremarkable blend of moments I wouldn't remember. But in one day, I broke a board with strangers, saw the biggest hole in the world (I think), and now I was falling asleep in a beautiful, cool campsite. Even better, our RV seemed to be on the mend.

So this was camping. My phone was off. I could see stars through my open windows. As people turned into their tents and campers for the night, all I could hear was the pine branches swaying in the breeze. I kind of thought RV parks were great before. Endless hot water for showers, pools, 50% off because of our Passport America membership. But I think that was my RV inexperience talking. Being new to this whole RV life thing, I didn't realize you could camp like this—completely surrounded by nature but still cozy in your home.

This was RVing. *Really* RVing. Just us and nature. And a mattress. And a shower and bathroom and the rest of the stuff we owned in our home on wheels. This I could get used to.

Well, as long as we could make coffee in the morning.

Chapter 11

Where am I?

I tried to picture what was on the other side of our windows but I couldn't recall where we camped. *What state are we in? New Mexico? Arizona?* I racked my brain but memories of a dozen RV parks and highways filled my brain.

I leaned over and lifted the corner of our blinds and peered out. Red dirt. Shady green trees.

Utah.

That's right, we left Jacob Lake without visiting the north rim of the Grand Canyon, which was closed because of wildfires. (We also walked to the Chevron across the street from the campground for some average coffee, in case you were wondering. We would figure out how the generator worked another day.)

Then we made it to St. George, Utah, and found a small RV park.

I knew absolutely nothing about St. George. Or Utah. I

picked it for our route since it was an easy detour between the Grand Canyon and Vegas. Although, when I called my mom last night to tell her where we were, she was thrilled.

"Oh, the headquarters for Moore Business Forms is up there!" She practically shouted into the phone.

"The place where you worked in the 80s?"

"Yes! They had a factory in Utah where we got all our forms. But they closed down back in the nineties when people didn't need to order business forms anymore."

You heard it here first, folks. The business where my parents worked in the 80s—and consequently met, fell in love, and had me—used to have a factory in the town of St. George that's been closed for over twenty years. I'd put this hot spot on your bucket list before the whole world discovers this fascinating tidbit. (It's also close to the world-famous Zion National Park, which is a much better reason to visit.)

Not that we had a ton of time to explore since we had a schedule to keep. If it feels like we are clipping through states, that's because we were moving along quickly. June looked like this so far:

June 1-3: Albuquerque

June 4-5: Prescott Valley

June 6: Mechanic's parking lot

June 7: Grand Canyon

June 8-9: St. George

Almost two weeks had passed since we left Austin, but it felt like longer despite our fast pace. Probably in part due to the fact that driving an RV takes way more time than driving a car. I don't quite understand how it happens because we end up driving at similar speeds. Yet we always arrived at our destination at least an hour after our original ETA. I told Heath that for every hour Google Maps says it will take to get somewhere, we needed to add 15 minutes for it to be accurate.

Don't tell my mom, but yesterday as we drove, we started calling this "round one." Everywhere we went, there were more places we needed to visit but missed because of time. So far we missed Carlsbad Caverns trying to make up for the day we lost because of the tow dolly and we would miss Zion National Park trying to make it to Heath's next job in time. And we would miss Arches National Park simply because we'd never heard of it until we crossed into Utah and everyone gave us this look that said it wasn't a road trip through Utah if you didn't visit Arches. During our two days in Utah, I learned that there were five national parks and I had somehow missed routing us to visit any of them—a rookie traveler mistake.

The list was growing longer, sparking a new dream to not only visit all 50 states but to keep traveling. We owned the RV outright, even though no one laughed at our joke that we were homeowners. Maybe this wouldn't just be a honeymoon. This could be life. We could wake up somewhere new every day. Meet new people. Explore new places. Grow. The dream simmered in the back of our heads, expanding with each state.

We'd only been on the road for two weeks, but it felt like longer. Heath already had a theory on this that he was intent on telling me first thing that morning. I had barely poured myself a cup of coffee and a bowl of cereal before he launched into his theory. I rubbed the sleep from my eyes and sat at the table as he talked excitedly.

"When you're going to the same job every day," he explained, "you run on autopilot. You drive to work without remembering the drive. You do your job but nothing about the day sticks out because it's the same as yesterday. But on the road, every day is different. We haven't slept anywhere more than two nights in a row. We've seen mountains and canyons and deserts and rivers and forests. Your brain is consuming so many new things that time feels longer because it takes more brain power to process everything new you're experiencing.

"I only found one article on Google to back up my theory, but I'm pretty sure it's true," he said confidently.

I leaned back in the plush blue dining chair thinking about the idea he just laid out in front of me. I didn't know if it was true, but the using extra brain power theory would explain why we collapsed into bed exhausted every night and slept in every morning.

"Whoa! What are you doing?" I asked Heath, noticing that he had leaned across the table and grabbed the spoon out of my bowl.

"Trying a bite of your cereal. I'm hungry. I haven't eaten anything yet. I've been researching," Heath said with his mouth full of my cereal. My milk dribbled down his chin.

"Make yourself a bowl of cereal, don't steal mine!" I reached across the table and snatched my spoon out of his hand.

Heath looked at me confused. "But we're married."

I paused. "Yeah...so?"

"So what's mine is yours!"

"Share the cereal box, not the spoon, weirdo. That's like sharing my toothbrush," I wrinkled my nose.

Heath blushed and looked down at the table.

"You used my toothbrush?!"

"It was dark! I didn't want to wake you up by turning on

the light and yours was right there! I was being considerate," Heath argued.

I burst out laughing. He was so earnest and so gross. I reached over from my chair and grabbed the box of cereal off the kitchen counter.

"Here," I said, passing him the box. "Please eat as much of this cereal as you want and promise to never steal food from me again."

"I didn't have to get up and grab a bowl when I ate your cereal," Heath grumbled. I always thought adjusting to life in the RV would be harder than adjusting to marriage, but no one warned me that my husband would steal food off my plate.

After eating our own breakfasts, we packed up the RV like a well-oiled machine, washed two cereal bowls, and cruised into town for Heath's third job. I was still dreadful at video, but I learned something new each day I filmed and even remembered the tripod this time. After a long day working in the sun, we settled down in an office to conduct the final interviews with Heath's coworkers.

I listened as Heath interviewed one of the workers, AJ, a soft-spoken man built like a tank. He shared his story of playing minor league football before an injury sidelined him. Then he started running his own tile company, but the recession hit and no one was building anymore. So he ended up picking up a few hours here at the Habitat for Humanity ReStore where he worked full-time and finally felt like he was actually making a difference.

"Running water doesn't grow stale," he said as if this explained why he had the ability to get back up every time life knocked him back to square one.

His words pierced me. It's a common phrase, I think. It sounded familiar, like something my dad would've said to me as a teenager to get my nose out of a book and exercise.

But hearing it from AJ was like someone finally articulated the inner dialogue that pushed me to quit my job, to buy the RV, to not give up on this silly dream to visit all fifty states after every setback.

Stale.

That's what life felt like before we decided to pursue this adventure.

To stay meant being stagnant. Like a Texas pond breeding mosquitoes with a hint of West Nile.

But running water doesn't grow stale.

So, I wanted to live a life worth writing about?

That meant I needed to move. To do something. To do *this*. To come to this moment and hear his words, even though it involved Heath working during our honeymoon and I was vehemently against that idea for a while.

I mean, don't get me wrong. I wish getting here didn't involve the two straight weeks of desert and a breakdown and that one terrible showering experience and the obvious reality that everything ahead of me was only going to get more difficult.

But running water doesn't grow stale.

Hardships are part of it. Pivoting, finding a path forward, pushing yourself to find a solution—that's the good stuff. That's how you make it to where you were meant to be, like AJ said of finding his job at the ReStore. Was it a bit of a cheesy cliché? Maybe. But he wasn't wrong. If we wanted more out of life, continuing forward on this journey would be the only way to do it. Maybe this was why we needed to film a documentary instead of just traveling to all fifty states for fun. To meet people like AJ, to learn about life and what it means to strike out on your own and take a big risk.

"Hey, babe?" Heath asked softly.

I lifted my head and raised my eyebrows, spectacularly failing to pretend like I had been paying attention to AJ as he continued answering Heath's questions and not lost in my own ocean of emotions.

"I think that's good unless you have any other questions," Heath interrupted my potentially life-changing epiphany that would forever alter how I approached living and traveling and filming this documentary.

"No. That was great. Thank you so much, AJ."

The humble man shook Heath's hand and we all got back to work.

I think we are getting the hang of this RV thing.

It's easy to think you have the hang of things when you're drinking wine in a hot tub with palm trees swaying overhead. It sounds like a classy vacation when I say it like that, but I'm drinking from a plastic cup, and this bottle of wine cost less than three dollars. It tastes a bit like spiked fruit punch, but with my legs floating in the hot tub, everything is perfect.

In addition to finding an RV resort and feeling on top of the world, we finally figured out another massive RV mistake we made. For our first two weeks on the road, we had constant stomachaches. At first, Heath said it was because of the daily gelato sandwiches and making s'mores. What else should you eat while camping? I argued. Then one night I boiled broccoli for dinner.

"Ugh," I coughed, spitting it out on the plate. "This tastes like plastic!" Before you think I sound like a four-year-old, I love broccoli. And this wasn't the first vegetable of our trip. But without a doubt, this broccoli tasted like licking the inside of a water hose.

"It's not that bad, babe," assured Heath, the dutiful I-love-your-cooking-no-matter-what newlywed.

"No, something is wrong. I think it's the water."

Heath argued the water was fine, we were at an RV *resort* for goodness sake.

A quick Google search would confirm that you should not drink water from a water hose and that RVers buy *drinking* water hoses—a huge distinction that a smarter woman might've researched weeks earlier instead of prioritizing finding waterfall hikes in the Columbia River Gorge. Our stomachs were instantly better once we stopped casually poisoning ourselves.

With a new water hose and cheap wine, I felt like Heath and I really had the hang of RV life. We knew how to find decent RV parks with clear water that didn't break the bank. We camped without hookups for the first time. We visited a national park. We were basically pros at this point, I thought, leaning my head back in the hot tub.

"Oh if you're going to all 50 states, you have to drive the Al-Can," said a friendly RVer in the hot tub with us. The older man leaned back with arms outstretched taking up half the hot tub when we climbed in. We swapped RV life stories—well, we shared our one interesting story about breaking down outside the Grand Canyon and getting to break boards. He didn't find that nearly as emotionally charged and life-altering as we did and he eagerly started sharing his own travel trips with us.

"The what?" I asked. Alcan sounded like a kind of bird.

"The Alaska-Canadian highway. Most gorgeous drive there is and a big bucket list trip for RVers. You'll want a rock guard and a good camera though. It's basically dirt roads and grizzly bears for days."

I didn't know driving to Alaska was a thing. Sure, theoretically you could drive. But it must be thousands of miles. And only be an option in the summer. Heath and I didn't know when we would make our way up north to Alaska. December after we finished the lower 48? No thanks. I will happily wait until the snow melts. I knew enough about RVing now to know Alaska in the winter would freeze our tanks—and likely us, too!

"If you head up in the summer, the sun never really sets so you can drive all day without ever being in the dark," the friendly stranger chattered. "Or you can ferry up if you have a small enough rig. What kinda rig you got?"

In my experience, this is how every conversation goes with RVers. There's a certain flow:

1. Where are you from?
2. Vacationing or full-timing?
3. If full-timing, oh what do you do for work?
4. Where have you been?
5. Where are you heading next?

Somewhere in there, you get asked what kind of rig you have. If you've remodeled your RV or the person finds your home interesting, they will ask for a tour. Sometimes they won't ask, but your husband will be so proud of the renovation work he did that he will invite them inside anyway. So, it's best to always do your dishes and make your bed so your home is presentable to strangers.

Random conversations with RVers around the campground are how we find all our best travel tips and learn important things we should already know, like the 30-foot vehicle limit on the Pacific Coast Highway. When we told the friendly hot tub guy we were heading to California next, he explained how intense the coastal road would really be and gave us tips to navigate the winding cliffs.

Listening to hot tub guy's advice, I picked up my phone and opened Google Maps, smiling because the RV park Wi-Fi actually worked, and typed in a route between Seattle and Anchorage. 42 hours across what looked like mountains the entire way. And you drove through the Yukon! You were practically at the north pole at that point.

I raised my eyebrows at Heath who was still chatting with the stranger in the hot tub.

"What?" he asked.

"We should totally drive to Alaska from Seattle. We could probably do it in two weeks," I reasoned. I mean, we could drive 10 hours a day for four days to get there, spend a couple of days exploring, work a job, drive back down. Okay, two weeks might be cutting it close. Alaska was huge! And there was so much to see. Never mind, this plan probably wouldn't work, my realistic mind concluded. Of all the states to rush through visiting, Alaska wasn't one of them.

"I'm down," Heath agreed before I could take back my suggestion. "Let's find a way to make it happen."

Chapter 12

Hemingway once said, "Never go on trips with anyone you do not love."

To this I would add, especially if you're on a tight budget and gas is $4/gallon and you're willing to take people up on their offer to "crash on their couch" for a few nights.

California may have the most national parks in the country, but the state isn't very camper-friendly. Especially in southern California. RV park prices were easily triple my we-can-only-afford-$20-a-night budget, and tons of parks posted: "no RVs over ten years old." Twenty-year-old Franklin did not fit in and we had no options on where to stay.

Which is how we ended up parked on the street outside of Jace's house, Heath's brother's former roommate. Staying in the RV wasn't technically allowed and since I wasn't thrilled at the prospect of waking up to a cop banging on the door in the middle of the night, we crashed on the black leather couch. In my mind, this was a practicality and the only way we could hang out in LA for a few days. After all, Heath raved about how if he could live anywhere, it would be southern California. And the official goal of the trip was to find a place to live—although I had half-forgotten that goal once we got swept into the speed and excitement of sleeping somewhere new every night.

We parked our RV on a residential street in Redondo Beach, which was actually two miles from the beach, and carted a fresh change of clothes inside every day. Other than parking at Granny's for a couple of nights, this was our first shot at saving on camping fees for a few nights and it didn't matter that the couch was actually a tiny loveseat and a chair. It saved us over $100 and, with the higher gas prices in California, we had to pinch pennies where we could.

Plus, Jace worked in film and offered to give us some tips on our documentary. He installed a video editing program on my computer and taught me how to use it. To practice, Heath and I pieced together a short video recap of our first five states, which ended up being more discouraging than anything.

I knew I wasn't going to be great at filming yet, but the footage was shockingly horrible. Blurry. Dark. Shaky. When Heath worked his 4th job as a lifeguard in Vegas, I apparently had the GoPro in photo mode instead of video mode so I had a hundred pictures of Heath swimming and zero video clips. That was next-level bad.

I tossed and turned on the couch thinking about our documentary. Heath and I both knew we were clueless about video and what it took to make a feature-length film. We also knew that everything about RVing and travel would be new to us, but I thought we'd catch on to all these new skills more quickly.

Something about watching it all play out on the screen in front of us in hard-to-hear, out-of-focus, shaking video clips made our inexperience readily apparent. I cringed watching the video of the many U-turns we made on our way to Heath's first job and the interviews I filmed in Buffalo Wild Wings where you can hear baseball announcers on TV louder than the waitress Heath interviewed.

Perhaps it's my youth showing, but I thought once I was moving—running water as AJ would say—that I would shake that *what am I doing with my life* feeling. Now that's my guiding thought at 4:00 AM while I'm tossing and turning, missing my home.

Home.

Did I really just think of my RV as home? That's new.

I missed my bed, with the two bottom corners of the magenta mattress awkwardly missing. I had used scissors to cut down a mattress topper to match the mattress once it was clear it was impossible to find a new mattress the exact size of the RV bed.

When did those 200 square feet become home in my mind? Nevada? New Mexico? Maybe it was that night in Utah when we realized that while one person made stovetop popcorn, the other should just stand under the smoke detector waving a tea towel because even if the popcorn isn't burning, the smoke alarm will go off every time and need to be fanned. It seemed like a more prudent decision than simply removing the smoke detector and throwing it out the window.

Or maybe it was in west Texas when I drove for the first time and we named the RV Franklin. Was it weird to name your home? I wondered.

Home.

I like the sound of that.

"This is the most beautiful place I've ever seen!" I exclaimed, opening the door which instantly slammed back in my face from the wind. "Okay, we might want sweatshirts."

Before escaping Los Angeles, Heath worked as a groundskeeper for a baseball stadium, we took one last hot shower, and we packed everything back into our home to head north on Highway 1. Of all the destinations on our route, this I looked forward to the most. Days of winding ocean views and hidden beaches. Plus, that famous California coastal weather—exactly what I needed after filming Heath's past five jobs in 100° temps.

A cool breeze sent my hair flying and I grabbed the camera to film the cliffs and crashing waves below. I pulled on the hoodie the sensei at Project Dojo gave me after that first day of filming. I certainly didn't think I'd wear it so soon.

We planned for at least a week to take the coastal route from LA to Portland, stopping at Redwoods National Park along the way. Since Heath already finished his job in California, we had a full week with no work. Just the gold coast and a 1,000-mile journey to enjoy. I peered over the guardrail at the steep drop below and thanked whoever it was who recommended we drive the highway north and not south. My stomach lurched at the idea of being inches away from that drop. I will take the inside lane, please and thank you.

After driving slowly along the coast talking and stopping at every scenic overlook, we abruptly found ourselves in standstill traffic inland. Everything was brown, the warm air blew in our open windows, and we noticed the engine beginning to overheat.

"Where are we?" I asked. "How did we get off the Pacific Coast Highway?" I grabbed our atlas and tried to pinpoint where we ended up. Once we hit Santa Barbara, the highway wove inland and we apparently needed to exit to stay on 101. Or 1. Why did the highway have so many names? 101 meant coastal, 1 meant coastal sometimes. I think. Why was there no "take the scenic route" button on navigation apps? That's a good business idea right there. I turned off the GPS and examined the map, giving Heath directions. Heath took the next exit, turned around, and backtracked a few miles to the exit we missed.

Quickly, the outdoor temps dropped, the ocean came back into view, and our engine temperature went back to normal. Looking closer at the map, I now realized that the highway didn't hug the coast all the way to Oregon. We would come inland again soon and have to find our way back to the coastal road. Navigating would be more of a full-time job than I imagined, I thought as I marked on the atlas which exits we would need to take to stay on the coast, but I was getting better at it. I was grateful that I followed the advice to pick up an atlas for traveling, even though I didn't think we would realistically use it.

We left Los Angeles before lunch and strolled into downtown Pismo Beach at sunset—taking a full nine hours to fully appreciate the regularly three-hour drive. The Pacific Ocean stretched out for miles on our left, shimmering in the afternoon sun. Most of the drive felt strangely remote after we escaped the sprawling expanse of Los Angeles. We could drive for an hour without seeing anything but the soft green coastal mountains dipping down into the deep blue water. Then again, we were driving really slowly according to all the cars that passed us.

But why would we speed through the Pacific Coast? I could stare out my window for days at the waves and the shore and the magical yellow and purple flowers that miraculously grew out of the sand. My phone was full of blurry photos snapped from the passenger seat that wouldn't do the landscape justice. Heath and I continued to pull over to snap photos—and let the line of cars behind us pass by—as often as we could while the sun made its way across the sky.

Sunset is the best time to roll into a beach town. Everyone else has packed up for the day and is headed off to dinner. We slid into four empty parking spots, a strategy we learned could guarantee that we could get out of the parking lot when we needed to. But this only worked if the parking lot was empty enough to have four spots in a row or in a square.

Stepping onto the asphalt I leaned back into the RV to grab my sweatshirt off the dash again. It was strange to think that less than 24 hours ago I was in 100-degree weather sweating without reprieve in the California desert and here I was shivering on the beach. That was one of the unexpected parts of RV travel that I quickly learned to love. In Texas, the temperature was consistent even if you drove three hours away. Being on the road, the temperature sometimes swung 50 degrees in either direction as we moved. From the desert to the coast and back again. It made it hard to dress for the day but it also meant a little more adventure with every passing mile.

Walking down the wooden path to the beach, we watched kids feeding seagulls and vacationing couples standing along the waves.

"Babe!" Heath shouted. "Look!"

He pointed directly at the setting sun, which I was already being blinded by. *Dude*, I wanted to say. *We just stopped at the beach in order to watch the sunset. I'm clearly already doing that.* But I followed his pointed finger to the water and saw a small splash. Seconds later a whale crested the top of the ocean and spouted water into the air.

"Whales!" I squealed, getting the attention of the kids playing on the beach. We all stood there for ten minutes, us and the few families and couples still enjoying the beach, shivering as the sun went down and a pod of whales swam toward deeper waters, giving us a show on their way out.

I leaned my head back on Heath's chest as the clouds lit up gold and pink and the sun sank too quickly over the Pacific. This was a true honeymoon moment, I thought, admiring the glowing clouds. Heath wrapped his arms tightly around my waist, either because he loved me or because the temperature was dropping rapidly in the absence of the sun. I felt our relationship growing stronger as the miles ticked by.

In the past month, Heath and I had spent every waking moment with each other. Because we ditched our tow car, it wasn't like one of us could even drive to the store or a coffee shop without the other. We went from working two jobs in two separate cities to being within 29 feet of each other at all times.

Some of the people we talked to laughed and scoffed at the idea of being in such a small space with their partner. And maybe it was because it was our literal honeymoon, but I didn't understand this idea. I loved Heath. Why would I want to marry someone who I couldn't be around at all times?

Instead of getting married and spending one week together before we "got back to our daily lives," Heath and I were being pushed closer together. Showing up at random businesses with a camera and awkwardly trying to adapt to a new day of challenges as a team, then piecing together footage. Dealing with a breakdown in the middle of nowhere. Sleeping on a friend's couch in LA and navigating countless miles of highway and city streets in an RV.

While some moments made me question our craziness, others (like this one) reaffirmed this wild idea. I never doubted that Heath was my person, but watching him dutifully dump the black tank and take on this journey with me solidified it. I pulled his arms tighter around my waist, grateful to have him as a partner on this grand adventure.

"If I tell you to tuck and roll, don't question it. Just open the door and jump."

Heath's tone made it clear he was not messing around. Our engine, which spiked in temperature occasionally, was starting to stay a little too hot and we still had a few hundred miles to our ultimate destination of San Jose where we planned on meeting a friend in a few days. There wasn't much between here and there. Hugging the coastal route was no longer the beautiful option. It was an engine-needs-cooler-temps requirement.

The engine overheating was getting to our heads and Heath

was having visions of the brakes going out and the RV plummeting to its death hundreds of feet below.

"You really think we'll lose the brakes?" I questioned, still knowing absolutely nothing about how engines work.

Heath shrugged. "We've already broken down once and don't have any idea what other things might go wrong on a rig like this. I just want you to be prepared. So if I say so, don't even think about it. Just open the door and jump." He paused. "Try to tuck your shoulder and roll. We aren't driving too fast so you should be okay."

I waited on the punchline of what I was sure was a joke that only Heath thought was funny, but the lingering silence after his sentence told me this was no joke. Cool.

I gulped and sat still in the front seat sending up a little prayer for safety. My eyes were wide open because every time I blinked I saw our house flying over the cliffside. I leaned forward to see how high up we really were and saw nothing but big black rocks and white water crashing. No one could survive that fall.

"You're not kidding, are you?"

"Which would you prefer, jumping out of a moving vehicle or flying over a cliff and drowning in the ocean?" Heath asked.

How are these my only two choices?!

Tuck and roll, I repeated to myself. I took a deep breath and exhaled slowly. When we dreamed up a life of travel and adventure, I didn't think we would spend our drives strategizing how not to die. After the RV broke down in Arizona, we were mentally prepared to deal with continuous engine trouble. But the hot engine and the chance of overheating our brakes had us on edge as we slowly drove the highway with cars piling up behind us. There weren't any towns for hundreds of miles, so we couldn't pop over to a mechanic to check out the engine. We were on our own.

All we have to do is survive…oh, and find camping.

Just as an extra precaution, we stopped on every extra-wide shoulder and scenic overlook to give our engine time to cool off. We stretched our legs walking along sandy beaches and short coastal trails. At lunchtime, I opened every window in the RV and grabbed our only pot from the bottom drawer. I flipped the water pump switch like a pro, filled the pot with water, and lit the stove. The waves crashed below and seagulls squawked overhead as I pulled a box of mac and cheese from the cabinet for a very cheap meal with a billion-dollar view.

"Where are we going to camp tonight?" I casually asked Heath as he climbed back inside with our camera in hand after capturing more footage of the coast. While we were discouraged watching the footage for our documentary, we still loved being able to record home videos of our adventures and capture the beautiful places we found on the road. Not to mention, filming on the coast was a thousand times more exciting than filming Heath mopping locker room floors at his last job.

"Every place we've passed so far has said full, not that I'm ready to stop yet. We've got a few hours till sunset. We'll pull into everywhere we see and try to find a spot. But if we don't, we might have to travel inland."

In Pismo Beach, we attempted camping in a Walmart parking lot, but were confronted with a barrage of "No Overnight

Parking" signs. This didn't fit with what everyone told us about RVing: you can always camp for free at Walmarts. We parked and walked inside to ask the manager about the signs.

The store manager explained there was a county law against overnight RVs and that while the store's policy didn't mind if we stayed the night, the sheriff might.

While it might be obvious to you, we were unaware that camping along the coast of California is popular (we found that out when it took 30 minutes to find an open campsite last night). Every mile brought us closer to the iconic Big Sur. We pulled into every single national forest and state park campground we encountered over the next few hours, but every place was full.

"These sites book out six months in advance," one ranger explained. *Grrrrrreat.* With no cell service, we couldn't even search for campgrounds nearby. We kept our eyes peeled for blue signs with the tent symbol.

The sun hovered just over the horizon when Heath pulled over to the side of the road.

"I'm just going to run across the street and check out the campground right back there."

"The one with the emphatic sign that said full, full, and FULL?"

"You never know!" Heath slammed his door and jogged across the empty highway with a smile on his face. His optimism never quit. The road was busy all day, but everyone had traveled to their home for the night, probably too afraid to take the winding road in the dark. In addition to stopping at every campground, we checked every parking lot and scenic vista, always seeing signs displaying NO CAMPING in bold letters. I saw a long night of driving ahead of us.

I gazed at the quickly setting sun and impatiently swiped across the screen on my phone. Still no signal.

Hearing the crunch of gravel through the open windows, I saw Heath running across the highway in the rearview mirror. He pumped his fists in the air like a teenage quarterback throwing his first touchdown.

"I talked to the ranger," Heath said breathlessly. "And someone booked three nights..." Heath gasped between every few words after sprinting back up the road. "...and never showed up..." gasp "...and it's the last night of their reservation..." gasp "...so he said we could have it!"

"What!"I squealed, admiring the views to my left even more. "Wait. If it's already paid for, does that mean we can stay for free?" #budgetmode

"Ha, I asked and he said no. It's only like 25 bucks though. Let's hurry up and get set up and eat dinner while we watch the sunset."

"Yes, please! Get in the RV!"

Fueled by excitement, Heath jumped up to climb in through his open window. I burst into laughter at the sight of his legs flailing wildly in the air as he tried to squeeze into the window.

"Owww," Heath groaned as he pulled his body through the window with his face now inches from the floor of the RV.

"Why," I asked between laughs, "did you think that would be an efficient way to get in?"

Heath continued to groan, rubbing his stomach. "In my head, it looked a lot cooler."

Turning on the engine, Heath made a six-point U-turn to get

into the entrance of Kirk Creek Campground. He pulled down the one-lane road to the only empty campsite, passed it, and backed in. I pulled some leftover queso from a jar in our fridge and heated it on the stove. I grabbed a bag of chips and a bottle of $3 wine we picked up at Walmart and set it on the picnic table outside. The sun was minutes away from disappearing completely and the air-cooled off significantly. I grabbed my trusty Project Dojo hoodie and pulled the bubbling cheese off the stove. At some point, we needed to improve our budget diet, but hot cheese seemed fitting for this celebration.

"RV site is paid for! I made the check out to Camp Awesome because look at this view!!!" Heath said, sitting at the picnic table. You could hear the exclamation points punctuating the end of every sentence. Our table faced the ocean, which crashed loudly roughly 100 feet below the bluff where we sat. "Oo-ooh! This dinner looks amazing. And this weather!" Heath raved. "No air conditioning needed tonight. I could get used to this boondocking thing."

"This what?"

"Oh, that's what the ranger called it. I'm pretty sure it means the same thing as dry camping."

I shrugged, dipping a chip into the spicy cheese. "Pour the wine?"

"Gladly." Heath sighed contently with a mouthful of chips. "This is it, babe."

"This is what?"

"I think this is why we needed to do this trip in an RV. I mean, we kind of chose the RV for budget reasons, but we never would've gotten this experience if we did our Airbnb plan. I know we already broke down once and the engine keeps randomly overheating, but I think this moment makes it worth it. There will always be hard moments in life, but these are the problems we chose. You just need a few moments like this to remind you to keep going."

"Wow, not even a drop of wine yet and you're already getting all sentimental. You know we still have 45 states of this to go," I teased.

Laughing, Heath stole a kiss as the sun sank over the calm waters.

Chapter 13

The rest of California went by just as beautifully outside our windows.

As we continued up the coast, we scooted inland in San Jose to grab lunch with Jia Jiang—the donut guy who gave Heath the idea for our documentary. He was surprised to hear that Heath actually took his advice. After his viral video, he explained, tons of people reached out to him for advice. Rarely did he hear from those people again. But here we were two months later actually doing it. His compliment boosted our confidence that maybe this 50 state adventure wasn't so crazy after all.

Jia also suggested we meet up again soon. He was traveling to Portland, Oregon—our next official stop for *Hourly America*—in a few weeks to attend the World Domination Summit. Tickets sold out months earlier, but he urged us to find a way to attend anyway.

World Domination Summit is hosted by Chris Guillebeau, a *New York Times* best-selling author who visited every country in the world. The conference was built for unconventional thinkers (like weirdos living in an RV, perhaps?) and some seriously amazing people I followed online were speaking—Jeff Goins, Pat Flynn, Elise Cripe, Michael Hyatt, the list went on. They weren't all travelers, but they were all creative entrepreneurs who created a life that allowed them to do work that they loved.

Following Jia's advice and with his pitch all rehearsed, Heath sent a Hail Mary LinkedIn message to Chris offering to volunteer at the conference for his sixth job.

Chris replied 16 minutes later:

"What's your email address? I'll forward your note to our volunteer coordinator in case he's interested. Most roles have already been filled, so it will be up to him."

An hour later, Heath was pacing the campground laughing on the phone with a guy named Wes. He ran the video team for the conference. "They could use help on the video team," Heath relayed to me after the call. "So we will be filming all week, but we can still sit in on most of the sessions."

"I'm totally in," I agreed. I mean, as long as they know I'm not very good at video. And that I will be that person who is awkwardly starstruck by every single speaker even if I've never heard of them before. Conference tickets cost over $500 per person so if we could get in for free, of course I would go for it.

I was excited about Portland before hearing about the conference, but after seeing the speaker lineup and learning that most of the attendees were people who wanted to travel *and* do their own thing, I felt like this event was made for Heath and me. We had the travel part down, but the working remotely bit was still a mystery. This conference couldn't have come at a better time.

After our inland detour to meet with Jia, we had time to kill before the conference so we decided to use the opportunity to slow down. We holed up in a tiny campground outside of Redwoods National Park to catch our breath after covering over 3,000 miles in the past four weeks. Rain tapped gently on our roof day in and day out while we sat on the Klamath River, the top of the trees hidden in the low clouds. The endless green was a far cry from everything we'd experienced so far in our travels.

I snuggled up on the couch with a fuzzy blanket and balanced my laptop on my knees to get some work done.

Now that we had a taste of true travel and the burgeoning idea to make this round one, we needed to get serious about finding ways to support ourselves on the road. Sure, we hadn't found anyone else under 65 who actually affords full-time RV life. But making money and RVing had to be possible. We hadn't even attended World Domination Summit yet, but knowing it existed solidified this truth for me.

Heath was busy writing blogs for Snagajob about each job he worked, but he also found an RV website that was looking for articles on RV renovations. The editor said he would pay me 8¢ a word for my story but now the cursor on my screen blinked mockingly. If I could get this article published, I...well I probably wouldn't even be able to fill up the gas tank. But it would prove that making money while traveling was at least possible.

I felt the pressure mounting.

Last week, we overdrew our checking account. That's

another reason we stopped at this cheap campground in northern California for a few days. The gas prices killed our bank account this month and cost us over $1,600. That's double what we estimated our first month would cost us and it really set us back financially.

We needed this article.

We also needed this article to be about 10,000 words long to make up for how much we spent in June.

But the editor only wanted 1,000 words and $80 for an article wasn't too bad.

I looked out the window at the fog floating on top of the river. I knew actually writing this article wouldn't be hard. I skimmed other renovation articles on the site and they were all very "here's the paint I used and here's the flooring I used." Simple and to the point.

It was the pressure that this had to work that I felt tightening the muscles in my shoulders.

Otherwise, we wouldn't make it.

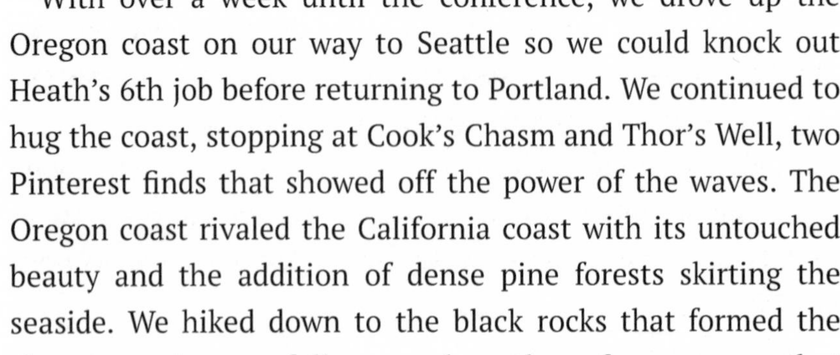

With over a week until the conference, we drove up the Oregon coast on our way to Seattle so we could knock out Heath's 6th job before returning to Portland. We continued to hug the coast, stopping at Cook's Chasm and Thor's Well, two Pinterest finds that showed off the power of the waves. The Oregon coast rivaled the California coast with its untouched beauty and the addition of dense pine forests skirting the seaside. We hiked down to the black rocks that formed the shore, stepping carefully around swathes of green moss that made the jagged rocks slick.

Here, the waves powerfully crashed on the rocks creating piles of sea foam. It looked like mounds of frothed milk piled up on the dark rocks. The churning waves hit land with such force that water spouted high into the air, quickly soaking us. We carefully hiked along the rocks mesmerized by the power of the breaking waves.

Snagajob lined up work for Heath at a Domino's, so we needed to leave the coastline, pop up to Seattle so Heath could toss some pizzas, and then make the drive back to Portland for the conference. It meant a few extra days of driving, but after that, we would be in Portland for a full week to make friends, enjoy the conference, and film, of course. Heath drove us up the interstate, reaching out his hand for a high five as we crossed the Columbia River and saw an "Entering Washington" sign on the bridge. Oregon was technically our 6th state to visit, but we decided to check off states as Heath worked his job, making Washington our "official" 6th state—and the first state where we didn't get to stop and take a picture with the state line sign.

After a day of making pizza, we started our engine in downtown Seattle at 4:00 PM on a Thursday and found ourselves in stop-and-go traffic. Other than LA, which we strategically drove through early in the mornings, this was our first major city and first rush hour of the journey.

Traffic in an RV really isn't that bad. We can run to the bathroom or grab snacks if we need to. I could pop a pizza in the oven and have dinner ready by the time we made it to our destination.

But our engine hated it.

Once again, the temperature started creeping up until it was dangerously close to overheating. This happened a few times once we left the coast and required breaks for the engine to cool off so we didn't completely overheat. Unable to find a campsite in Seattle (and clearly not learning our lesson about needing to make camping reservations yet) my old roommate saved the day by offering up her parents' driveway just north of the city.

The free place to stay was amazing, but the wisdom of a father? Invaluable.

"Oh, you probably just need to flush the radiator," my roommate's dad, Jerry, said with an easy shrug after we casually mentioned the engine getting a little too hot.

Not sure what a radiator does, but okay.

He drove Heath to the local auto shop to pick up some radiator flush fluid and they popped the hood. I cooked dinner inside the RV while they worked, grateful that we weren't making this journey alone. Every time something went sideways or we needed help, someone appeared with the exact knowledge we needed to continue pushing forward.

For $10 and an hour of Heath's time, our engine was fixed and our stress lowered back to the normal "no idea where I"m going to sleep tonight, but I'm used to it now" level.

Confident once again that our home on wheels could hit the open road, we departed on Friday morning and decided to take the weekend to drive the long way back toward Portland. The funny thing that happens when you're traveling every day is that you tend to forget about the calendar days.

Which is how we ended up spending a magical July 4th driving the scenic roads through Mount Rainier National Park. Every campground was full of course, but that couldn't stop us from touring the park. On one mountain pass, we passed snow on the ground. Snow? In July?! Perhaps it's my small-minded southern thinking showing, but I'm pretty sure snow on the ground in July is an impossibility.

"I have an idea," Heath said. At this point, I've known Heath long enough to know this is his signature catchphrase.

He pulled over at a scenic overlook and turned off the engine. Climbing up the step from the cab into the house of the RV, he started rummaging through cabinets.

"Where's that metal pan we cook with?"

"The pan I roast food in the oven with?" I asked. Tall pine trees, sparkling snow, sun on the mountain. This was definitely a gorgeous stop to whip up some lunch.

"Yeah, that one," he smirked.

"Right cabinet over the couch behind the olive oil. Wait. Why?"

"Because we don't have any other way to sled down that snowy hill right there!"

In our short-sleeved shirts and shorts, Heath and I stood in the snow taking turns sledding down the 50-foot slope stretching toward the forest. We slid down the hill until Heath ran into a tree stump and permanently dented the cake pan. Grease would splash out of that dent for the next few months since we couldn't afford a new one, but it didn't matter. The memory of snow sledding on July 4th was worth it.

Chapter 14

Between Heath's job for Oregon and the conference, we needed to stay in Portland for a week—our longest stay anywhere. We didn't have any reservations—okay *technically* we hadn't made a single reservation for any of our travels—but we needed to camp *in* Portland to be nearby for the conference and we quickly learned that finding an RV park in the city was not the same as finding an RV park anywhere else.

"Okay, I finally found a place," Heath announced after more than an hour of reading reviews and calling parks. "It's called Columbia River RV Park—"

"Ooh is it on the river?" I interrupted excitedly.

"Well it's near the river, but it's on the other side of the road. So no water views. But it's $36 a night and they only had one site left for two nights. Then we have to find something else."

"36 dollars?! Is there a pool?"

$36 would be the most we'd spent on any single campsite. If I was going to pay that much, I expected a hot tub. Or at least reliable Wi-Fi. Frugal Alyssa was spoiled knowing there were $13 parks out there, even if they did have brown water.

To make up for the expensive campsite, I got an alert from Paypal:

Someone sent you $79.48

I leaped internally. That article payment would cover our two nights here, and the website editor even sent me a note saying to reach out if I ever wanted to write more pieces for his website. It may not have added much to our bank account, but we swelled with hope seeing even a little money come in.

As we made our way inland toward the city, the temperatures were rising. We timed our arrival to Portland with a heatwave that sent temperatures into the mid-90s. But the city did look beautiful glittering in the sun. And as we drove down the interstate en route to the only RV park with any availability in the next seven days, we had a great view of what we would later learn was Mount St. Helens. It's not every day you look out your windshield and see an active volcano. Well, unless you live in Portland.

We pulled into a packed, neatly manicured RV park. Even without a pool, it was nice and quiet. If they had availability, we would've stayed longer, but every single park in town was booked out. We called all of them. We needed to find a place to boondock. However, we only had two nights of dry camping under our belts so far, both in remote landscapes. Rumor was we could boondock in cities too. Or "stealth camp," as it's called.

Sleeping on the side of the road in your RV isn't exactly legal in most places, not to mention it sounded sketchy. I pictured homeless men trying to break in in the middle of the night or sirens blazing by at 2 AM. But after calling every single RV park and campground in the area with no camping options, parking on the streets felt like the only option. Finding and booking campsites was quickly beginning to feel like a full-time job.

Heath, being the resourceful guy that he is, called up Wes who was heading up the film crew for the World Domination Summit and explained our dilemma. After Jace offered his couch when we couldn't afford a campsite in LA and when Jerry flushed our radiator when we couldn't figure out why the engine was overheating, we didn't underestimate the power of simply asking. People were always kind and eager to help.

"Why don't you try parking at Concordia University?" Wes suggested. "It's summer so the lots are all empty and I can get you in touch with their security team. One of our event planners is also a professor, so we've been renting out rooms at the college all week for our meetings. That's where the volunteer meeting you need to be at tomorrow will be."

Heath got the email address of a security guy named Todd and wrote:

> Hi Todd,
>
> This is Heath Padgett. I left a voicemail for the department yesterday but also wanted to reach out over email as well. (Happy 4th of July weekend by the way!)
>
> Wes from World Domination Summit passed along your email to me. My wife, Alyssa, and I are part of the film crew for WDS and we're traveling to Portland in our motorhome from Texas. There aren't a large number of places to park in the city, so we wanted to see about the possibility of us parking our RV at Concordia for a few days during the conference.
>
> Alyssa and I are both Concordia Texas Alums (2012 & 2013) and Alyssa was also on staff at Concordia Texas after graduation.

I'm sure you won't get this until after the holiday weekend but I wanted to try and get in touch with you anyhow. We would be very grateful for any type of parking whatsoever. We're self-sustained in the RV so wouldn't need any kind of electricity or water.

Lastly, the President of Concordia Texas is a very close friend/mentor of mine and would be happy to provide a reference for both Alyssa and I if you see fit.

Cheers,

-Heath

The man pulled out all the stops in a show of great desperation (or just solid proof that we aren't some random kids). I mean what are the odds that one of our university's sister schools happens to have parking right where we need it?

On Monday, Todd gave Heath a call and said we could park next to the baseball fields for the week. A week! That would save us hundreds! Not to mention save us the stress and would be exponentially safer than taking a chance on the streets.

So after our two-day stay at the $36 a night park, we filled up with freshwater, dumped our black and grey tanks, and lifted the jacks. Time for our first parking lot camping experience.

"Dude, this is awesome," said Wes, ducking his head into our RV after the volunteer meeting. At 6'5″ he couldn't stand up inside our house without bending his knees and tilting his head sideways. At 5'2″ the low ceilings in our home never crossed my mind.

"Thanks, man," Heath said. "It has everything we need. Sorry it's so hot in here. Let me crank on the gennie again."

The Portland heatwave only intensified in the two days since we arrived in town. With every window and ceiling vent open, the indoor temperatures hovered at 98°. Heath held down the start button and after a few seconds, a loud rumble shook the RV as our generator cranked on. A few minutes later, we had power to the RV and the A/C started blowing at full blast. Yes, it only took us a little over a month to realize that you needed to hold down the start button to turn on the generator. 100% should've been able to figure that out sooner.

After the 30-second tour of our 29-foot home, we stood outside chatting with Wes and his wife, Tera, who were heading up the media team for the conference. Wes films; Tera photographs. They were kind and funny, with thick Alabama accents, and they supported us immediately. They were new parents and had spent the first few years of their marriage traveling as much as possible. They encouraged us to keep traveling together and pursuing something different. And with their expertise, Wes shared quick video tips with us so we would be prepared for the week of filming ahead of us. We instantly loved them.

Because we were volunteering, this couldn't count as one of Heath's jobs. Snagajob lined up a job at the art museum in town for tomorrow, then we would film pre-conference activities for two days, attend the conference for two days, and then film post-conference workshops for two more days. In retrospect, Wes smartly assigned Heath and me to film everything before and after the official conference days. What with the fact that I had exactly six days of film experience under my belt, that was wise. Don't give me anything *too* important.

With a little encouragement and a few things I didn't know about film explained to me (DSLR? Exposure triangle? I just hit record, dude), Heath and I were ready for a good night's sleep and a week of craziness.

We said good night to our new friends, walked back into the RV, and found that it was roughly one degree cooler than it was when we cranked on the generator. The sun blazed through all the windows—and it was almost 9:00 PM! I had no idea just how long summer days up north could be. Hopefully, the eventual sunset would bring cooler temperatures.

This was our first time really using the generator, so when we laid down in bed, sweating on top of the sheets in our still bright bedroom, we weren't sure what to do. Leave the generator on all night? Would that run us out of gas? The generator's gas line is connected to the engine.

Wasn't that rude? Past campgrounds posted generator hours, probably due to the noise. Or maybe the pollution. You could smell the faintest whiff of exhaust billowing outside our now closed windows. We had quickly closed them all after cranking on the generator and getting hit in the face with fumes.

"It draws attention to us," Heath added as we discussed what to do next. "If we have the generator on, people will know we are inside."

"I can't decide if that's a good thing or a bad thing. How can we cool off otherwise? It's still so hot outside."

"I have an idea, but it might not be appreciated and it's too late to ask for permission."

"I'm all ears," I said, hoping for any kind of respite from the current 97° inside our home.

"I saw an electrical outlet on the baseball fence back there. We have a 75-foot extension cord. We can just plug in and run our A/C."

You might be thinking, wait a second, you can't just plug an RV into any old plug. And you would be right. But at this moment, we are only six weeks into our adventure and haven't learned that yet. We are about to.

"Yes, please!" I agreed to Heath's plan. Free electricity? That's my ideal parking lot camping experience!

I turned off the generator and Heath connected and started unrolling our extension cord. I opened our kitchen window and watched as Heath pulled the cord along, stopped, looked at his feet, looked at the outlet, and jogged back to the RV.

"We have to back up literally one foot to reach," he explained.

He climbed in the driver's seat, cranked on the engine, played with the joystick that controlled the leveling jacks for five minutes until they all lifted, and finally we inched backward a few feet. Heath ran out and plugged in our extension cord and I flipped on the fan for our A/C. Because our RV was so old, cranking on the A/C always sounded like it might explode the RV. So to keep the RV alive, I typically turned on the fan for a few seconds to let it pick up speed before I challenged the machine to switch to air conditioning.

After thirty seconds of sticking my face under the fan like a dog panting with its head out the window, I turned the knob over to A/C. It cranked on for a split second and shuddered off. See? This is why I have my special crank-on-first plan. I turned the knob off for a moment, got the fan to turn back on, and tried again.

The A/C cranked on for a moment and shuddered off again.

"Heath?" I called out. He was still outside trying to move our cord to be as inconspicuous as possible. "The A/C won't stay on."

"I'll try to unplug it and plug it back in."

He jogged back to the outlet and I worked through my short sequence again, but this time, not even the fan powered on when I twisted the knob.

"Um, babe?" I whispered loudly through the open window across the empty parking lot. "I think we blew the breaker."

"Oh. That's not good," Heath muttered. "Hmm...I will look for a breaker box?"

Heath walked around the parking lot looking for breakers or other outlets while I opened every window and vent in the RV and prayed for a light breeze. The sky was orange and fading slowly while the temps stayed constant.

The lack of temperature control in the RV is one of the things I least expected about RV life. Although, that might partly be due to my own misconception that every place in the country is less hot than Texas in the summers. I mean I knew it would be hot in the desert, hence why we knocked it out of the way first and fast, but the heat in Oregon? That surprised us. I really should've known more about my own country before leaving on this adventure, but there's no education like experience.

"Okay, so..." Heath whispered through the window as if plugging into electricity was an illicit crime. Wait. Is it? Theft maybe? I mean how much does one night of A/C in an RV really cost? $1?

"Couldn't find a breaker box, but I did find another outlet—"

"Great."

"—on the other side of the baseball fence."

"Oh." I pondered the dilemma. "So you would have to hop the fence." Hopping the fence definitely made plugging into electricity seem like a bad idea. Like we were clearly taking advantage of Concordia's hospitality. They agreed to let us park for free for a whole week and meanwhile we steal electricity. (I mean, technically we spent tens of thousands at the Concordia in Texas, so I feel like they owe us a little free electricity. It's not like I'm asking for student loan forgiveness or something substantial). I glanced at our atomic clock to see it still read 97° inside. If it said 85, I probably would've told Heath to not worry about it. It will cool off.

But 97 is miserable. 97 makes you do questionable things.

"Is there anyone around?" I asked in my best spy voice.

Heath looked left and looked right. If a cop drove by right now, he'd surely think we were casing the place. He shook his head, walked across the sidewalk, and hopped the six-foot fence with relative ease. I mean, Heath played baseball in college so he'd probably done that once or twice before. That or I married a skilled criminal.

A few seconds later, our fan in the RV kicked on. I forgot I left it switched to fan mode from when we blew the breaker a few minutes ago. I waited while Heath climbed back over the fence—this time slightly less gracefully so I'm 60% sure he's never committed a B&E now. Flipping the knob over to A/C, I heard a pop followed by a click.

Heath froze outside and looked over his shoulder.

Half of the lights in the parking lot went out.

Heath locked eyes with me. His were wide as if to convey

shock and a string of expletives. He quickly spun on his heels, hopped back over the fence, and retrieved our cord. He pushed the cord through the metal bars of the fence, climbed back over at breakneck speed, and hastily stuffed our cord back into the storage bay under the RV.

I stood in the RV with my hand over my mouth and all the windows still open.

So we definitely just popped a breaker. Or we did something worse and broke their whole electrical system. Given our utter lack of understanding of how RVs work less than two months into full-timing, I would not be surprised if we broke everything. *This is why you shouldn't buy an RV*, my mom's voice told me in my head.

Without saying a word, Heath and I looked at each other unsure of what to do. Call someone? Drive away and pretend nothing happened?

"So," Heath began slowly. "Think they will know it was us?"

"I think there's a good chance."

We stood in silence for a minute, trying to decide what to do. The sky was nearly black now, so leaving wasn't really an option unless we wanted to roam Portland in the dark. We already knew every RV park in the area was full. We didn't have many options other than climb into bed and try to sleep in the now slightly darker parking lot.

"So this is parking lot camping," I said, breaking the silence as we lay in bed on top of our comforter.

"This is parking lot camping," Heath repeated.

We are, without a doubt, the worst campers of all time.

Chapter 15

"Heath?" said a friendly voice on the side of the street.

"Jedd?" Heath replied.

I looked at Heath, then at the supposed Jedd, and then at the woman I assumed was Jedd's wife who looked as confused as I was. They were climbing out of a cab while we stood on the street corner waiting to go inside for the next session.

"Great to meet you, man!" Jedd said, giving Heath one of those handshake hug combos that men do so easily. At first, I thought maybe Heath had a fan who knew about our documentary, but since Heath knew Jedd's name too, I was really confused as to how these two guys became friends.

"Babe, babe," Heath said excitedly. "This is the couple I met on Twitter. They just finished a year in the Peace Corps and now they are traveling the world together."

"Hi Alyssa, I'm Jedd. This is my wife Michelle," Jedd said, extending his hand.

We all shook hands and swapped life stories so Michelle and

I could be brought up to speed. Apparently, the guys had been chatting on Twitter and planning to meet up for a few days, but they are both men, so telling their wives slipped their minds.

Only a few years older than us, Jedd and Michelle were the first couple we met who dared to live the same full-time travel lifestyle as us. Digital nomads, they said it was called. I didn't know what that meant but I pictured laptops and travel which wasn't too far off from our own time on the road. Jedd and Michelle spent most of their time traveling overseas and doing freelance work for clients around the world. The four of us instantly had so much in common and swapped travel stories and blogging advice.

Along with Wes and Tera, who we already planned to visit once we made it to their home state of Alabama, we'd now met two married couples running a business and traveling together. These people were living my dream!

We would see them again. I felt it in my bones. As much as we tried to stay in touch with friends back home, everything had shifted. As our physical distance widened, we had less and less in common with our friends in Texas. Walking around the streets of Portland, we found people who inspired us.

We said goodbye to Jedd and Michelle after exchanging numbers so we could grab dinner together during the conference and Heath and I got back to filming. We were tasked with filming academies—aka workshops that occurred before and after the conference. I was tackling blogging, travel hacking, and a learn-any-language course while Heath ran around filming an outdoor fitness workshop and a business startup lecture, each of us choosing the academies that were most interesting to us. We were given bright orange name badges that acted like backstage passes to get us into any part of the event, but once we were in the room, we faded into the background filming short clips for a recap video of the workshops.

Or sometimes not filming, as I found myself frequently pulling out my phone and typing notes on what credit cards could get you free flights and how to make money as a blogger. My fingers couldn't type fast enough as I tried to absorb everything I heard.

Heath and I ping-ponged around the city bouncing from workshop to workshop and ran into each other more than once on the streets unexpectedly. The summer heat didn't relent and my feet ached from the miles I covered. Yet, this was so much more fun than filming Heath standing still in the corner of a museum for an hour...which is literally what I did when he worked at the Portland Art Museum.

There was an energy and excitement here that couldn't be matched. So far on the road, we met plenty of retirees and, of course, Heath's rotating coworkers. But we hadn't met anyone else chasing the same dreams as us—work for ourselves, travel the world. Here, everyone was chasing after bigger dreams than we were. We met world travelers, best-selling authors, and so many entrepreneurs.

I instinctively shrank back, intimidated by everyone around. *I don't fit in with people like this,* I caught myself thinking after I interviewed a woman who shared her "Year of Fear" where she pushed her comfort zone by doing new things every day—like beekeeping, a police ride-along, and driving a race car. Everyone I met had a story and a mission.

You do too, I kicked myself mentally.

Oh, please, I argued back with myself. *I slept in a parking lot last night and also probably committed a felony. Would "it was an accident" work on the FBI*? These are the questions I pondered while not falling asleep in our sweatbox/RV.

I was an imposter.

I stood outside the open theater doors while the blogger's workshop took a lunch break. I grabbed a few people on their way out to interview for the recap video. A month ago, this alone would've intimidated me but after filming seven of Heath's jobs, asking random, slightly uncomfortable people if I could record them was now normal.

"So how did you end up filming this?" A guy named Marc asked after I thanked him for letting me ask him questions about the workshop.

"It's kind of a long story," I said, pausing without launching into the details. He raised his eyebrows as if to say he wanted to hear it. I shared how I was on my honeymoon and we were trying to go to all 50 states. How we decided to film a documentary and reached out to Chris Guillebeau about volunteering at his conference. How Wes called Heath and let us film even though we didn't have a ton of experience.

"That's awesome," Marc said, sounding genuinely interested. "Do you have a blog? I want to follow along. You said you have 43 states left?"

I was taken aback. Before taking off on our trip, people asked about our honeymoon with the same tone as a stranger asking "what do you do for a living?" It's that detached politeness where you knew they didn't really care about your answer. The conversations here were different. I told Marc my website address and watched him pull my site up on his phone and follow it. I struggled to pick up my jaw off the floor as we said goodbye and he sauntered off for lunch.

I may have been standing in the back of packed theaters filming, but I realized I didn't have to fade into the background too. Emboldened by one tiny act of encouragement, I continued running from venue to venue filming and interviewing speakers and attendees.

Sure, I was mentally preparing to return to my RV to see a note on the door from the security team asking us to explain why the lights in the parking lot were out. But, just like everyone else here, I was chasing after a dream that was always slightly out of reach. It was up to me to figure out how to make those dreams a reality.

I resolved to make the most of the opportunity.

Camera in hand and orange badge around my neck, I had access to everyone.

I interviewed Darren Rowse who started an obscenely successful website called ProBlogger. I chatted with Pat Flynn of the Smart Passive Income Podcast on how to find success as a blogger. I would later look at the footage and think "wow, this lighting is horrible" and "could I have just gotten the shot in focus instead of being so starstruck?" But I now had direct, practically personal advice from the best in the business on how to make my dream of becoming a writer true so I could continue a life of full-time travel.

I looked down from the balcony at the crowded auditorium where the last speaker of the day was talking about making money from a blog. I didn't have a pen to take notes, but I did have a camera. I balanced it on the back of the chair in front of me and let it record as much knowledge as it could while I rested my feet. My head was already spinning from everyone I'd met and learned from.

We had an idea—travel to all 50 states.

That idea morphed into the goal of making some money so we could keep traveling indefinitely.

As I looked around and recounted the dozens of stories I'd heard at the conference, our dreams felt a little closer.

Sure, our bank account was still shrinking and Franklin would probably break down again soon. But seeing all of these people filling the theater beneath me—taking notes, asking questions, laughing—proved that this impractical dream was possible.

Chapter 16

Oregon left us fortified and buoyant but physically and mentally exhausted. We spent six straight days filming and attending the conference and then had two days to make the nine-hour drive to Missoula, Montana. I'm older and wiser now, so when we hit the heat of eastern Oregon, I boldly walked to the back of the RV and held down the start button to crank on the generator to run the house A/C in the RV while we drove. Now at least the house wouldn't be stifling hot when we arrived at our destination…if only we learned this back in New Mexico, but now is better than never.

As we drove farther from the city and closer to the Rockies, I felt myself unconsciously relaxing. The green trees and the surrounding mountains rejuvenated us in a way that we didn't know we needed, restoring our energy after go-go-going in Oregon. All that time in the fast-paced city starkly differed from the expansive lands of Montana.

In Missoula, Heath worked for the city which happened to be throwing their weekly "Downtown Tonight" event with food trucks and live music down by the river. We left work at sunset with tons of free food and a couple of bottles of wine as gifts from Heath's kind bosses.

"We need to start writing this down," I told Heath as we drove north out of the small town.

"Writing down what types of wine we like? You're the one who always buys the $3 bottle at Walmart and lectured me when I picked out one that cost $5."

"Okay, do you want to go to Hawaii? Because that is going to be crazy expensive and we can use all the $2 savings we can get. When you sell our documentary for millions of dollars, then I will let you pick out the wine."

"How did this turn into a fight about money?"

"I don't know. I think you started it. Oh!" I remembered. "Okay, my idea. About money but in a more positive way. Lately, it's been evident just how many things we've gotten for free because people are nice. We had all those free meals during the conference. Plus free conference access. Free lunch and dinner today, free wine, free places to stay. We should make a list of all the free things people give to us and write down how much it would've cost us otherwise. I think it'll keep us grateful and it'll remind me of all the ways we've saved money."

"That's actually a really good idea."

"The surprise in your voice is insulting, but thank you," I said smugly. I grabbed a red notebook from the cabinet above my head. I flipped to a clean page and started writing.

July:

- free night in Washington at roommate's parents' house ($30)

- not having to go to a mechanic to fix the radiator ($?)
- free nights in Portland at Concordia ($150)
- Too many free meals/snacks/drinks to count during WDS
- World Domination Summit tickets ($1000)
- Michelin from Santa Barbara who gave us some soap at last night's campground when we realized we were out and couldn't do dishes
- Wine, a box of hamburger meat and fixings, and free lunch from Missoula

"We should crack open that wine when we get to the campground," Heath added. "We'll be at Flathead Lake in less than an hour."

"Absolutely," I said looking up from my journal and taking in the view through the windshield. The green grass waved in the breeze and the mountains glowed pink with the setting sun. "Wine would work perfectly with this."

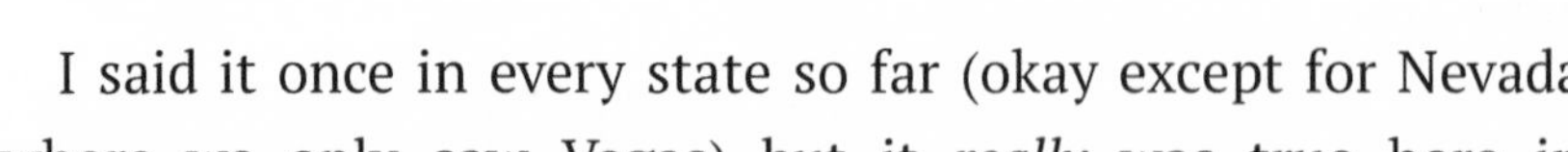

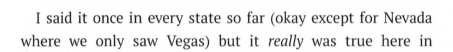

I said it once in every state so far (okay except for Nevada where we only saw Vegas) but it *really* was true here in Montana.

"This is the most beautiful place I've ever seen."

The national park bus drove us up the road past all ten miles of Lake McDonald, curving along rocky mountains with streams of water rushing down them. Colorful flowers were bursting out of cracks in the rocks contrasting with a sky filling up with grey clouds. We drove along the lake, then a river, and finally into the trees to our trailhead. The soft red dirt and imposing trees reminded me of the Redwoods.

The bus dropped us off in a parking lot across the street from the Trail of the Cedars, the short loop trail that accessed the Avalanche Lake trailhead. Families pushed grandparents in wheelchairs and kids in strollers along the elevated wooden path. We crossed a bridge with powerful white water cascading through the gorge beneath our tennis shoes. A sign ahead pointed us up a very steep staircase to begin our hike to Avalanche Lake. 2.3 miles to go.

I was out of breath and beginning to feel nervous about attempting a five-mile round trip hike when a four-year-old rushed past me on the trail. Okay, no need to make me feel so out of shape, kiddo. With all the miles we blazed through behind the wheel, I spent too much time sitting in the passenger seat.

The steep ascent ended and the path opened up with a forest to the right and a rushing creek to the left. Families and hikers spread out and a gentle wind blew my ponytail across my face. I zipped up my jacket. With every step, the statement became more true:

This is the most beautiful place I've ever seen.

Purple and teal rocks smoothed by the rushing glacial creek sparkled next to the trail. The water and the breeze rifling through the trees provided a constant peaceful hum. Heath and I hiked quietly, passing families hiking with babies strapped into complicated backpacks and older couples with hiking sticks.

Heath and I talked about everything and nothing as we walked through the trail. (Most common topics of conversation: Can we come back here ASAP? How can we keep traveling like this indefinitely? This is amazing!) The further we hiked, the other hikers thinned, leaving us to hike through sections of the trail completely alone.

"Stop," Heath said firmly, as if I was singing an annoying song instead of quietly walking behind him through a narrow point in the trail. "Back up slowly."

I peeked around him to see an elk not 10 feet in front of him. We were hiking through tall bushes on a narrow, curved part of the trail that unknowingly led us right to the giant antlers of the bull. We made eye contact, the elk and I. He just kept chewing on his grass while we stood frozen, not backing up like we should've because moving at all when you're that close to a giant animal is intimidating as all get out.

All of the bear-aware signs had me mentally prepared for what to do if I encountered a bear. Play dead if it's a grizzly. Be big and loud and throw rocks if it's a black bear. Make noise as you hike so you don't surprise a bear. The information for elk was to stay 100 feet away. How do you do that when you just turn a corner and bam! There he is.

Fortunately, he stood alone, with no family members to make him feel protective. We broke our eye contact and Heath and I backed away, waiting for him to pass so we could continue to the lake. A moment later, a big family hiked up the trail on the other side of the elk, loudly oohing and ahhing and prompting the bull to move further into the forest away from us.

Continuing down the trail, we soon ended at a large stretch of rocky beach and the blue waters of Avalanche Lake. Walls of stately Christmas trees (the scientific name for the familiar shaped green tree) lined the water with a staggering embankment of rock rising up behind them. The mountains were so rocky and steep almost no trees grew on the nearly perpendicular mountainside. I counted no less than seven waterfalls racing down from the mountain tops past banks of white snow.

The glacial water was so clear, you couldn't tell how deep it was, but you could see logs littering the lake bottom, a by-product of avalanches, I assumed. We sat on a large rock at the edge of the water each munching on a granola bar and silently judging the hikers who were sharing their snacks with the chipmunks.

"I think it keeps going," I said to Heath pointing to the thick forest of trees where I could see occasional flashes of bright red and orange hiking jackets.

"I'm down if you are. I thought we were already at the end, but we can keep going for a little while. If you're not too tired for the two and a half miles back."

"The first part of a trail always takes longer than hiking it back. Plus now it's more downhill."

"Very true. Let's go then."

We stuffed our trash into our hiking backpacks and made our way through the trees back to the main trail. Everyone else seemed to hop off the trail here to hang on the beach, but the dirt path continued into the darkness of the trees. You couldn't see the lake through the trees, but every 100 feet or so we'd come across a fallen tree giving us a clear view of the bright turquoise water. If I cropped out the mountain views and pine trees and didn't mention the cool air, you might think we were in the Caribbean.

We had the trail to ourselves until we came to a sign:

End of Trail. No camping. No Fires.

Off to the left, a rocky beach beckoned us. Unlike the first beach we encountered which was full of families and hikers, we were the only ones here. All you heard was water lapping against the shore and wind rustling the trees.

I'd like to tell you something profound or wise that I learned about life in this moment. But all I could think about as I sat on a log memorizing the ridges around me was how rare this is.

How rare it is to find a moment of such uninterrupted silence. To be alone. To give yourself the chance to sit and be. To not have your phone out, because you definitely don't have service so there's no point in even carrying it with you. Never when I worked full-time and lived in an apartment and did the whole normal adult life thing did I have a moment like this. There was always music playing, TV in the background, cars driving by. Here you could think. Breathe.

I tried to think of another moment in the past eight states where we just sat outside. Not moving or hiking or exploring. Not eating a meal. Just sitting and appreciating where we were. Slowly we were shedding our vacation mentality to see it all, do it all, rushing everything, checking off the boxes of all the cool things we wanted to see and do on our trip.

"I hate calling this a trip," I blurted out to Heath who wasn't following the thoughts in my head and needed a second to catch up. "Everyone always asks how the trip is going, but trips end. You get back and life goes back to how it was."

"You don't want to go back," Heath said more as a statement than a question.

"Do you?" I asked, gesturing my arms toward the beautiful expanse of Avalanche Lake.

"Since WDS last week, or I guess that was only a couple days ago—wow. We've already done so much since we left Oregon. But since WDS, I've been thinking about that more too. We met so many people who are traveling all the time like it's no big deal but before meeting them, it felt like a big deal. Like it would be too hard to find a way to make money and work remotely. Now that we've actually met people doing it and we have the RV, all we need is income."

"Totally. I keep thinking about what the manager said when we checked into that first RV park in Austin. Everyone was all crowded around us and she said how smart we were to do this now and not wait until we're retired like they all did. And yeah we are doing it, but if we *keep* doing it beyond just this quote-unquote trip, I don't even know what you'd call that."

"Full-time traveling?"

"We could travel full-time," I tested the words on my tongue. "That sounds like a dream."

"It's not a dream if you actually do it," Heath pointed out. "Come on, the sky looks like it's about to let loose. Let's head back."

The words lingered in my mind.

There was something undeniably sexy about full-time traveling. Or being location independent or a digital nomad or any of the catchy ways of saying "working traveler" that we learned at the World Domination Summit. It evokes images of white sand beaches and lush green mountains and a certain carefree attitude.

That's what I pictured when I heard full-time travel at least, even though that was nothing like our experiences traveling so far. There were mountains and beaches, often in the same day, but it was so much more than just beautiful scenery.

The return hike was less eventful—except for seeing a single deer from 200 feet away—and by the time we made it back to the wooded trail through the cedars, the rain started to pour. We jogged across the road to the picnic area where the bus would pick us up to return to Apgar Campground and our rolling home. I pulled my jacket hood up over my head and wanted to hide under the cover of the trees, but more hikers appeared so we stood our ground in the rain to make sure we made it on the next bus.

I shivered in my wet clothes and after a long 20 minutes, the bus finally appeared. Being the end of the afternoon, the bus coming down the mountain was mostly full but we squeezed on to make it back to the campground. We hung our wet jackets up in the RV shower to dry—rain jackets didn't make the shortlist of packing supplies, a small oversight—and settled in for the night.

When we finally departed Montana to head south, the stunning views didn't end. We weaved down highways along green mountains and shimmering lakes dotted with giant log cabins sitting on acres of open land. Yellowstone and the Grand Tetons wowed us with waterfalls, sparkling blue waters, rocky mountains, and summer crowds. We saw a bear, a moose, and I swear a wolf sprinted in front of our RV one morning.

Other than biting our nails up the 10% grades of Teton Pass, our time in the mountains passed without incident. We plugged our noses as we explored the unbelievable sights and smells in Yellowstone. We hiked mountains where we shouted conversation at each other so we could scare off any bears. Heath "showered" in Jenny Lake when we dry camped without hookups while I barely waded in past my ankles in the glacial waters. One morning in Wyoming, we even cranked on our furnace to warm up from the 39° frost only to realize we had no idea how to use the furnace and it never warmed up. A minor hiccup and a problem for future Heath and Alyssa to figure out.

By all accounts, the Rockies sailed by smoothly (and much too quickly). Heath worked at a music shop in Idaho, a bakery in Wyoming, and a coffee shop in Colorado, and we gained confidence as we crossed off each state.

In the three weeks between Oregon and South Dakota, we hiked, spent every day outside, and even though we were regularly offline in the mountains, Heath and I took time in the mornings to write blogs for a few websites—slowly adding to our monthly income. Other than replacing a cracked sewer hose, our woes with the RV were seemingly behind us and we felt at home on the road. This RVing thing is a cinch, we thought, as we settled into new campgrounds every night. Life was perfect.

Which explains why it was all about to go sideways.

Chapter 17

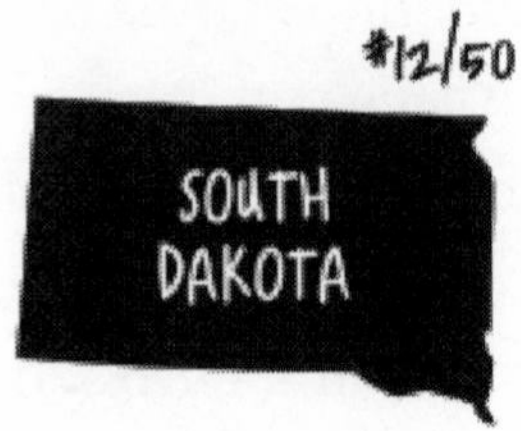

South Dakota is a hidden gem. After endless prairies from Denver across eastern Wyoming, rocky black hills entered the landscape in South Dakota. Along with a shocking number of signs blinking: Look Twice, Save a Life. It's the more memorable way of saying watch out for motorcycles.

And there were a weird amount of motorcycles for being in the middle of nowhere. Every few minutes, someone clad in black leather sped past us. We wound our way toward Crazy Horse Monument, escorted by a hundred Harleys, and couldn't figure out why. Is there some motorcycle culture thing that involves visiting Mount Rushmore at the beginning of August?

A vinyl sign above a bar answered our question: Welcome Sturgis Riders!

Every year, according to the quick Google search I did on Heath's phone, Sturgis, South Dakota hosts the largest biker rally in the world, attracting over half a million bikers and prompting the many "look twice, save a life" signs. Our route to Crazy Horse and Mount Rushmore would keep us over 50 miles south of the actual town of Sturgis, but we couldn't tell from the traffic on the roads.

Tiny towns three blocks wide were clogged with bikers. We eked by at 10 miles an hour surrounded on all sides by pedestrians and motorcycles. Hundreds of bikes lined the roads while their owners milled around, beers in hand. Apart from the Pacific Coast Highway, I'm not sure I'd seen Heath this nervous while driving as he maneuvered our RV around pack after pack of motorcycle groups.

Pulling into Crazy Horse Monument, we waited in line to pay the entrance fee. $20 would be steep, but a few people told us that Mount Rushmore was nothing compared to Crazy Horse and it would be worth the stop. We scooted forward slowly before stopping at the booth.

"Hi, it's the two of us," Heath said.

"Well hi you two," a friendly older man said. "What brings you out here?"

"We're on our honeymoon actually," Heath said, looking back over his shoulder to smile at me.

"Your honeymoon! Well, go on in then! It's free entry for honeymooners today." He clearly made this up on the spot, but we wouldn't question his kindness. I would add it to the gratitude journal. The gate agent smiled and wished us congratulations before giving us parking directions.

"Thank you," we both called out as Heath pulled away. I put up my hand and without looking, Heath gave me a high-five. Sometimes it's the little things.

Crazy Horse, we would learn over the next two hours, is way better than Mount Rushmore. It's been in progress since the

1940s and won't be finished for decades to come. Eventually, the monument will depict Crazy Horse, the famous Native American from the Battle of Little Big Horn, sitting on a horse and it will be 563 feet tall. In comparison, the heads on Mount Rushmore are 60 feet tall. Which is why when we pulled into the gate at Mount Rushmore and saw the tiny faces, we just snapped a quick photo of the presidential busts from the passenger window and continued on. Crazy Horse took the cake.

You hear about all these great American landmarks growing up, like Mount Rushmore, but only once we started traveling did we start hearing the inside scoop on lesser-known, but well-loved other attractions. We met half a dozen people before we made it to South Dakota who urged us to skip Mount Rushmore in favor of Crazy Horse. We decided to make it our first official travel rule: If we hear a destination suggested more than once, we must visit.

We pulled back onto the highway and I started calling RV parks to find us a spot for the night. We thought once we left the popular destinations in the west that finding RV sites would be easier. With summer winding down, fewer people would be on the road, we reasoned.

Only problem: the unexpected biker rally.

We finally found Heartland RV Park with one campsite left for the night.

"Yes, we'll take it. We're on our way!"

Turning into the RV park an hour south of Sturgis, we stood out like sore thumbs with no motorcycles and no cool toy hauler. We walked around the park during the afternoon to stretch our legs and heard stories from the many people attending the event. Accountants, government workers, bankers, grandparents—the motorcycle event attracted people from all over who bonded over their love of biking.

Despite being in the middle of nowhere in South Dakota, we found ourselves at an RV park with good Wi-Fi for the first time on the road. Great Wi-Fi. Can-stream-Netflix Wi-Fi. With dark clouds on the horizon, we decided to cuddle up in bed and stream a movie.

Well, we moved to the bed after sitting on the couch for five minutes and feeling drips of rain hit our knees. We looked up to see little drops dotting the ceiling around the handle where you could crank up the four-foot-long antenna on the roof to connect to local TV channels. (Or at least that's how the ancient 1994 technology was described to me.) The unused antenna now boasted our first water leak. I grabbed our only mixing bowl and wedged it at the foot of the couch, adding a hand towel on the seat to absorb the rain before our couch was soaked.

So we relocated to the bed and the rain poured while we watched Russell Crowe fight in the Colosseum.

Back in May while Heath lived in the RV leading up to the wedding, thunderstorms rolled through Austin. Spring is prime storm season in Texas, with tornados, high winds, and lightning storms. One particular night, Heath texted me frantically about the lightning. He couldn't sleep. The rain and thunder shook the RV all night. He paid for a couple of apps on his phone to show high def radar and real-time lightning strikes. Little red lightning bolts flashed right on top of the blinking blue dot that showed his location. The next morning, he learned the Airstream trailer parked not 50 feet away was struck by lightning, frying the electrical system so badly that the RV and every device that was plugged in was destroyed.

Which is all we could think about when we couldn't hear *Gladiator* over the sound of the rain on our roof and the thunder rattling our windows. Heath opened up his lightning tracker app and saw lighting striking all around us. A dark red mass moved slowly east, encroaching on our location.

"I think we should seek shelter," Heath said, angling the phone screen toward me.

I'd never sought out shelter from a thunderstorm before. I remember my mom always telling me to not shower in a thunderstorm for some reason. But it was a general rule that you were safe inside. With the RV rocking from the wind and the rain, it didn't feel safe inside.

I leaned over to our bedroom window and pulled our shades up. It didn't look safe outside either. "It's pouring buckets. Look, the gravel roads are rivers. Where will we even go?"

"There's a bathhouse at the end of this road. I think I see people standing under the awning of it actually," he said, joining me at the window. In the distance, I could see porch lights on a small building. Thunder boomed overhead. Running through water in a lightning storm didn't sound smart, but with the most intense part of the storm looming, we had to make a decision fast.

"So make a run for it?" I asked Heath.

"Do we have rain jackets?"

"Nope."

"Rain boots?"

"Flip flops."

"Our options are get soaked walking over there, or stay in

here and potentially get struck by lightning," Heath pointed out.

"I feel like you're discounting the option that we get struck by lightning on the sprint to the bathhouse. It is not close."

"Your call."

I weighed the options quickly. With the dark red portion of the storm drawing closer and closer, taking shelter was the right choice. There's just a terrifying sprint through dark stormwater to conquer first.

"Let's go."

Forgetting to close my laptop and leaving Russell to fend for himself, we jumped off the bed and headed for the door. I slipped on my flip-flops, looking for a jacket to protect me from the rain, but Heath was already opening the door and climbing out.

"I've got the keys," he said as if someone would try to break into our RV during this storm.

"Leave 'em," I replied, but Heath was already jogging away. I hopped down our rickety metal steps, pushed the door closed wondering why Heath grabbed the keys but didn't intend to stick around long enough to even lock the door, and ran after Heath who was 50 feet away from me already. Well at least with the way he was already rushing away, only one of us would likely get struck by lightning and die.

I jogged as fast as I could in ankle-deep water in my flop flops—which should be an Olympic sport for the level of difficulty and skill it requires—and was completely soaked when I joined Heath and a crowd of biker girls taking shelter. We all squeezed into the hallway out of the wind and the rain while the lightning picked up. Everyone exchanged glances and small comments about the weather the way you do when you're stuck in a small space with strangers.

"I should've brought a towel so I could at least shower while I wait in here," I told Heath, forgetting my mother's advice.

He laughed. "Go ahead. You don't need a towel. We'll get soaked when we walk back to the RV anyway."

"Fair point." Once we were inside, the situation didn't seem that scary at all. The building stood firm and we were surrounded by friendly chatter that drowned out the commotion from the raging storm. After fifteen minutes, we could see through the tiny window on the bathhouse door that the flashes of light shifted mostly off to the right side of the park and we opened the door to check out the storm conditions.

Which is about when I realized we were the only sober people in this bathhouse.

I'm not entirely sure how I didn't notice it before. But the blonde woman was shouting and flashing someone outside, so it became pretty obvious. I couldn't tell what the blonde was slurring, but the fact that she started taking off her clothes toward whoever she was yelling at told me that at least it was probably happy yelling?

The bikers wandered off in the direction of the men they were yelling at, all standing in the rain oblivious to the storm, or simply not caring that wet leather isn't comfortable, leaving Heath and I alone in the bathhouse while the skies continued to dump. Poking our heads out the door, Heath checked his app again to see the storm had fully moved east past us. Other than overflowing the mixing bowl on our living room floor, the rain alone didn't pose much of a threat. So we walked back to our house and I held my flip-flops in my hand this time, moving faster and getting less wet without them slapping water all over me.

When we opened the RV door, we instantly knew something was wrong. The microwave was flashing 12:00—the international sign of a temporary loss of power. The coffee pot wasn't flashing the time at all. The international sign for no power. *Gladiator* was still playing on my laptop, which I had learned from the Airstream incident to keep unplugged during a storm, and some of our lights were on. But definitely fewer lights than before.

"This is weird," Heath said. We didn't lose power in the bathhouse during the storm, so we assumed we hadn't lost power in the RV. But clearly, something electrical was tripped. We walked around flipping light switches and testing outlets. No outlets or lights on the front half of the RV worked, except for the light under the microwave. The refrigerator was off—or at least the little green light looked off and when we switched it to propane mode like we do whenever we don't have electrical hook ups, nothing happened. We decided we'd have to test the temperature in the morning and keep the doors closed as much as possible until we could figure that out. We cranked on the generator to see if that could give us power back in the RV, but the machine shuddered and shook the RV before failing to turn over.

None of it makes sense, we thought as we double-checked outlets and unplugged everything for the night just in case more storms blew through. Why would only half of the RV be messed up and the back half be fine? And why would the generator not turn on?

I laid in bed unable to fall asleep as I tried to figure out what could possibly be wrong this time. We checked everything twice. Luckily, we moved the coffee pot into the bedroom and it instantly lit up 12:00 when plugged into a working outlet, so at least our only way to make coffee survived the storm.

I saw another mechanic shop in our future.

The next morning, the RV engine cranked on with a whine that caused Heath and me to give each other a look that said "Can we pretend that we didn't hear that sound and that everything is totally fine?" We pulled onto the highway determined to finish South Dakota by exploring Badlands National Park on our way to Sioux Falls for Heath's next job. But when we turned left out of the campground and started to ascend a hill, the panorama of South Dakota came into view and the sky was a wall of black. Without a word, Heath pulled over and whipped out his phone. I saw him open a very colorful weather radar app. The main color was an intimidating line of crimson slowly moving toward our location.

"This is a nice campground. How about we stay for another night?" he suggested.

I nodded in rapid agreement, noticing we were the only vehicle on the road as we made a U-turn and headed a mile back to the campground to lock in another night. Despite our phones alerting us to daily tornadoes in the area, we survived three stormy nights at the RV park before we had to get back on the road. The roof kept leaking, but we did find a GFI switch hidden in a cabinet in our bathroom. We clicked reset and regained power to our fridge and outlets. The lights flickered back on too, though they were abnormally dim. The generator stopped even trying to turn over.

Short on money and time, we continued east ignoring our ongoing electrical issues for the time being.

Which is why the sign for "free donuts and coffee for honeymooners" caught our eye. Cruising down Interstate 90, hand-painted signs punctuated every few miles.

Free ice water, Wall Drug.

5¢ coffee, Wall Drug.

Homemade ice cream, Wall Drug.

It's a blast, Wall Drug.

At this point, we had no clue what Wall Drug actually was. Gas station? Restaurant? Store? Ice cream shop? Giddy over the promise of free homemade donuts and coffee, I searched for Wall Drug on Google Maps to make sure we wouldn't miss the exit. Although at that rate, we could probably expect another 100 signs letting us know where to turn without a GPS. The billboards worked like magic and, free donuts or not, we were too curious not to stop.

We pulled into the roadside attraction—Wall Drug, the largest drug store in the world—and found that it's a little bit of everything. Restaurant. Store. Museum. Chapel. A mining area. A water show. At one point there's a T-rex jumping out at you. Oh, and a tiny little drug store where you can actually get medicine. It was curious and odd and wonderful.

We wandered around getting lost and wondering what on earth we stumbled upon. We grabbed our donuts and coffee and snapped a selfie at this bizarre little attraction before hopping back on the road. I recorded in my red notebook "free coffee and donuts ($3)" as Heath pulled back onto the highway. We already filled up half a page with free food and free camping nights. I found myself re-reading the list to get my mind off our increasingly stressful travels when we pulled under an overpass after a loud beeping came from our phones alerting us of yet another tornado in the area.

Growing up in north Texas, tornados every spring are just part of life. But in Texas, I was in a real house with brick walls and a foundation. I'm pretty sure a tornado could hurl our RV halfway across the state. While the motorhome presented an incredible amount of freedom, South Dakota revealed the RV's major weakness. There was no way to feel secure in critical weather. You just hoped and prayed you could find shelter nearby. The stress of being exposed to the elements compounded as we moved across the midwest.

Every day was more of the same. Heath worked a job, we drove in the rain to the next job.

We made cupcakes in South Dakota, poured beer in North Dakota—where we couldn't find a campsite so we drove into Minnesota, making North Dakota our first state to not spend the night in. Heath poured wine in Minnesota and milked cows in Wisconsin, which meant waking up at 3:00 AM to work on the farm all morning in the pouring rain.

Now the RV was beginning to have a slight mildew smell from the humidity and the roof leak, but we couldn't air it out with the endless rain. Our yellow towel and blue mixing bowl had become a permanent fixture on the floor next to our couch. Not that that means I hadn't tripped over it every day for the past two weeks. I had. But there was no point in moving it since the rains hadn't stopped.

And they had to stop sometime, right?

Chapter 18

"Are you still awake?" Heath whispered from the pillow next to mine.

"You must have me confused with the amazing Alyssa who can sleep through chainsaws and sirens and rock concerts," I retorted.

Rain. Acorns. Small branches. They all beat against our roof at a deafening roar. We didn't turn on the lights—no need when there's that much lightning happening—but looking outside showed the dirt around our campsite was now a small pond.

We chose to camp at Cunningham Lake just north of Omaha because it sounded beautiful. It even looked beautiful when we arrived at sunset. But parking so close to a lake suddenly became our stupidest decision yet. I couldn't tell how high the lake was, but there was nothing but standing water outside every window of the RV. How much rain would it take for the lakeshore to reach our tires? Could the water wash us away?

The rain fell in sheets and the weather apps showed rain for the next few days. Not hours, days without reprieve. The storm raged on.

We weighed our options.

Option 1: Drive away and find a safer place to park on high ground.

This would mean Heath going outside to unhook our power cord while standing ankle-deep in water during a lightning storm...okay scratch that plan. We can't leave. There was so much standing water outside now that we probably wouldn't be able to see the difference between roads and mud and would end up stuck.

Option 2: Find shelter and leave the RV to fend for itself like we did two weeks ago in South Dakota.

Except we weren't in an RV park or even a state park. There was no map given out when we pulled in and we didn't spot the bathhouse as we found an open campsite. So we would be splashing around the campground in the dark hoping there's a shelter around somewhere. Scratch that.

Option 3: Wait it out.

Our safest option. Our only option really.

It was far from ideal and we'd already taken turns every ten minutes of the last two hours asking each other if we were still awake. The branches of the giant tree we parked under loomed over us, casting shadows in the lightning and threatening to blow over and crush us.

"What are the odds that a tree branch falls and crushes us and our home?" I asked.

"Why would you bring that up? I was just about to go to sleep!" Heath moaned.

"I'm being serious. You can hear that tree creaking in the wind!"

"The tree is not going to crush us," Heath reassured me, flipping over to attempt to sleep once again.

I got up and paced the RV, double-checking once again that everything was unplugged. Did I unplug and put away all the camera chargers earlier? I pulled out the camera bag from behind the passenger seat to check.

"Oh no. Oh no, oh no, oh no, Heath." I groaned. I hate the midwest. Can we please go back to the Rockies when life was simpler?

"What?" Heath asked with a sigh, climbing out of bed and finally resigning to the fact that neither of us would be sleeping.

"Turn on the lights and grab some dry towels. The camera bag feels completely soaked," I said as I pulled out piece after piece of equipment. The bottom, top, and sides of the camera bag were soaked through. The inside was damp. Closer inspection showed that the equipment itself was mostly dry, except for a few smudges of water on the bottom of the camera that I wiped off with my sleeve. *Thank God.*

"How is it that every side of this whole bag is soaked and everything inside is fine? This isn't a waterproof bag," I wondered aloud.

Heath flipped on the flashlight on his phone. "It was sitting behind this chair, right?" He asked. I nodded. He squatted down and started feeling around the floor. "There is just a puddle of water right here. Where is it coming from... The walls are all wet too. And soft when I press on them. I think...yeah. Crap. I'm pretty sure this window is leaking."

Water damage is cancer to an RV. Those words we heard while RV shopping flooded back to me. We dried everything best we could, storing the camera gear far away from windows, and leaving a trail of bowls and towels all over our floor. Two water leaks. No generator. Questionable power that had our lights flickering. The RV still made a screeching noise when we turned over the engine. So much was breaking on the RV, I wouldn't be surprised if the roof caved in.

This is not the glamorous travel lifestyle I was promised.

Well, I guess no one ever actually said RVing would be glamorous. Except there was that amazing windshield view when we camped at the Tetons. That was a million-dollar view for sure. And camping to the sound of the waves in California? Pure magic.

That's the thing about living in an RV. Stuff breaks just like in a house, but it's almost immediately offset by the most gorgeous views of mountain vistas. Or a moose ambles past your window. Or you spend a day with your jaw on the floor driving around the Grand Canyon.

However, the midwest hadn't offered us anything but storms since we crossed into western South Dakota.

Finally, around 4:00 AM, the storms began to slow down. We no longer needed to discuss hypothetically what would happen if/when the RV was struck by lightning or where was the best place to sit in case the tree blew over or what we would do if the RV started to float away. We drifted off to sleep for a couple of hours before our easily snoozed alarms started reminding us every nine minutes that we had a job to get to.

We moved like jello through the RV, tossing wet towels on the shower floor and securing anything that might move while driving so we could make it to our job at the brewery in time. Between yawns, Heath drove us through sprinkling rain, although the skies threatened more. I miss the sun, I thought, even though we saw the sun in between storms yesterday. It was brief and muggy and not appreciated fully.

The day passed in a blur. Devouring a bowl of cereal in the parking lot. Heath sweeping. A machine filling bottles of vodka. The smell of beer. Tasting a thimble of rum and thinking that would be all it would take for me to fall asleep on the freshly swept floor. The smell of alcohol all around made it feel like we were stuck in a hangover even though our lack of sleep was flooding-related.

We wrapped after lunch and drove, in the rain, back to the lake. Either because we are gluttons for punishment or because all the RV parks were filled. My sleep-deprived brain couldn't remember. We fought through Omaha traffic, parked at a different campsite further away from the water and not under a tree, and collapsed into bed to nap.

I woke up an hour later, only knowing that I fell asleep because of the clock. My brain was groggy and exhausted and Heath continued to snore on top of the covers next to me. I pulled a bag of off-brand Cheerios from our cabinet and poured myself my second bowl of the day, too tired to think about making real food. Plopping down at the table, I started backing up our footage from the past two days of jobs.

I leaned back in the chair, letting the computer do all the work while I spooned down my snack. After every job, I spent at least an hour copying the memory cards from each camera to my computer and then copying the files from my computer to my hard drive. It was a simple process that paired well with eating a snack.

Phwoomp. That's the best way I can describe the "your files finished copying" sound my laptop made. Kind of like a landing thud, but with a little oomph to it. I sat down my bowl to the side of my laptop, wiped the SD cards clean, and plugged in my hard drive to back up the files. Right-click, new folder. I typed:

17 Hog Stop BBQ – Iowa

18 Lucky Bucket Brewing – Nebraska

So close to halfway. When we were done with the midwest, we'd be on the home stretch. Summer and its monumental thunderstorms will be just a memory. I couldn't believe when I planned our route that I thought to avoid hurricane season and winter temps but never even Googled tornado season.

I scrolled through the folders on my computer to drag the video clips into their new folders on my hard drive.

I scrolled.

And scrolled.

And scrolled.

I buried my head into my hands. *This did not just happen.* I fiddled with memory cards and folders searching everywhere. My heart pounded. I kept searching in vain but knew it was gone.

"I just lost it," I said, shaking Heath awake from his nap.

"Lost what?"

"All of the footage from the past two days." My voice quivered.

"What do you mean you lost it?"

"I mean it was right here. I imported it to the computer, then wiped the cards, then plugged in the hard drive because I only have one port on this laptop and I can't fit all these things in at the same time, and when I went to move the footage from the computer to the hard drive the same way I always do, it was gone. Just gone. I've looked everywhere. Recent imports, recent folders, trash. It literally disappeared." I felt tears building up behind my eyes and tried to push them back. I assumed Heath would be upset. I was upset. Would we have to find and work two more jobs so we could have footage from every state? Would Snagajob be mad when they realized we had no photos or video clips for Heath's blog recaps? I couldn't believe I messed this up.

"And you're sure it's not on the cards anymore?" Heath said, leaning his elbow on the table and scrolling through the empty folders on the screen.

"I checked."

"And it's nowhere on the computer? You didn't save it to a different folder?" he questioned.

"I've done this after every single job the exact same way. It just disappeared! I don't know what happened. Two whole jobs. Gone. I didn't bother to back up yesterday's job yet since I knew we would be working again today. I thought it would be faster and easier to just wait and do them both at once." Footage from two states was gone forever.

Heath sank into the couch and ran his fingers through his hair with a groan. The storms, increasing number of RV leaks, and lack of sleep were wearing us down a little more each day, but this felt like rock bottom. This was 100% my fault and we needed this footage for our documentary and for our sponsor—AKA our biggest source of income. I couldn't believe I screwed this up.

We were quiet for a long time before Heath picked up his phone. "If we leave right now, we can make it to your parent's house by 1:00 AM. We haven't paid for this campsite yet. We could just head south and take a break for a few days. Maybe figure out why half of the stuff in the RV isn't working."

"Leave? Right now?" I asked, surprised at his response to realizing that I lost our footage. I expected him to at least be a little mad at me, but he seemed to know that at this level of sleep deprivation, a fight would be brutal. Instead, he was on my team, supporting me at this low point when he had every right to be furious. "It's 4:00 PM. We barely slept last night and that's a lot of driving." My words were skeptical, but internally, I was already picturing how nice it would be to go back to Texas. Sleep in my old bed. Shower every day. No leaks. No tornados. Not to mention my mom could cook us a few meals, adding to our savings. Maybe my dad could help us figure out what was wrong with our RV. We hadn't taken it to a mechanic to be diagnosed since that monster storm in South Dakota.

I sat on the couch next to Heath and looked out the window at the gently falling rain and the black horizon, knowing that at some point soon lightning and wind and who knows what else would likely terrorize us again all night. He put his arm around my waist and leaned his head against mine.

"It's been a hard few weeks. I think we both want a chance to reset," he said.

"Let's go."

Chapter 19

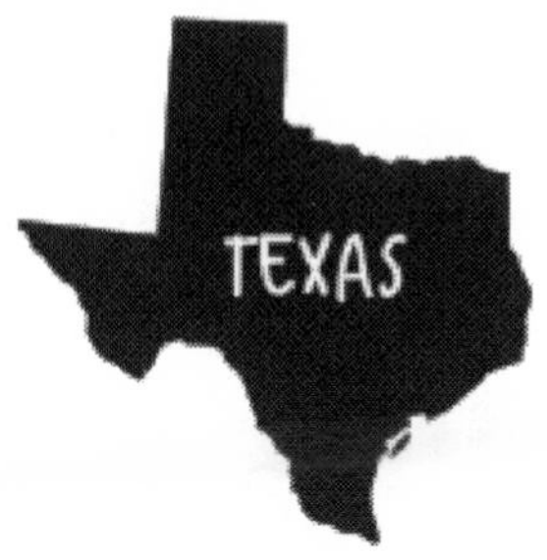

"You were definitely struck by lightning."

"What?!" Heath and I said in unison to the mechanic.

Taking shelter in South Dakota was the right idea.

"If not struck, it was close enough to melt your house battery. Totally destroyed. Connections were melted." I gulped listening to the mechanic casually recounting the damage to our home. "We replaced the battery and, after that, the generator and everything worked fine. For now at least," the mechanic said, eyeing our old home with a shrug.

On the ride from the mechanic back to my parents' house, Heath and I threw around our options.

As we made our way south down I-35 toward Texas, I had worried that taking this break was the wrong decision. I almost told Heath to stop driving more than once. What if we got a $1,000 mechanic bill? What if we had to stay in Texas for a while to refill our bank account?

If we took this break, would we be able to get back on the road?

I feared that stopping not even 20 states in might mean we would get comfortable. Too comfortable to get back out on the road and finish our 50 state goal.

But we could afford the $200 mechanic bill even if it meant our bank account was getting closer and closer to zero. While our house sat in the shop, Heath and I were both blogging on our personal site (making $0) and for a few companies (making less than $150 a month). We hustled as hard as we could, but writing just didn't make much money. And we were dangerously close to being completely broke. Our resolve weakened as our reality became clear. We were *maybe* two weeks away from hitting zero. If we hadn't stopped in Texas and saved on gas and campgrounds, we would've hit zero this week.

"Do you want to stay longer? We can park in your parents' driveway and take a couple more weeks to see if we can find remote work. Or write a few more blog posts," Heath offered as we inched forward in Dallas traffic.

"What about Snagajob?" I asked. They surely wouldn't be happy about us delaying our plans and breaking our contracted dates.

"They probably wouldn't pay us our monthly payment on the 1st, but they might be okay with shifting dates around."

"They are paying us $1,000 a month for their blog posts and the documentary. Realistically, you and I would have to write at least 15 blog posts for other companies to even come close to that much. Or find another way to make money. Video maybe, since we have cameras?" I rambled, my mind getting lost in the logistics. The fear of ending up penniless in a broken-down RV grew in the back of my mind. I wanted to make it to all 50 states with Heath. I wanted us to figure out a way to financially make this possible.

I tried to think back to life in New Orleans. I think my biggest worries back then were missing my long-distance boyfriend and boredom, but life was so different now that it was hard to picture that I once spent most of my days sitting still in one place.

Life certainly wasn't boring any more. And I definitely didn't miss Heath considering we were within 20 feet of each other 24/7.

I smiled thoughtfully and looked over my shoulder at our home on wheels.

So far, our trip around the country challenged us more than I thought it would. I knew things would get hard, but I kind of imagined a flat tire here, maybe a tense bear encounter there. The tornados and getting struck by lightning and weeks of losing sleep from thunderstorms didn't cross my mind.

Maybe we just needed this respite in Texas to remember why we started this adventure in the first place. It's hard to remember why you chose RV life when it's 4:00 AM and you're drying off camera batteries and the RV is shaking from the wind...but you're also wondering if it's shaking because the lakeshore finally caught up to you and you're about to be swept away.

We wanted a life of adventure and we definitely got it. The first 18 states went above and beyond in delivering adventure and challenges and beauty, but we still had 32 more states worth of adventures.

The RV was good as new. Or at least the house battery was new. There were still innumerable leaks but we'd half-forgotten about those since we escaped the rains. Other than our shrinking bank balance, we didn't have a good reason to stop traveling. Being broke didn't feel like a good enough reason to stop.

We decided to press on. We just had to find a way to not be broke.

"Jim's parents are visiting him in Austin all week, so they said we can park in their driveway and stay inside if we'd like," Heath said, hanging up the phone.

"Yes!" I replied. "What side of St. Louis is it on? Missouri or Illinois? Because we need the Missouri side for your next job. The Italian restaurant in Chicago counted for Illinois." Heath double-checked the address was in Missouri and secured our parking until his job over the weekend. Every free night of camping felt like buying another day out on the road. We realized that if we could spend most of the next month free camping, we could keep extending our bank account.

We pulled our RV up the inclined driveway and parked, partially blocking the sidewalk in the tiny suburban subdivision. Our ratty old RV stood out against the green lawns.

"Should we drop our jacks to level out? Or plug in our extension cord for the fridge?"

"Nah," Heath said. "I don't want our jacks to scrape up their driveway and I don't want to run our long extension cord into their garage. Feels weird since they aren't here, you know?"

I agreed and packed up a reusable grocery bag with toiletries and clothes to move into the guest bedroom. I dumped everything on the bed and went back to the RV to refill my tote bag with some food to cook inside the house.

The thing about traveling is that you become intensely adaptable. No matter where you are, you develop the ability to make yourself at home, even when you're in your husband's college roommate's parents' house instead of your home on wheels. We were so comfortable coming back to the house after Heath's job in the city that we forgot about the RV a little bit.

Until the morning we planned to leave for Indiana.

I repacked my reusable grocery bag with the random foods we brought in a few days earlier. Shredded cheese, ketchup, carton of almond milk, a half-eaten bag of broccoli florets. I folded the bag against my chest as I stepped out of the front door into the cool fall air. Being from Texas, fall was a foreign concept. It applied to a three-week period in November when everything turned brown and it was 70 degrees every day. This mid-September chill was different. A single deep breath outside and you instantly started craving hot apple cider and pie. I don't know how the air did it, but I wanted cinnamon-flavored anything and the satisfying crunch of stepping on a particularly good leaf.

I unlocked and climbed into our RV, which felt just as chilly as the Missouri morning air. Plopping the grocery bag down in the chair, I opened our fridge to restock. Huh, I wondered. *Is it that cold outside that I can't feel a difference between the fridge and the air, or is our fridge off?* The little green light on the propane setting was still on. A quick opening of the freezer confirmed my worst fear when my nose was assaulted with the rancid scent of decaying meat.

Our refrigerator was toast.

I carted my groceries back inside to break the news to Heath. Living without a few lights working? No big deal. No generator? We can survive without it. No fridge? Deal-breaker. We needed food.

Heath and I started running down the checklist to figure out how to get the fridge back up and running.

House battery: charged and operational, not the problem.

Propane: still plenty in the tank, not the problem. Tested for leaks, no leaks.

Plugging into electricity and waiting overnight: still a room temperature fridge, not the problem.

Google gave us two options:

1. Buy a new RV fridge—which starts at around $1,500
2. Burp the fridge

"I don't know what you're saying right now." I sat on the couch staring at our fridge. "$1,500 for a fridge? That's like 10% of the whole value of the RV. And burping? What is that supposed to mean?"

"I'm just repeating what this RV site says. Burp the fridge," Heath repeated. "Take it out, flip it upside down and let the chemicals all redistribute and then flip it back up and it works."

"None of that makes any sense to me," I shook my head.

"Just come look at the back of the fridge," he said, leading me outside and pulling off a panel that revealed the back of the fridge. It wasn't pretty. Twisted copper (or formerly copper) pipes were crusted with dirt and I didn't want to guess what else, but it was chalky and blue. "I think that's our only option. From what I've read, if the propane fridge runs when it's unlevel, these coils back here can explode. Something about the chemicals not being able to move like they are supposed to. Look at all this gunk. I'm pretty sure that's what happened."

"Explode?"

"I think they just burst and that's where all this paste stuff came from."

So in exchange for a free place to stay, we created a small chemical explosion and broke our refrigerator? Shouldn't RVs come with a warning or something so you don't do this by accident?

"And it's a thousand dollars for a new one of these fridges?" I asked.

"More like $1,500 for a cheap one. Plus labor for someone to install it."

"We really can't afford that," I said. Only a few days ago everything was looking up. TV reporters came out to interview us at a bike shop in Oklahoma. Readers of our blog started reaching out to express their support of our crazy dream and how, despite all of our challenges, we were still moving forward. But this was an immovable wall. A very expensive, very necessary immovable wall.

Our bank account confirmed it with a balance of $82.71 in our checking account. Between the maintenance and paying off our credit card expenses for the month of August, we blew through the $1,000 monthly payment from Snagajob for our sponsorship. I had a little money I knew would come in before the end of the month, but certainly not enough for us to make another big purchase. Forget the problem of where to store cold food. How would we even afford food?

"So here's what I'm thinking," Heath said with confidence, bolstering my spirit. "We need a fridge."

I looked at him, waiting for more. He stood with his hands on his hips staring at the back panel of our fridge, but he didn't say a word.

"That's it? Your plan is just that we need a fridge? I know we need a fridge!"

"Well, what's your plan?" He argued.

"I don't know!" I replied, defeated. "Cause I don't know a lot about refrigerators, but I know that they are supposed to cool things and that when they stop cooling things, that's usually when you have to buy a new one."

"You just said we can't afford to buy a new one."

"I know what I said, Heath!" I bickered.

"We should go inside the house," Heath said, not wanting to cause a scene in the tiny neighborhood.

I spun on my heels and marched back into the house in frustration just to collapse on the couch and bury my head in my hands in defeat. *What do we do?* The obvious choice would be to find a video client and buy a fridge with the money we make. But we had no leads on clients, no paid experience, and video is definitely an in-person thing. Other than the people we met at the ice cream shop for Heath's 21st job, we didn't even know anyone in Missouri. Or I could find 20 extra writing gigs, a seemingly impossible feat.

Heath sat cross-legged on the floor next to the fireplace scrolling through his phone—something I found deeply annoying. *We are only at the pinnacle of crisis here, but be sure to check Twitter!* I rolled my eyes, not that he was looking at me.

Everything was packed in the RV. The food was the last thing to put away and we were ready to make the easy drive to

Indianapolis. Less than 30 states to go. And now we had been defeated by a fridge.

What do you do when you lose your fridge, have no money to replace it, and just got back on the road freshly determined to not give up?

No really, someone please call me and tell me because I'm stuck here.

Years later, I would ask myself why I never called my parents to ask for help. I mean, a fridge is a necessity. We needed food to live and while we could switch to canned goods and more dry foods, we still needed milk and eggs. Surely our families would've helped us out. But at the time, the thought never crossed my mind. This was our pickle. Heath and I needed to find our way out. We had made it this far. We couldn't end at 21/50. No way.

"There's not a chance the two of us can lift and flip that fridge over," I said to break the silence.

"I know," Heath said, leaning his head back on the couch. "I already tried to see if I could move it and it's insanely heavy. We would need multiple people."

"We only have one option from what I can tell. Turn the freezer into an icebox. Buy ice every day and use it to keep the essentials cold. No more frozen foods or foods that need to stay super cold. We'll probably have to go to the grocery store every single day because there won't be room for much more than eggs for breakfast and whatever we buy for dinner. Definitely no room for Tupperware with any leftovers. We don't have any other choice."

"We do have one other choice," Heath countered. Please don't say go back home, I pleaded internally. Don't let this be the straw that broke the camel's back. Don't say we can go back to Texas, stay with family, find a way to make money, replace the fridge, then trudge on later. Please don't let us lose momentum. If we go back now, we will never get back on the road. It'll be too hard.

"We could go to Nashville."

I blinked at him slowly. "How does that fix our fridge?"

"It doesn't. We will just have to do what you said and save money for a while and maybe in October, we can get a fridge. But here's the thing, you and I are alone right now. Sure we have friends or family we can call and tell them what's going on or we can even drive back to Texas. But I think if we went back to Texas again right now, it would be too easy to give up.

"Chris Guillebeau is doing a book signing in Nashville tonight. I just saw it on Twitter. And we both said that we felt like we finally found our people at his conference in Oregon, right? It's five hours away. It's not that big of a detour from Indiana. And to be honest, I feel like quitting right now. Like every time we start gaining momentum, we get slammed to the ground with fuel pumps and lightning, and now this.

"I need," he took a deep breath. "I need to just feel like we're not crazy for doing this. Because no one would blame us for quitting right now. I'm pretty sure after hanging out with friends and family last week that no one really expects us to actually make it to all 50 states. And I think we both need to be around people who won't let us give up."

As you can see, Heath has a thing for speeches.

I traced the goosebumps on my forearm with my fingertips. Five hours away. That's a $125 gas tank detour, based on the past few months. Our cashback credit card offered bonuses on gas this month, but that was pennies on the dollar. We needed income. Badly.

But this wasn't a detour about money. Heath was right. We were alone in this at the moment. But we didn't have to be.

"I tweeted at Chris to see if we needed tickets or anything to attend so I could convince my wife that we should drive to Tennessee," Heath continued.

"You didn't!" I laughed.

"See?" he said, angling his phone toward me, showing me a growing thread of people hopping into the conversation encouraging us to drive the RV out. Even just seeing thoughtful comments from people who were excited for us to attend felt so good. Even though they didn't know it, a simple "Yes you should come and you can park your RV here!" was infinitely encouraging. It made me realize how often in life we have no idea what kind of obstacles people are facing and that even the smallest moments of kindness are amplified when people need it.

Heath looked at me hopefully. The RV could still drive and we couldn't stay in St. Louis forever.

"What time does it start?" I asked.

"6:30. And I already asked if there was room in the parking lot for our RV and someone replied and said yes."

"Adding 15 minutes to every Google Maps hour for RV time..." I calculated in my head. "We need to leave in the next 30 minutes and not hit any traffic."

"You already packed the RV. Let's go."

Chapter 20

Before the RV became our honeymoon plan, Nashville made our list of possible places to live because of the creative community. Sure, everyone knows country music. But there was also a huge community of writers, bloggers, and artists filling the room to listen to Chris speak.

We pulled into the parking lot at sunset with a little time to spare. The Nashville Entrepreneur Center was an old brick building downtown next to a fancy bowling alley. Someone from the Twitter thread named Andy saw us pull in—apparently arriving at business events in an RV gets people's attention—and came over to greet us. He led us to a turf-covered courtyard filled with people and…is that a hot tub? That's weird. I curiously dipped my fingers in the water. We leaned against the edge of the hot tub and talked while Andy bought us a drink from an Airstream turned food truck. We'd only just arrived but instantly felt like this was the right call. Five hours ago, it felt like the wheels were falling off our trip. Now even just being around people who were in our corner felt huge.

Someone made an announcement and the group wandered inside to a large gray room filled with chairs. Every seat was taken with more people standing in the back, affirming our assumption that there's a large community of creatives and travelers living in Nashville.

Chris was touring to promote his new book, *The Happiness of Pursuit: Finding the Quest That Will Bring Purpose to Your Life.* For years, Chris pursued his goal of visiting every country in the world. (Yes, as soon as I heard he visited every country, I added that to my bucket list.) In his book, he shared stories from his own journey but also stories about so many other people he met along the way all pursuing some great goal. As I listened to him speak, his words perfectly described our trip.

The more people he met, he realized that people found more happiness in pursuing their goals than in completing them. Pursuing the goal gave meaning to someone's life. It gave them "something to be about" and in that they found meaning.

I thought about our journey. Broken fridge notwithstanding, I agreed. Pursuing our goal to visit all fifty states was thrilling. When we talked about continuing to travel, we even tried to brainstorm our next goal so we would have something to work towards. It was that stated goal that thrust us forward and gave us direction. It felt like Chris was talking straight to us. *Today may be a hard day, but your goal is worth pursuing.* I looked over at the table in the back of the room where a young couple stood ready to sell copies of Chris' books. We'd have to buy one. I had a feeling this book was precisely what we needed to read.

Before the night ended, Chris asked people to raise their

hands if they drove in from out of the city to attend. He called us out personally and shared our story since he had replied on Twitter and knew we were coming. We sat in the back row, so everyone in the room turned around and looked at us while I waved awkwardly. Chris shared more about our mission to visit all 50 states, making it sound epic and noble that we were attempting this voyage and documentary. (He did not get the memo that I had nothing more than a bag of ice, shredded cheese, and some broccoli in my freezer box at the moment. There was no room for luxury items like refrigerated ketchup, which we left in St. Louis.)

I don't remember what he said about us. No one does, probably.

But whatever he said changed our lives.

Because instead of ducking out so we could make it to our campsite for the night, we stayed for hours. For the rest of the night, person after person came up to say hi.

There was James, whose three kids would later beg to the point of tears to be allowed to join us in the RV after they learned Disney World was on our route. There was a different Chris, who casually invited us to park in his driveway after knowing us for ten minutes. Of course we immediately accepted, perhaps because of low funds or perhaps because we no longer had standards for who we trusted enough to stay at their home. (He owns an Airstream, so apparently that was connection enough to say "What's your address? We'll be right over.")

And then we met Kara and Nate, the couple standing in the back of the room selling books for Chris. Unlike every other adventurer and traveler we'd met on the road, they were actually our age. Kara worked as a nanny—just like I did to save up money before we hit the road. And Nate ran his own t-shirt company—just like Heath did in college. What are the odds? They were weeks away from their first long-term trip abroad to Europe and Asia and we were halfway through our first big trip. It was kind of like meeting the international traveling versions of ourselves. In our 10 minute conversation, as the evening wrapped up and people started stacking chairs around us, we made plans to meet up again in November when we intended to stay in Nashville for more than 48 hours.

Before heading out to the RV, we unexpectedly ran into Wes and Tera again, who drove up from their home in Alabama to attend the book signing.

"Y'all *must* come to Florence and stay in our driveway when you come to Alabama!" they said.

"Absolutely," we agreed, racking up more free night's stays. Only 100 more and we can afford cold foods again.

Nothing that happened that night fixed our fridge. Even the different Chris, who had renovated his Airstream and worked as a contractor, came out to the RV and shrugged when we mentioned the issue with our fridge saying that we would ultimately need to replace it.

But Heath was right in choosing to surround ourselves with other travelers to distract ourselves from the morning's disappointment. They encouraged us and shared their own travel stories, reminding us that bumps in the road are simply what give travelers so many good stories. We may have eaten popcorn for dinner before we walked into the book signing, but surrounded by this community, we knew we would continue on our quest.

"I just got off the phone with Jia," Heath announced, hopping back up the stairs into our RV. He had been pacing in Chris' backyard on the phone all morning. We barely fit down Chris' narrow driveway, but he let us stay for free and even had an electrical outlet for us to plug in the rig during our one-night stay. So far, we had driveway camped with so many people that it didn't even feel strange to park at a stranger's house.

"Didn't you just talk to him like three days ago?"

"I did and he called me again because he's looking for someone to help him with a 50 state book tour. And he saw on Twitter that we went to the book signing for Chris last night. And he thought, who better to plan his book tour than a guy who's already going to all 50 states?"

"Wait, what? You're going to plan his book tour? Does he know that you don't know anything about planning a book tour?"

He laughed. "Yeah. But I know travel, he says. And it would be my job to find him speaking gigs, places to hold signings, get him on podcasts, stuff like that. I told him I'd never done any of that before and he said that didn't matter. He said he's sat down and given lots of people advice in his career, but it's rare to actually see someone take it. Seeing us still working on *Hourly America* convinced him that I'm the guy he should hire."

"Babe!" I squealed, hopping out of my chair to give him a hug. "This is huge!"

"If it goes well," Heath continued, "then I can work with him through his book launch in April. But since I'll be busy working jobs through the end of the year, he said he only needs me for about 10 hours a week and he'll pay me $20/hour."

"That's..."I calculated in my head. "$800 a month? For the next few months? You told him yes, I hope."

"I told him my wife probably wouldn't go for it," Heath feigned disappointment.

"Oh you did not," I said, punching him on the arm.

"Are you kidding? I made sure he was cool with my hours being flexible while we traveled and said yes immediately. We could actually break even through the rest of the year with the money from Snagajob plus your writing plus this. And this would give us our first client if we start a business together. I already threw out the idea of filming a book trailer for him and he wants to film a course in the spring too."

Heath and I celebrated, jumping up and down as we saw a glimmer of hope that we could keep traveling.

My head was spinning. Heath and I had been brainstorming how we could find client work that would allow us to write and make videos. Planning a book tour certainly never came to mind, but the theme of this trip seemed to be learning how to say yes to anything and everything. When people recommended a place to visit along our travels, if we could make it, we said yes. If people offered up a place to stay, we said yes. Random jobs we'd never done before? Sure. Plan a cross-country book tour? How hard could it be?

The unexpected opportunity would add to our workload, but it would keep our bank account from hitting a negative balance this month and ease a little of our financial stress, extending our runway just enough to keep traveling.

Chapter 21

Before getting married, we heard two basic responses to what our first year of marriage would be like.

"Oh it's the honeymoon year," people crooned. "Everything is rose-colored and you're still so in love. Oh, to go back to that time!"

Others took a different route.

"The first year is by far the hardest. You're getting used to all these things about the person that you didn't know before. And you're trying to balance marriage on top of everything else in life. We fought more that first year than the whole rest of our marriage."

Which is exactly how you could split our trip.

The first half was the honeymoon period. Everything was gorgeous and new and intriguing. Problems arose often, but we tackled them together. When our phones started screaming tornado warnings at us while we drove down the interstate in South Dakota, together we navigated to safety to wait out the storm. In Arizona, we climbed on top of the roof of the RV to watch the sun sink over the desert. We drank $3 wine out of plastic cups while walking around Jenny Lake at Grand Teton National Park.

But now we were definitively in the second camp. The first-year-sucks camp—even if we were technically still on our honeymoon.

With the mounting stress of not having a fridge, a growing balance on our credit card, and a growing pile of work to be done to pay off our credit card and buy a fridge, little things like Heath leaving his shoes in the middle of the floor *again* had me lashing out in frustration. Tensions were at an all-time high in the still-leaking RV.

The long list of problems was beginning to fracture our partnership. It's Heath versus Alyssa versus this fridge. Heath versus Alyssa versus our dwindling bank account. Heath versus Alyssa versus the fact that Heath's having a hard time finding jobs for our documentary.

Heath.

Versus Alyssa.

Versus the toilet deodorant.

"I have to have internet at 4:00 PM for my kick-off call with Jia. I *have to*," Heath emphasized. "It's a video call."

"Yeah. But it's not even noon. So why don't we drive for a few hours and find a place to stop on the way," I advised.

Heath exhaled. I could see his nerves about getting started with his first client. The pressure to do a good job and make that extra bit of money to allow us to keep traveling weighed heavily on his shoulders. But I wasn't going to sit in a gas station parking lot for five hours just because we knew it had a cell signal. As September winded down, a deadline threatened us. While we had a little flexibility when it came to when we visited each state and worked Heath's job, the northeast came with its own timeline: October 15th.

The general rule, other RVers advised us, was you had to be south of Boston by Columbus Day weekend because that's when every campground closed and the nights started to freeze. We saw snow on the ground in Washington and woke up to a 39° house in Wyoming one morning, but we hadn't yet hit a true freeze. With October right around the corner, we had roughly three weeks to clear nine jobs, traverse hundreds of miles, and try to enjoy seeing our first ever fall colors along the way.

So we needed to hit the road and head north.

But have you driven through Indiana?

At 3:15 PM we'd been in the middle of nowhere for a while. Heath was freaking out. "I have to have internet, Alyssa. I can't miss this call, Alyssa."

So, I found us a Walmart off the interstate up ahead—this many months into travel you know that a Walmart off the interstate is almost guaranteed to have some cell signal—and I took over driving so Heath could start prepping for his meeting. I could hear him sitting at our dining room table clacking away on his keyboard with loud sighs, like working from our home on wheels was a grave inconvenience.

I shook my head in the driver's seat. We'll arrive at Walmart just in time, he's already all set up, there's no need to stress.

But we had never worked on the road. Not really. Not while

being beholden to clients and meeting times and needing consistent internet. Our ETA of 3:57 PM did not stress me out. Three whole minutes before his meeting! Easy!

Heath was navigating me from the backseat, counting down the miles to my exit with increasing anxiety, as if my driving the speed limit was stressing him out and it was all my fault that we'd park only three minutes before his meeting started. Wait, maybe two minutes. A little patch of yellow appeared just up ahead.

Finally, I exited and pulled up to the red light to turn right. I could see Walmart not even a mile up the road. 3:58 PM. *Easy*, I thought again. Heath was booting up our hotspot in the back, tsking as he waited for it to connect to the cell signal and worrying aloud that it wouldn't.

"If your phone has a cell signal, the hotspot will have a signal," I reassured him, finally turning right. I cruised along the main road toward the Walmart when Heath started shouting at me.

"Turn right! Turn right!"

"I can see the Walmart right there!" I said, lifting my hand to point half a mile in front of the RV where the giant blue sign marked the parking lot entrance.

"The GPS is saying turn right now! Slow down! Turn right here."

Of course, I was not planning on turning there, so I was not going slow enough to turn. I flipped on my blinker and hit the brakes hard to turn into the empty parking lot adjacent to the Walmart. I could've had a nice right turn lane and red light up ahead to easily cruise into the Walmart parking lot. Instead, I'm Vin Diesel squealing into the empty lot going way too fast while Heath is trying to catch his laptop from flying off the table in the back.

"You're going too fast!" Heath yelped.

"You made me turn!" I screamed back.

I slowed to a stop while Heath grumbled in the back about why this is why he always drives the RV. (Yes, it is Heath. Because you're a terrible navigator who gives me two seconds heads up to make a right turn.) At 3:59 PM, Heath was connected to the internet just fine, and I heard the familiar sound of Skype booting up. *Easy*.

I didn't know why he was stressing. We were parked. I was putting up our front window shades and the RV even smells amazing. Actually, wow. The RV smells really good. Clean.

"Heath!" I screeched as I looked behind me to see that our entire floor, our new vinyl wood flooring installed just a few months earlier, was dark blue. Heath was sitting cross-legged in our dining chair, unaware of the clean chemical smell filling our house.

"Agh!" he shouted over the sound of the Skype ringtone. "I told you that you were going too fast! You made the toilet deodorant spill everywhere!"

"You poured it in the tank before we left this morning!" I shouted back. "Did you remember to put the lid back on? Because that bottle has tipped over every day and never poured out all over the floor!"

Heath wasn't listening. He was twisting around his computer and switching seats so he wouldn't have the inside of the RV in the background of his video call. He answered with a smile as if absolutely nothing chaotic was happening all around him while I tiptoed through the thick dark blue liquid coating my feet. I pulled all the dirty towels out of our laundry hamper and tossed them on the floor before pulling a stack of clean towels from the cabinet. The thick blue liquid covered every inch of the floor from our bathroom to the cab and it was going to take every towel we owned to clean it up.

I stifled a cough as the formerly clean smell suffocated me. I quickly opened all the windows and the door to air out our home.

A mop! That would've been a useful thing to have packed at a time like this.

Slowly, the laundry basket was filled with heavy blue towels and I switched to hand towels and washcloths to finish cleaning the sticky floor. While Heath and Jia talked business, I was on my knees scrubbing our beautiful white kitchen cabinets until I realized that the baseboards would forever be blue. There's no amount of cleaner or elbow grease that could take this off.

The toilet deodorant, a previously full bottle we picked up in Texas, still, somehow, had a little of the chemical product inside. I screwed the lid back on, which after close inspection wasn't broken or cracked at all, giving weight to my theory that someone who isn't me forgot to put the lid back on properly.

Heath finally hung up his call over an hour later. "It smells so bad in here," he said. Which is kind of like saying "Thank you for cleaning up, honey. I hope the blue stain comes off of your feet and knees!" Except that it isn't a thank you at all. I glared at the back of his head while he walked by.

When we were dating, I used to love going to Heath's

apartment on the weekends to make pancakes for breakfast together. Now we argued over whether the freezer stayed cool enough from the mostly melted bag of ice to not get food poisoning from our breakfast staples.

It's not exactly the ideal way to start the day.

Two weeks after our fridge's death, we pulled into an RV park in Ohio with a service shop out front. We'd called multiple service shops as we made our way from state to state, but most were booked months out for repairs. The unexpected little service shop was a surprise. The owners, probably seeing the state of our rig from the outside and taking pity on us, promised to come by our RV and help us burp our fridge even though they were closed for the day. Burping was our last resort, although two weeks after the incident I wasn't holding out much hope.

It took three grown men to lift and flip the fridge. The group briefly considered letting the fridge burp outside but it quickly became apparent that the fridge wouldn't fit through the door. How did it even get in the RV? I looked around at the layout and the size of our windows. I think they built the whole house around the fridge itself.

With no hope of getting it out (and increasing worries that replacing our fridge would never happen), our fridge sat upside down in the middle of our living room/dining room/kitchen with all our food sitting in one side of the sink covered in a layer of ice. I graduated college and quit a good job to end up adding questionable milk submerged in melted ice water to my morning coffee.

Please no one tell my mom.

In the process of removing the fridge, the guys disconnected the propane gas line that powers the fridge while boondocking. As soon as they lifted the fridge, they nicked said gas line releasing propane into the air. I climbed out the front of the RV to turn off the propane tank from outside before we all asphyxiated on gas in the tiny space while the men fumbled with flipping over the heavy fridge. Thankfully the kind Ohioans grabbed a couple of parts from their shop to help us plug the leak, literally saving our lives. We rubbed dish soap over the pipe to watch for bubbles showing us any gas escaping. No bubbles formed and we rested easy that night...with the windows cracked just in case.

The guys came back the next day to flip the fridge back, eliciting a rushing water sound as something moved around in those pipes, and together they helped Heath hoist it back into place. We were to let it cool for 24-48 hours with electrical hookups to see if it would start working again. They wished us luck and rejected any payment for their help. I scribbled their names into my red notebook of free kindness we accepted on the road.

We continued across Ohio for Heath's next job. Meanwhile, the leaves outside started to change. The weather became open-your-windows-all-day-and-night weather. We walked from our campsite down the road to the shores of Lake Erie to watch the hot pink sun sink over the water.

"That fridge is never going to work again, you know," Heath said after 24 hours and the fridge still hadn't cooled at all.

"Yeah, I know," I sighed, staring at the waves lapping the rocky shore. There were a lot more dry cereal dinners ahead of us.

"We do have one other option. We can buy an apartment fridge," Heath suggested.

"What's an apartment fridge?"

"You know, just like a fridge but it's not full size."

"So a mini-fridge."

"Bigger than a mini-fridge, smaller than a normal fridge. It wouldn't have power any time we are driving, but we aren't really driving for more than 5-6 hours a day anyway. We can just keep the doors closed so it stays cold enough for the food to be okay and then always have electrical hookups overnight. Then we can have a fridge again, stop dealing with ice which is really getting messy, and not keep dealing with running out of food because we don't have a way to keep it."

"How much is an apartment fridge?"

"Like 200 bucks."

"200 is doable." At this rate, we'd spend $200 on ice over the next couple of months anyway.

"Agreed," Heath said as a final sliver of the sun dipped over the lake.

"I'm not entirely sure that fridge is going to make it out of the RV though," I said, slumping my shoulders.

"We'll find a way because we have to. Even if it's in pieces."

With a possible solution decided, we spent the next week driving past stunning lakeshores and growing green mountains as we made our way from Ohio to Niagara Falls to the apple orchards of Vermont to the White Mountains of New Hampshire. Everything was picture-perfect. The slowly changing leaves. The old colonial-style homes with giant maple trees out front. Fall decorations gleamed outside every store and house. The air smelled like apples and cinnamon. The tiny towns felt like walking through a postcard.

Inside the RV was a different story, what with the whole no-working-fridge saga living on. Heath and I were still arguing more with the added stress of the fridge. I was pretty sure he was still mad about the toilet deodorant. That was six states ago yet the RV had a fresh, clean scent.

As soon as October first rolled around and we got paid, we would buy a fridge and put this headache behind us.

Chapter 22

We pulled into the Home Depot parking lot in Portland, Maine and took up four parking spots.

"Do you think it will stay cool while we are driving?" Heath asked John who worked in the home appliance section.

"With as small as it is," he began, pointing at the apartment fridge, "I would guess it'll stay cool for 6-8 hours. Any longer than that and you'll want to hook it up to power or use your generator."

Heath gave me a look that conveyed eight hours was longer than we would probably ever have the RV unhooked. (He would be wrong, but with lows in the 30s, we set our food outside overnight because our ice melted and the RV park didn't sell any. We had reached a new level of desperation.)

At $228, we could buy this fridge without overdrawing our account and gain back a little bit of our humanity, my eyes said back to Heath.

The residential fridge would only run while we were hooked

to electricity, making it harder for us to dry camp or take advantage of free nights in driveways. But it would mean we could go to the grocery store only once a week again and always have food on hand.

"We'll take it, John," Heath said. John scuttled off to find our fridge in the back.

"I'm very excited for a fridge, babe. But what are we going to do with the old one? You have to specially dispose of fridges. You can't just drop it in a dumpster."

"Who is going to know it's us if we just drop in a dumpster? We'll be three states away by then," Heath smirked.

I raised my eyebrows. You learn so much about a person during your first year of marriage, namely which crimes they are unrepentant about committing.

Luckily, John rounded the corner with our fridge and interrupted our criminal planning.

As the three of us walked to the front of the store, with John towing our refrigerator on a dolly, Heath and I realized a few problems as we discussed our situation.

Problem #1: Our broken fridge is still screwed into the walls of our RV.

Problem #2: The freezer is full of room-temperature food that probably isn't good anymore.

Problem #3: The old fridge is too heavy for Heath and me to remove on our own.

Problem #4: How are we going to get the old fridge out if it doesn't fit through the door?

Problem #5: Where are we going to fit this new fridge until we can get the old one removed?

Problem #6: What recycling laws are we going to have to break to find a place to dump this fridge?

I Googled "where to recycle your refrigerator in Maine" which yielded a lot of confusing web pages when John, a true angel from the heavens, spoke up.

"I'll take it," he said, as if reading my worried mind. He explained he works on refrigerators in his spare time and he could try to fix ours and resell it. "We'll put it in the bed of my truck." Once again, the kindness of others saves the day.

That solved our problems with recycling the fridge and getting help moving it.

"Use the blue credit card," I instructed Heath so he would use the card that gave us up to $20 cashback every month, a small money-saving hack of mine. "I'll get the RV ready." Heath continued to the register and I rushed out to the RV to get the old fridge ready to be taken out.

I pulled the few not-even-cold-anymore groceries out of the freezer and dropped them in the sink. Half-eaten bag of shredded cheese. Tiny carton of almost-empty half and half. I stood there pondering for a moment before dumping them in the trash. The few bucks it would take to replace the remaining groceries was worth avoiding the inevitable stomachache that would come with keeping this junk.

Foodless and a little smelly, it only took unscrewing one screw for me to free our fridge. Which is when I remembered our biggest problem.

Problem #4: It's too big to fit through the door.

John rolled the giant box carrying our new fridge out to the RV and the guys climbed inside. After a few minutes of trying, it was clear: This broken, smelly, terrible fridge was an inch too wide for our door frame. Plus, with the awkward angles in our front cabin, we couldn't take the fridge out our front doors either. The hallway was too narrow to make it to the emergency exit behind our bed. It was stuck in the middle of our kitchen, with no way out.

"What about that window?" I spoke up, pointing to the window behind the couch. "It's the only one that opens all the way."

John whipped out a tape measure from his orange apron.

The window: 25.5 x 24 inches

Our fridge: 25 x 24 inches

Barely enough, but enough.

Red-faced, the two men slid out and lifted the fridge from its perch in our kitchen. They grunted as they shuffled two feet across the floor toward the window. I grabbed the top to help them tilt the fridge to lower it toward the window. In the process of trying to wedge it into the open window, we rammed into the dark blue accordion blinds and busted them into two hanging pieces. A minor casualty.

The screws anchoring the blinds held firm in the wall and the broken blinds blocked half an inch of the window, making it impossible to push them out of the way enough for the guys to navigate the window opening.

"Hold on just a sec," I said, grabbing the keys off the dash and crawling out the front. I unlocked our storage bay, grabbed our power drill, and hopped back inside where the guys held the heavy fridge with it semi-resting at an angle at the top of our couch waiting to slide it out the window. I hit the screws with the drill and tossed the pieces over my shoulder until the blinds were free and out of the way.

No more than a quarter of an inch of space remained on any side of the fridge. The rubber window seal squeaked as they started to push the fridge out the window.

"Wait, right there!" said John suddenly. "Someone has to catch it from the other side."

Heath and I balanced the fridge on the window frame, hoping the wall wouldn't give out while John repositioned. We pushed until the fridge was almost out and teetered on the edge of the window. Heath hopped out to join John in setting it down on the pavement while I gave a final push from the inside.

I exhaled and wiped the sweat from my brow. Finally, the fridge saga was over. The monster was out of our house and never coming back. John wandered off to bring his truck over to load up the fridge to take home while Heath and I easily maneuvered our shiny fridge into its new home. It looked tiny in the giant hole where our RV-size fridge used to rest.

We thanked John a thousand times before cranking on the engine to head to an RV park for the day to plug in and let the fridge cool off before heading to the grocery store. As Heath turned right out of the parking lot, we heard a crash in the kitchen. The fridge tipped over and fell out of its cubby. I yelped and hopped out of my seat to right the fridge.

I gave Heath a look of horror when I returned to the passenger seat and buckled up.

"I have some zip ties in a box somewhere. Once we get to the RV park, I'll make sure it stays," Heath assured me.

He turned onto the highway. Then the fridge tipped over again, wedged between the cabinets and the kitchen counter.

I spent the rest of our 40-minute drive sitting on the floor next to the fridge pushing it back into place after it tipped over again and again with every curve and turn of the road. We would need lots and lots of zip ties. And a new set of blinds.

But we would have food.

Finally, our problems with the fridge were over.

We cruised into Massachusetts with confidence. Someone who followed my blog—yes, someone follows my blog!—offered to let us stay for the night and said he could even give us electricity so our new fridge would work. Plus, he found us a job for our documentary in his town, saving us a few days of cold calling businesses. Heath hopped on a phone call with Steve to make sure he wasn't a wacko, but with the goal to free camp as often as possible, we probably would've ended up in his driveway no matter what. Staying with him for two nights would save us good money and we felt safe in our RV.

Everything was looking up again. We were enjoying life together, taking scenic drives through the stunning colors of a northeast fall and walking the scenic beaches. The days were sunny and cool, perfect for a little driveway camping.

We slowly crept down a very steep driveway, nervous about the angle. We *just* bought a working fridge. We couldn't break another one! But at the end of the sharp hill was a small flat area where a tiny Casita trailer sat. We parked next to it. Mary Ellen, Steve's wife, wasn't home yet and Steve gave us the keys to his car and directions to "Prospect Hill" nearby. I think we showed up too early and he just wanted us out of the way so he could prep dinner and his wife could come home without two strangers in her house, but we gladly accepted the keys and his local suggestion.

We drove eight minutes to the local park and parallel parked along the main road. A low rock wall no higher than our knees bordering the park reminded me of how old this part of America is. The rocks were jagged and mish-mashed together marking the perimeter of an open green field. The field sloped downward toward a thicket of orange and yellow trees which gave way to an expansive view of eastern Massachusetts. For miles, we could see the gently sloping hills and distant mountains peppered in greens and reds. The sun was sinking lower over the horizon setting the trees and clouds aglow with color.

Heath and I sat on the rock wall soaking in the views with the pointed rocks poking our bums as we watched the sun go down.

It's funny how no matter how much you may travel—across 28 states and counting—the world still possesses the power to awe you. This was a simple city park, not Yellowstone or the Grand Canyon. But the raw beauty humbled me, forcing me to still and take in the moment.

Visiting the northeast in the fall was my biggest goal when I routed out our fifty-state road trip. We were halfway through October and following the leaves south as they changed color. Come to think of it, that's probably why I failed to research what the weather was like in the midwest in August. I was blinded by one superior goal: make it to the northeast in September and follow those leaves south.

It didn't disappoint, I thought as I watched a yellow leaf

flutter to the ground. You never saw colors like these back in the south. The leaves turned brown and crunchy.

Here, they lit up the landscape.

This was what RVing was about, I thought once again. Since making it to this part of the country, we donned blue plastic parkas on the Maid of the Mist as we ventured toward the truly massive power of Niagara Falls. We picked apples and ate (way too many) apple cider donuts on a farm in Vermont—both free to us since we strategically found jobs for our documentary that could give us regional experiences without hurting our pocketbooks. We purposefully got lost in New Hampshire just to take tiny roads through miles of forest and rivers. And we wandered through this beautiful park with endless views.

For the first time since Missouri, I felt the tension building in my shoulders release. Outwardly, I may have seemed fine with buying ice and going to the grocery store almost every day. But I think the uncertainty of if and when we could afford a new fridge weighed on both of us more than we realized. The tiny fissures in our relationship over the past few weeks instantly disappeared once the tiny apartment fridge was zip-tied into place.

Heath and I lost ourselves in conversation recounting the magic of our travels the past few weeks when Steve texted us that dinner was ready.

After enjoying a delicious Moroccan dinner with Steve and his wife—who seemed perfectly normal and not at all like serial killers—we climbed into the RV, agreed to keep all the windows open so we could smell the fresh fall air, and went to bed expecting to have the best sleep of our trip.

Instead, we woke up with splitting headaches. We dressed

slowly, already dreading a day of filming when we both felt so sick, and wandered into our new friend's home to cook breakfast and make coffee.

"Do you take cream in your coffee? We don't have any," Steve said.

"We have some. I'll go grab it from the RV," I replied.

Before I got to the door, I smelled it. I only needed those few minutes of fresh air to realize what was wrong, but now the odor was pungent. Deadly.

Propane.

I carefully stepped into the RV. Our carbon monoxide detector works, as we learned from once leaving a window open while running our generator. If we had a major gas leak, surely it would alert us. When I walked into the RV, the smell disappeared. I checked our stove, double-checking to make sure no knobs were turned on and no gas was leaking. Nothing. Hot water heater wasn't on. Where was the propane smell coming from?

I shrugged it off thinking I was insane. Our fridge is electric now, the stove isn't on, the hot water heater isn't on, the furnace isn't on. There isn't anything using propane.

An hour later after breakfast as I walked back into the RV, I could smell the odor again. Unmistakeable.

Maybe it's because the tank is almost empty, I thought. We'd tried to fill our propane tank a dozen times lately, but every RV park we visited couldn't fill our tank or didn't have the proper person on staff. We were nearly empty and hadn't filled up since July in Idaho.

"Heath?" I asked. "Do you smell that?"

Heath sniffed the air inside the RV. "Smell what?"

"Propane?"

"Hmm. Not really."

"Here, step back outside," I motioned. "Now smell."

Standing at the base of our steps, Heath took a deep breath. "Oh yeah, I really smell it now. That's weird." He looked around over his shoulders as if he might see a propane tank lying in the driveway to explain the smell. "I wonder where it's—oh God."

"What?" I asked, my stress level rising.

"Grab the dish soap." Heath started unlocking and removing the panel where you could access the fridge from the outside. I handed him a bottle of yellow Ajax. "Remember how when we took out the fridge in Ohio, we busted the propane line and capped it?" He spoke as he squirted soap all over the golden hose. Bubbles started appearing instantly betraying the hidden gas leak.

"It busted again," he said, looking at me.

"So our propane is leaking?"

"Yep." Heath walked over to the one storage door without a lock and lifted it up to reveal our onboard propane tank. He twisted the valve closed to turn off the propane. "We are going to have to get the propane line fixed again. Or since our new fridge runs on electricity, they may just take out the whole line so we don't have to worry about it busting again."

"Wow. Okay..." I paced back and forth outside while Heath spoke. Thoughts turned in my head. "So when we both woke up with splitting headaches this morning...?"

"Yeah."

Our words hung in the air heavy with implication.

"And if we hadn't opened all the windows last night?" I asked.

"Yeah."

We looked at each other and at our home on wheels that seemed determined to fight us at every mile. It's actively trying to kill us now. This propane line was the last remnant of the old fridge. Perhaps with it gone, the fridge saga could finally, really be behind us.

"Okay," Heath began. "I'm going inside to ask Steve if there's a good mechanic he recommends that can fix this today."

"Good call."

After a couple of calls and a few dramatic comments about the dangers of propane leaks, a mechanic finally said we could bring the RV in. They couldn't fit it in a bay and they would have to work on it in the parking lot, but they would take care of us. We called Heath's job for the day to let them know we'd be late. We drove to the mechanic and watched from our dining room table as a guy shimmied under our RV in the misty rain to remove the propane line.

Now, the fridge saga was finally over.

Chapter 23

With fresh air in our RV, we cruised down the coast feeling lighter. With our refrigerator woes behind us and stunning fall leaves everywhere we looked, RV life was an adventure again. We involuntarily pulled over on the side of winding northeast roads captivated by the explosion of vivid red, orange, and yellow leaves. It was Columbus Day weekend and we only had a few days to enjoy Massachusetts, Rhode Island, and Connecticut before making it south to New York City.

"I just had an interesting phone call with CNN," Heath said nonchalantly, stepping back into the RV after pacing around Normandy Farms, a giant campground right outside of Boston.

"CNN?"

"They found our story on Twitter and want to interview us while we are in the city. They want to hear more about our honeymoon and how we're filming this documentary while we travel."

"Ah! That's amazing!" I squealed as I stirred rice on the stove.

"Yeah, I called Jon over at Snagajob to let him know and he said Fox, Huffington Post, and Business Insider are all interested too."

"In us?" I questioned.

"In us," Heath confirmed, glowing with pride and excitement. "So we are going to need to stick around New York City for a few days. Jon is going to get us a hotel room in the city so we don't have to commute every day for interviews."

I felt dizzy trying to wrap my mind around all of the major interviews we were about to do.

Our idea to visit all fifty states in our new-to-us RV wasn't cool in the beginning. It was an "oh, good for you" kind of goal where people silently wondered if we'd gone insane. But now that we were still traveling and sharing the ups and downs of the journey online, our friends and family started to recognize that this wasn't just the whim of two kids. We weren't traveling just because we were bored or hated our jobs. And we weren't giving up if we ran out of money or found something new to distract us. We were going to find a way to finish no matter what.

In spite of the RV's best efforts, we were still pushing forward. If living without a fridge for a month didn't stop us, it felt like nothing could keep us from making it to all fifty. I wondered if people somehow would find it inspiring or think that we were the example they needed to see to chase their own travel dreams. Although, we'd be a terrible example. Our bank account was almost back to zero again. Our roof and windows are still leaking. We regularly get lost driving around new places. Heath filled our entire gas tank with the wrong kind of gas the other day. Not really role-model material.

Maybe the news headline should be: "Newlywed couple too resilient or too dumb? You decide."

When we stayed with Steve in Massachusetts, we asked him how he found us and why he followed my blog. "You had a dream and you went after it," he said matter of factly. "And you're still going for it. I don't think you know how rare that is."

His words continued to bounce around my brain. I wondered if that's why all these news outlets were calling. Did they care about the documentary and Heath working? Or was it all about RV life? Or was it as simple as Steve suggested, two kids chasing a dream and trying to inspire others to do the same?

I didn't know, but I was excited to find out.

Now we just had to get to New York.

"What are you doing?" I snapped, looking up from my computer screen. I usually didn't work from the front seat, but since the next few days would be spent in the city, I tried to get ahead on writing. Plus, I'd already told Heath it was a straight shot from Hartford, Connecticut to New York City on the interstate, so I didn't think Heath needed my attentive navigation until I felt him beginning to exit.

"That sign said New York City," Heath replied as if my question was ridiculous. He drove under an unmistakably bright orange sign as he exited.

"So you did not see the 10 bright orange signs for the past

three miles that said 8-foot clearance, no exit for large vehicles? I noticed them and I'm looking down at a computer!"

"No-o?" Heath asked quizzically.

"HEATH! You JUST drove under one! It was right under the words New York City. I told you when we left Hartford, stay on I-95 until we hit the George Washington bridge. In Manhattan. Does this look like Manhattan? All you had to do was drive straight for three hours!" I rubbed my temples while every single car on this exit ramp passed us honking their horns and shaking their heads. *You're going to die*, the horns echoed.

"Well, what do you want me to do?" Heath shouted back at me.

"Follow simple instructions and read traffic signs for one!" I snapped back, pinching the Google Maps screen on my phone and trying to find a way off of the road Heath dumped us on before we took our roof off. Heath knew the low clearance was coming now, so I wasn't worried he was about to decapitate the RV. But when a road sign says no large vehicles in all caps, I wasn't sure if there would even be an exit off this highway that we could take that didn't involve a low clearance. Would we have to drive across the grass and find another road? Would we have to shift into reverse until we made it back to I-95? How do we get back to the interstate?

"I think this guy is forcing me off the road," Heath interrupted, looking in his rearview mirror. "He's honking and pointing."

"Well he reads road signs," I said under my breath, still trying to find an alternate route on the map. Why doesn't Google Maps have an avoid low clearances option? "Pull over."

Heath listened and pulled over into the grass on the side of the road while other drivers flew by looking at us like we were idiots. A white truck pulled over on the shoulder next to us and Heath rolled down the window.

"You know you're about to take your roof off, right?" said a man with a thick New York accent.

"Yeah, I know," Heath replied. All the honking and yelling seemed to finally get the message through. "We are trying to get back to the interstate."

"I figured," the man said. "Follow me."

He pulled back onto the highway with us not far behind and took what looked to be a shoulder but ended up being a very well concealed exit not far up the road. We wound through neighborhoods and past old shops and local restaurants before finally pulling up to a red light. The guy motioned out his window for us to pull up next to him so I rolled my window down.

"Turn left right here and you'll hit the interstate in a couple of miles."

"Thank you," Heath and I said as the light turned green and we drove away. The guy just shook his head, probably thinking something along the lines of "kids these days."

We drove in silence until Heath made it onto the interstate again heading south following the signs for New York City.

"Do not, do *not* exit again until I tell you to, okay?" I repeated to Heath. He grumbled something in response and I put my computer away to help him navigate through the rest of the city, which while not as deadly, remained stressful. Ever since leaving our car in west Texas, we had stressed over what it would be like to drive the RV to Manhattan. Steve and Mary Ellen had given us explicit directions when we stayed at their house. We had to take the George Washington Bridge. With propane onboard, we couldn't take any tunnels. We could've worked Heath's job somewhere else in the state since we'd both visited the city as tourists before, but all of the news outlets wanting to interview us required a trip to midtown, so we had to fight standstill traffic in the Bronx.

We slowly made our way to the upper level of the George Washington Bridge, following the semi-trucks who seemed to know exactly which level of the giant bridge to take. We rose to the top level surprised to see a forest of green waiting for us in New Jersey. There was only one good option for camping in New York City: Liberty Harbor RV Park. It was technically in Jersey City over the Hudson River. We had to drive into Manhattan, cross the bridge, and then navigate toll roads in the biggest city in the whole country while a hundred taxicabs simultaneously honked at us to get out of the way.

Cars, buses, and semis pressed us in on all sides and seemingly every single road was under construction, giving us tiny traffic lanes to navigate in our home. We squeezed through multiple toll booths, counting coins to pay for all the unexpected fees. At one point, we crossed a small bridge with concrete barriers on either side. I closed my eyes so I wouldn't see us scraping the sides of our house on the narrow road. But we made it through the tiny lanes, finally pulling into an asphalt parking lot peppered with electrical pedestals. We took a campsite where we could glimpse the Statue of Liberty through the masts of sailboats bobbing up and down in the harbor.

Heath backed in easily and leaned his head back against the headrest. "Please, please, tell me we have wine. I need a drink."

I wondered if these were the kind of stories journalists would be asking us.

"Alyssa, please tell me how many times you've almost died attempting this feat."

"Well Anderson, there was the nearly asphyxiating on propane incident and Heath almost decapitating me—and that's just this week! There's also a shrill high-pitched noise coming from the brakes, but we're ignoring that at the moment."

Those definitely weren't stories I wanted blasted across the national news, but it was a glimpse into our real life on the road. For as incompetent as we sometimes felt fighting with our RV, we had passed the halfway point on our journey. Somewhere in the northeast, it began to sink in that we were actually going to make it to all 50. Up until now, it felt like we were faking it when we assured everyone that we were going to all fifty states. It didn't feel like such a pipe dream anymore. With every state line we crossed, our confidence grew.

Six months ago, I was dreaming and planning a grand adventure that I wasn't entirely sure would happen. Visiting all fifty states this year felt out of reach. Now in state 31 and with cold food in the fridge again, I realized the tides were turning.

Forging our way across the country only served to inspire more dreams—dreams that didn't seem so impossible now that we had developed the grit required to push through the hard times. When the Indy Star interviewed us or the evening news in North Dakota, we felt like imposters sharing a fantasy. Going into the week ahead in New York, that discomfort of feeling like a fraud faded and was replaced with pride. We may have no money to our name and an RV determined to not make it back to Texas, but we were still moving forward.

I hoped our rusting old RV conveyed the same message.

Chapter 24

CNN is coming into my RV today.

They wanted to film our segment from the RV and edit it together with footage of our trip to be shown later on TV. After a couple of glasses of wine last night to unwind from the stress of arriving, we cleaned the best we could. But once I knew our RV would be on national television, cleaning didn't seem to make a big difference. You couldn't hide the 20 years of age. I kicked myself for not buying a couch cover to cover up the hideous, very 1990s, blue patterned couch. Lucky for us, the broken blinds haphazardly taped together hanging above the couch distracted from the vile fabric. All the blue at least matched the stained baseboards I created in Indiana.

There was nothing to do about it now. I vacillated between shaking with nerves to a veneer of nonchalance as I downed my second cup of coffee. This would air on CNN. *CNN.* This was now one of half a dozen news stories we'd be doing, but at least it wasn't live. We could mess up and they can edit it out later.

No big deal, I tried to convince myself. We don't even watch the news anyway.

No big deal except that it could potentially be seen by MILLIONS.

Half of the people who watch won't remember what they saw 30 seconds later, I argued.

Some people will think we're insane, I worried.

Some will probably think we're irresponsible kids, I knew.

Some will think it's awesome, I hoped.

And an hour after it airs no one will remember it at all. It's only a three-minute segment. Shake it off, I told myself.

It's no big deal. No big deal, I repeated as I scrubbed our coffee pot cleaner than it's ever been—as if the viewers would send me emails commenting about the coffee residue stains on the bottom of the pot.

Like I said, back and forth between freaking out and freaking out slightly less.

The cameraman arrived first, making small talk and asking us questions as we gave him a quick tour of the RV. We set up our camping chairs outside and let him have the RV to himself to capture shots of our house and download footage from our documentary to his hard drive. He wanted shots of the RV driving, national parks, jobs Heath worked, and us exploring to be added to the piece. I scrolled through my footage pulling some of my favorite clips I'd filmed.

Once the reporter arrived, the whole interview sped by in under an hour. She asked a few questions and had us do silly things like sit in the front seat of the RV and wave to the camera. And then it was over. The crew thanked us and left, promising to share the story with us once they edited the final piece together.

"How did that feel?" Heath asked after the crew walked back to the train station and into the city.

"Easier than I thought. You answered all the work questions, I answered all the travel questions. We had a good balance."

"I was worried I was talking too much."

"I was worried I was talking too little!"

Heath laughed. "Well, one done. I scheduled a cab to pick us up in a couple of hours to take us into the city. Ready for a bunch more interviews?"

"Ready as I'll ever be."

"You look great. Let me just vamp what you've already got going on," the makeup artist smiled.

In all likelihood, that is the nice television way of saying "let me redo your makeup completely before you go on camera" because I spent a solid 20 minutes in that chair while she brushed over what I brushed and re-curled everything that I curled. I watched a makeup tutorial on YouTube in our hotel room and felt pretty good about myself. But in those 20 minutes, that magician took me from everyday human to OMG. My skin was glowing, my eyes popped and my hair didn't look a tenth this good on my wedding day.

I strode back into the green room at Fox Studios with my head held high because this was definitely the most stunning I've ever felt. In the RV, it is all leggings and sweatshirts and comfy clothes we could move in. Now I was wearing high heels and pantyhose at 6:00 AM on a Sunday morning. Why did I even pack pantyhose to spend a year camping? I have no idea.

Heath waited in the green room—after less than five minutes in hair and makeup and now sporting a bronze glow—wearing the same suit he wore on our wedding day.

"Hey babe," Heath welcomed me as I interrupted his conversation with a family in the greenroom. "This is Travis Freeman and his parents, Mary and Larry."

"Hi," I waved, immediately feeling stupid as I realized I was waving at a blind man. The man in his 30s stood in a tan suit with a walking cane in his hands, flanked by his parents on either side of him.

"Hi," the friendly family replied with smiles. "Your husband was just telling us about your honeymoon. What a fun way to start your life together!" They settled onto the couch opposite Heath.

"Thanks," we said in perfect unison, the conversation sparking more butterflies in my stomach.

"We've really loved it. What are y'all in for this morning?" I asked.

"We've got a movie premiering tonight," Travis said.

"Well, we didn't make the movie," his mom popped in to explain. "It's inspired by Travis here."

In high school, Travis got a migraine that lasted for days. The migraine turned into eye pain that revealed a rare infection had created a clot in one of the veins at the base of his brain. He was rushed into surgery but the infection took his eyesight. Determined to get back to normal life despite his sudden blindness, Travis continued to play football. He wrote a book about being the first blind football player which Hollywood picked up to become a feature film.

It was the kind of story you actually like listening to on the news and I felt myself relax listening to Travis' story. As we waited and chatted with the family in the green room, they invited us to join them at the premiere.

"I don't know if it will count as your job for New York, but I'm sure they could use volunteers on the red carpet! Give me your email and I'll make sure y'all are added to the list."

"Really?" We both asked, incredulous. We've talked to this family for three minutes and they are inviting us to a red carpet movie premiere in Times Square? And we are on *the list*? *The list* is totally Hollywood code for "you're super cool and important." I mean, we definitely only got recruited as volunteers for the event staff, but hey. Red carpet? Movie stars? Author who had his life turned into a movie?

Could this morning *be* any crazier?

And just like that, the production assistant bounced in to walk us onto the stage for our interview.

"I was just there last weekend! They have the best fried clams!" Tucker Carlson boasted about Bob's Clam Hut—Heath's 27th job in Maine—before we went on air. Everyone was seated on a rounded couch. We were mic'd, told where to look, told where not to look, and had the next three minutes of our lives to not make fools of ourselves.

Fortunately, Tucker and Anna, who introduced themselves as we sat across from them, couldn't be kinder. I'd never watched Fox & Friends, but these were two camera-perfect faces if I'd ever seen them. They smiled and chatted with us during the commercial break, getting just a hint of our story while someone in our ears gave us the countdown to air.

And then the red light blinked on and the cameras turned toward us. Anna narrated from the teleprompter while we watched a montage of footage play across the live feed. Brewing beer in Indiana. Serving food in Wyoming. Playing with puppies in Kansas. Cleaning the baseball stadium in California. People were actually watching footage of our documentary. Things that I filmed!

Well, they were if they watch the news at 7:00 AM on a Sunday morning.

Heath and I twiddled our thumbs and looked at each other, nervously wondering when the montage would end and our faces would be live for the world to see. The 18 seconds ticked by slower than usual and then suddenly my face appeared on the live stream—still looking down at the preview monitor. My heart pounded in my chest. *Didn't the PA just tell us to keep our eyes on the hosts? Have I really already messed this up?* I popped my head up like a kid who got caught with her hands in the cookie jar.

Anna welcomed us to the show and we exchanged pleasantries.

"Thank you for being here."

"Thanks for having us."

A couple of days ago, a producer called us for a pre-interview. They said it would be a quick, easy way for us to practice our answers to the questions they might ask so we could be prepared, but I'm 90% sure it was so they could cancel having us on if we sounded like lunatics once we opened our mouths. We passed muster and were emailed a dozen different questions that the hosts might ask us once we were on air. I wondered why they couldn't just tell us the exact questions they might ask, so Heath and I could figure out who should answer what and make sure we hit all the key points. You see newscasters with papers in hand while reading off a teleprompter, so I assumed they would be given the exact questions to ask.

I swear none of the questions that came out of Anna's mouth were in that email.

Or if they were, any memory of what I was supposed to say flew out of my brain as soon as the camera zoomed in on my face.

Heath, always cool under pressure and well-seasoned at being thrown into new situations after 30 jobs, smoothly answered the first couple of questions with a smile. I remember laughing and smiling in genuine response to the conversation playing out before me.

And then Tucker said my name.

Tucker, I thought, *what are you thinking? Heath is nailing this. I'm nodding and mmhmm-ing in all the right spots. I appreciate you bringing me into the conversation, but I'm not sure I can form a coherent thought right now. My heart is pounding. I'm awkwardly sitting up straight with my elbows slightly out to air out my armpits because I'm sweating under these spotlights. This is like P.E. all over again. Please. Don't. Pick. Me!*

"Alyssa, what did you like?" Tucker said after asking which job was our favorite.

My brain raced to the place where I most wished I could be at that moment.

"My favorite was a little winery in Alexandria, Minnesota," I recalled, thinking a glass of wine sounded pretty good right about now.

Later when my parents called to gush over watching us on TV, they praised me for my answers about our documentary being "an American effort" and the people we met along the way feeling like family.

"I said what?" I asked, racking my brain and finding I had no memory of my three and a half minutes of fame. All I could remember was a blur of laughing with the hosts and smiling at the cameras while consciously trying not to fidget with the curl of hair that kept falling across my eyes.

The interview ended sweetly with Anna asking how we felt living in an RV and working together on a documentary had affected our marriage.

"It's helped, yeah," Heath said with a smile.

"It's been amazing," I said as I placed a hand on Heath's knee. *If you ignore the undeniable romance of waking up with a propane-induced hangover last week.*

We floated around New York City for the rest of the day hopping around studios for different interviews. For so many moments along our journey, there were doubts and breakdowns and low account balances that made me wonder if we had made the right decision. All fifty states, in a year, with a newlywed husband *plus* trying to film a documentary with no experience. Explaining it to the strangers we met on the road was often met with a look of confusion as we tried to share our story. But, for three and a half minutes, the morning show hosts boosted our confidence. We were doing something that mattered. We were impacting the lives of people across the country as we filmed their stories and shared our own.

And tonight we were walking the red carpet.

"Okay here's the escort list. You each have one or two people you're responsible for. You'll greet your person, first stop is photos, then video, then interviews. Guide them across the red carpet, stand out of the way so you aren't in the background of the photos or videos, and then take them upstairs. It's two escalators to the concessions. They can get popcorn and drinks with these tickets," the event coordinator spoke quickly, pulling a stack of tickets out from under her clipboard.

Heath and I looked identical to how we looked on Fox since we both only brought one nice outfit in the RV and had no idea what was appropriate for a red carpet movie premiere. Were we overdressed or underdressed? We layered on our heavy winter coats to ward off the frosty October chill. I was a little nervous once I saw the literal red carpet lined with velvet ropes hanging on golden stanchions to keep the press at bay. This may be even more exciting than being on TV, I thought. It was definitely less nerve-wracking.

"Then there's one more escalator to the floor where the theater is. There are assigned seats in the theater. Take your guests to their assigned seats. If they ask, the producers will say a few words before the film begins. People will begin to arrive in about 20 minutes. I suggest going upstairs now to familiarize yourself with the layout and where you'll be seating your guest. Any questions? No. Find me if you have questions." She spoke hurriedly and disappeared in a flurry of motion behind the step-and-repeat banner patterned with the *23 Blast* film logo where the stars would soon stand to have photos taken as they arrived.

We rode up the escalator and Googled the names of the famous people who would walk the carpet tonight. A few soap opera stars and a bunch of football players made the list. I was assigned a former Dallas Cowboy, a fact that would delight my dad. I'd never heard of him, but he was famous enough to have a Wikipedia page so I could brush up on my facts before meeting him. (And more importantly, memorize what he looked like so I could greet him by name when his car arrived.)

"Victor Garber…I recognize that name."

"Do you think we'll get popcorn?" Heath interrupted my Google searching and pointed at the concession stand as we made our way to the second set of escalators.

"Yes, we'll get popcorn. That's what the tickets are for. *Titanic*! Oh and *Legally Blonde*!"

"Can we get the popcorn now?"

"Heath. Focus." I grabbed his elbow and pulled him away from the smell of melted butter. "I'm trying to show you which super famous people we can meet tonight. You don't want popcorn butter all over your hands when we greet them. Look, this guy is coming. Recognize him?"

"Kinda," Heath said, glancing at IMDB on my phone. "I haven't seen *Titanic* in forever."

"He has touched Reese Witherspoon's leg, Heath," I said seriously. "We should try to be his friend."

Heath chuckled. "You were starstruck meeting Tucker and Anna this morning and you had never heard of them before."

That's true. "You're never starstruck by anyone, so I'm starstruck enough for the both of us," I reasoned. "I'm just trying to make the most of our first red carpet! Who knows if we will ever walk a red carpet again?"

"We can have a red carpet when we premiere our documentary."

"You think we will have a premiere?" I asked. The thought hadn't really crossed my mind. Editing the film was the next daunting task to tackle. I couldn't imagine sitting in a theater while people watched everything I shot.

"Of course we will. It might just be at one of our parents' houses. Probably your parents' house. But it'll still be a premiere. We'll tell Victor to invite Reese Witherspoon."

"Good idea. She might be busy though."

"Probably," he agreed.

We memorized where our guests would be seated in the surprisingly normal movie theater and descended the escalators returning to the red carpet. Slowly, media and guests began trickling in. The event staff we joined guided each starlet down the red carpet. We didn't recognize a single face, save for the Freeman family who looked just as gobsmacked by the flashing lights and red carpet as I was.

The red carpet was a commotion of journalists asking questions and flashing cameras while the actors, producers, and professional athletes all posed and smiled acknowledging that this was just another day of work for them.

Finally, just before showtime, my guest arrived. I'd tell you his name, but for the life of me, I can't remember. He was tall, well-dressed, and looked like someone who played professional football and probably modeled in his free time.

"Am I late? We came straight from yoga," said the glistening athlete in front of me. I couldn't tell if the glisten was from yoga or the fact that he and his friend jogged up to the velvet rope.

"Not at all. My name is Alyssa," I said. He and his friend introduced themselves and I escorted them across the red carpet, waiting as the press asked questions like, "what do you think of the film" even though clearly no one had seen the film yet. After awkwardly rocking back on my heels in the background while waiting for the last interview to wrap up, I guided the men up the escalators, to the popcorn, and to their seats, passing Heath along the way. Heath winked at me and continued riding the escalator upward chatting with some producer.

By the time we both made it back to the red carpet to see if the event staff needed any more help, most of the guests had arrived and the press was packing up. We asked a volunteer to snap our photo in our fancy clothes on the red carpet with the shiny step-and-repeat behind us. For a moment, we felt like movie stars.

My heels clacked loudly on the tile floor as I stepped off the red carpet and headed toward the concession stand so Heath could finally get his popcorn.

Today was perfect.

I shared our story on live national television.

I walked a real-life red carpet.

The Big Apple was delivering on all its glittering promises.

Of course, the bright lights kept us distracted from seeing what was waiting in our inbox:

URGENT: Cease and Desist.

Chapter 25

"He sent us a cease and desist? What does that even mean?"

"Basically it's the precursor to suing us if we don't stop," Heath tried to explain.

"Suing us? I don't understand. Don't stop? You can't sue someone for going to all fifty states. He didn't invent the idea!"

David—name changed because he would probably sue me if I printed it here—was a man on a mission. A few weeks earlier, I found a message request from him in my Facebook inbox with a simple message: "Just thought I'd bring it to your attention that the concept of working 50 jobs in 50 states has already been accomplished."

I'd rolled my eyes when I read it, perfectly imagining his arrogant tone as I clicked on the link included in the message. Going to space has been done before but it doesn't mean no one else can become an astronaut.

Years ago, David worked 50 jobs in 50 states and wrote a book about it. A book with a couple dozen reviews that was now ranked in the millions on Amazon. Not exactly a bestseller.

But the guy was adamant that we had to stop our own trip to all fifty states because he'd already done it and we were infringing on his business.

Before the cease and desist, it was emails, messages, and comments on our website, blogs, and social media spamming us with hate. Our stories on CNN and Fox & Friends took off and without even being interviewed, we were tagged in posts by Yahoo, the Daily Mail, the Bobby Bones Show, and Forbes. Our story was everywhere and almost always titled the same: 50 Jobs in 50 States.

David was pissed.

All the news stories featured new comments like "why would they even bother covering this? It's already been done before." David had at least gotten creative and made fake profiles (but not creative enough that we couldn't trace them back to his mom's email address in 15 seconds). He was an annoyance, but we weren't going to stop filming our documentary just because he posted rude comments on our Facebook page and blog. We deleted them and moved on.

The letter from his lawyers kicked it up a notch.

When you break out and try a new lifestyle, you open yourself to criticism from everyone who hears about it. I expected some negative or judgmental feedback. I didn't expect someone to hate us so much that he'd try to sue us.

"When Fox and Huffington Post live broadcasted the story, they both titled it '50 Jobs, 50 States' which is in the name of his book. That's what Yahoo put on their homepage too. You can't even copyright a book title, but that seems to be what's upsetting him. Basically, in his lawyer's letter, it says we can't say 50 jobs in 50 states."

"We didn't even say that? It's not even on our website in so many words," I argued. "And as if you can tell the news what to title their articles!"

Every single interview we'd done in the past week stuck with 50 jobs in 50 states for their headline. Of course they would—it's catchy. It's easy to grasp. We had already made sure our website said "working a job in each state" to avoid copying this guy after a month of messages from him, but we couldn't control other websites.

"I know. It's not on Snagajob's website either, but apparently, this guy found the CEO's phone number and left him an angry voicemail saying the same thing. That we're infringing on his business and have to stop."

"Crap. Is Snagajob mad? They aren't going to drop us, are they?" I began to panic. They were our only consistent revenue since the beginning of the trip.

"Jon said their legal team is on it and they will send a reply through their lawyers. He didn't seem too worried, more like just annoyed."

"I'm annoyed too," I whined.

And worried. You can't copyright actually working a job in all fifty states. What if someone moved a lot in their life and really did get jobs in each state? It was clear what this guy wanted. Stop at state 31, tuck tail, go home. Let him keep his ego intact and stop being overshadowed by our story.

After some Google searching and combing through our websites, it didn't seem like we were doing anything wrong. Reading through the cease and desist, we weren't using any of the taglines the lawyer claimed we were. We always clarified "working an hourly job in each state" and skipped using numbers at all. There was not a basis for these claims. A message from Snagajob's lawyers confirmed to us that we didn't need to be worried about any legal recourse.

But the constant barrage of hate from this guy took the wind out of our sails after floating through New York. Despite our best efforts, he was determined to tear us down.

I scrolled mindlessly through the comments on our news stories to see what he was saying about us, laughing briefly when I saw a comment on the Daily Mail that said "why does that girl look like a different person in each photo?" Makeup, my dear, makeup. Where did they even find these pictures? I wondered, considering that I should maybe make my personal Facebook account more private. They found way too many photos of me without makeup on that were never meant to be shared on an international news site.

On top of David's spiteful comments were dozens of comments about how it must be nice to have a trust fund to live off of and be independently wealthy. I looked at the photo of Heath and me in front of our RV. How could any of these people see *that* RV and think "wow these people are rich?"

They got meaner.

Just another entitled millennial.

How nice of mommy and daddy to pay for them to go play. Sick.

And, when the news outlets so kindly posted that photo of me driving the RV for the first time:

That guy looks like he's regretting marrying that girl.

They'll file for divorce before they finish.

The comments sucked me in, each one seemingly worse than

the last, with rants and stories from people with too much time on their hands.

Downtrodden, I closed my laptop and sank into the couch in our RV ready to lift the jacks and keep heading south.

Twenty-four hours ago, I felt empowered. After working in a grey office day in and day out, life was finally colorful. I was bursting with stories and new experiences and excitement to continue seeing America.

Now I felt foolish. People hated me for doing this. Strangers on the internet took their time to openly comment about how little they thought of the way I was living my life.

I buried my head in my hands and took a deep breath. I closed my eyes. I listened to my breath as Heath paced outside talking to the team at Snagajob to find a solution to the legal action.

For as often as travel brings you to mountain peaks, it also lays you bare. The excitement of chasing your dreams is met by a breakdown. The glory of watching the sunset on the golden fall leaves is stressed by work. The thrill of feeling like your story matters to the world is replaced by legal action telling you to shut up. It's never boring. Even driving across the flyover states of middle America was punctuated by stunning landmarks and the melting power of lightning.

In some ways, it's why we fall in love with travel. The unpredictability. The excitement. It's the complete opposite of life at home where I found myself recognizing other cars in traffic because we all left work at the same time each day. *Isn't this what I was seeking when I told Heath we should visit all fifty states? Adventure! Challenges! Beauty!*

I shook my head and looked up at the ceiling of our RV. There were brown spots around the roof vent where rains had seeped through the leak we still hadn't been able to fix. I shook my head again and opened my laptop, quickly closing the browser before new comments could load.

I opened the OneNote app and started journaling to release the stress and emotions bubbling up inside my head.

This is ridiculous.

Am I going to stop halfway through our journey to all fifty states just because of this one guy? NO. No. So why do I feel terrible? Reading comments was a terrible idea. Never do it again. Okay, what am I stressing about?

1. *Being sued.*
   Solution: Snagajob will resolve the legal issue. The lawyers are on it and commented that this was "the weakest cease and desist they'd ever seen." Note to self: don't worry about this.
2. *Comments.*
   Solution: People on the internet don't get to validate how I live my life. I mean, they kind of do if I'm going to write books, but that's a totally different ball game. People are way meaner on news websites than they are anywhere else. Don't listen to the haters. Listen to Taylor Swift's new Shake It Off *song instead. Haters gonna hate. Just don't ever check the comments again, okay future Alyssa?*
3. *Our toilet keeps clogging.*
   Solution: Okay, a quick Google search says to boil water and flush it down the toilet to clear out the clog. Let me go try that.

I popped up from the couch distracted by a project. Clearing a clogged toilet wasn't the distraction I hoped for after getting pulled down by the events of the morning, but it was something I could actively solve right now.

I filled our only pot with water and lit the stove. My thoughts bounced around while I waited, ping-ponging back to the comments I read. People saying that I was ugly or looked like a 12-year-old or was a brat. "Nope," I said aloud, shaking the thoughts out of my body. *We're not going to focus on that*, I told myself. *We're going to focus on the toilet.* Should I pour the boiling water in and then flush the toilet? Or should I hold down the foot pedal and then pour it directly down the drain?

I weighed the pros and cons. Keeping the toilet open while I poured would allow a lot of unwanted smells into the RV, so option one won out. Grabbing a potholder to hold the warm handle steady, I walked slowly to the bathroom trying not to spill. I really should've opened the toilet seat *before* picking up a heavy, boiling hot pot of water. Leaning over with my eyes on the pot, I slowly lifted the toilet lid with one hand and poured the water into the toilet. Thank God we only have a two-quart pot because I hadn't even considered that filling the pot all the way might've overflowed the tiny toilet bowl.

With the pot empty, I pressed the foot pedal to flush. The clogged toilet paper created a sort of suction in the pipes and the sudden rushing of water somehow forced a huge bubble of air to pop in the toilet. Hot water splashed on my legs.

Hot water. From the toilet. Just burned my legs. I shuddered and gagged instinctively at the feeling.

And then the *stench*.

The steam wafting up from the toilet clung to my face and

assaulted my nose. There's a standard black tank odor all RVers have smelled. It lingers at dump stations and rides with you down the highway if you forget to add your toilet deodorant to your emptied tanks.

This was worse.

This was the smell of cooked poop. Not even fresh cooked poop. Cooked poop from days ago, before our hotel stay, and dating back a full week to when we last dumped our tanks in Connecticut. The smell of week-old, steamy poop filled the air.

I raced out of the bathroom, closing the toilet seat and the door in a rush, gasping for fresh air.

I was starting to understand some of the comments that didn't understand my life choices. Starting to question them myself at the moment.

Chapter 26

"Do you want to too?" Karl asked unexpectedly.

"Oh, I don't work the jobs. Just film," I replied nodding toward the camera hanging around my neck.

Karl made a face. "That's not what I asked. Do you *want* to? We could always use more," he raised his eyebrows mischievously. I had only known Karl for an hour, but somehow the head of Six Flags America was acting as if he knew me. Or maybe he could see in my eyes that I was a little jealous of Heath's job...

"Yes, I want to be a zombie!" I blurted out.

Karl chuckled.

"Go on then," he said, motioning toward Heath who was pulling on tattered clothes from an oversized bin labeled ZOMBIES. Halloween was last night and this was the last day of Fright Fest at Six Flags in Maryland—Heath's 35th job.

Heath and I didn't get to celebrate Halloween. Instead, we went to Walmart and bought a strand of Christmas lights and a one-foot-tall tree because we are *those* people. But this was our chance to dress up like monsters and run around the park terrorizing children.

I put on a frayed threadbare men's button-up shirt over my t-shirt and joined the line behind Heath.

"Look at you finally working," Heath teased.

"You *know* why I haven't worked any of your jobs so far," I replied haughtily, adjusting the settings on the camera for the dim lighting of the yellow-tiled room.

"Oh yeah? Why's that?"

"Because I'm going to be way better at it than you."

He laughed. "Let's see it."

I smiled as I panned the room with the camera. The employee locker room was packed with clowns, monsters, and mummies. All of these employees auditioned to join the ranks of the undead and we were crowding the locker room waiting for two things:

1. For the sun to go down so the monsters could officially be released (giving families with young children a chance to leave the park)
2. Makeup

The artists airbrushed face after face in shades of green, brown, white, and black depending on the character. I watched as one makeup artist picked up a roll of toilet paper. I assumed she would create a mummy, but instead, I filmed her ripping off a piece of toilet paper and gluing it to the zombie's face. *What is she doing?* I wondered. Blowing on the glue to make sure it was dry, she airbrushed the toilet paper black and began to rip a hole in the center, creating a little crater inside the rough toilet paper edges. She picked up a bottle of what appeared to be fake blood and squirted it inside the little crater. It dribbled slowly down the zombie's forehead. Satisfied with her work, she sent the zombie on his way and called up the next person in line. As the zombie walked past me, the toilet paper didn't look like toilet paper at all. It looked like rotten flesh flaking off of his face. It was both brilliant and disgusting.

After a few minutes, Heath sat down in his chair and his artist went to work. There were six chairs set up in the tiny room and at least a dozen people rushing in and out. I tried to stay out of the way while he got his makeup done. This was a far cry from getting our makeup professionally done in the green room at Fox. Heath looked terrible when she was finished, so I knew this artist was good at her job. Blood appeared to pour out of his mouth, down his chin and even dripped onto his clothes.

I passed the camera off to zombie Heath and sat in an open chair awaiting my gruesome transformation.

"Do you want me to film you?" he asked.

"Nah, we don't need me in the documentary. But take a picture! I want to see my zombie-ness," I replied, settling into the chair. There was only one big mirror on the other side of the locker room so I wouldn't be able to see what the artist was doing to my face as she worked.

"Hi, my name is Jada," the makeup artist introduced herself as she refilled her airbrush. "I don't recognize you. What are you?"

"Zombie," I replied. "It's my first day," I added, borrowing Heath's usual line and shooting him a wink.

She nodded. "Hold your breath, okay? This stuff smells like apples but you shouldn't breathe it in."

Resisting the urge to smell it, I held my breath while she sprayed my forehead, nose, and cheeks a shade of dark green. But it took a while, so by the time she was airbrushing my neck I had to take a breath. It did smell like apples.

I sat patiently while she glued two giant pieces of toilet paper on my cheeks, painting them and ripping them and adding blood. She applied purple lipstick and extra dark makeup around my eyes.

"It's time!" someone called out, creating a whirlwind of motion until only a few monsters remained in the locker room with Heath and me. A distant sound rang out and I could imagine the gates opening slowly as 100 costumed actors unleashed themselves on the park guests. Screams echoed all the way back to us in the locker room.

"Good?" She asked, holding up a mirror.

Good is not the word I would use.

Cast me in *The Walking Dead,* because I am a zombie. I barely recognized myself. The (toilet paper) flesh peeling off my face and the black under my eyes was enough to convince you that I hadn't slept in a decade.

In full dress, Heath and I made our way out of the locker room and back into the park. Karl gave us a tour of the park when we arrived earlier this afternoon and pointed out where the zombie section of the park was. I walked backward in that direction while filming Heath as he shared the details of his job for the night. Between the dark night sky and the dark makeup, you could only make out shadows—punctuated by teenagers shrieking and running past us.

We made it to our section and could see a dozen zombies skulking around. Consumed by the excitement of putting on costumes and getting our makeup done, we forgot to clarify exactly what we were supposed to do. Hide and jump out to scare people? That wasn't very zombie-ish. Follow people around? Maybe.

We stood awkwardly for a moment getting our bearings. We had to get release forms signed by anyone we filmed, which wasn't a problem for filming employees, but would be a problem for filming the park guests we interacted with. We were trying to decide logistically how to actually film Heath doing his job without showing the faces of people he scared.

"You know what?" I asked Heath. "It's almost too dark to film and we have footage from 32 other jobs already." Purposefully not mentioning the two jobs where I lost the footage. "I've already got your makeup and commentary filmed. Why don't I put the big camera away and let's just be zombies?" Without the cameras, we didn't have to worry about filming people without their consent and we could just have fun.

"I like that idea," Heath said looking relieved that we wouldn't have to chase down innocent park guests to get their signature on a release form. I jogged off to lock up the camera in our RV which was parked just behind the back entrance to the park. People gave me a wide berth when I hurried past them, reminding me how I must look to them. Ratty old zombie carrying a fancy camera.

When I returned, Heath was standing in a circle with a few other zombies, the most terrifying of whom was a waif of a girl wearing a ragged white shawl draped over her shoulders and white contact lenses that made her look truly zombie-like. She held an old porcelain doll in the crook of her arm and absent-mindedly stroked its hair. Even from afar, she was terrifying.

"No, no, like this," I heard her say as I approached the group. She cocked her head to the side and widened her eyes. She made eye contact with Heath and slowly closed the gap between them. He instinctively took a step back.

"Okay, yeah that works," he said with an unsure laugh. I joined his side and Heath flinched. "Oh, hey babe," he introduced the zombies to me. "They're teaching me the best way to be creepy and they are really, really good at it."

"You can't just walk normal," a guy Heath introduced as Shawn instructed me. "Pretend like half of your bones are broken." He collapsed his spine to the left side and bent his right leg at an awkward angle before shuffling forward on his left foot and dragging his right leg behind him.

"Ah, good tip. You look very dead," I affirmed.

"Thank you," he beamed. "I see a group heading this way. Let's make 'em scream."

Equipped with the professional zombie instruction, Heath and I dispersed in the open area. The sky above was black and the only light came from the windows of restaurants and gift shops in the area. I wandered into the shadows, finding a landscaped portion of the walkway with big trees and benches that I could duck behind. A group of three middle school aged girls walked by with their arms linked. After they passed, I slowly started following them. One of them sensed movement behind her and looked over her shoulder and saw me. She started walking faster, trying to pull her friends along, but her friends spotted Heath and Shawn up ahead and were trying to slow down.

I closed the gap between us quietly until I was close enough to breathe on the girls' necks.

Am I supposed to be this close? Karl mentioned something about how they are known for their Fright Fest and that the park gives explicit instructions to anyone attending that you will interact with the actors. I wondered what interact meant. I definitely felt creepy walking inches behind these very oblivious girls. I decided I should alert them to my presence to feel less like a stalker. I let out a low, guttural moan trying to harness my inner zombie.

The girls whipped their heads around—with one of the girl's ponytails whacking me across the face—and shrieked. They took off sprinting right into the waiting arms of Heath, Shawn, and Vanessa (the hair-raising doll-holding girl). I tried not to laugh as the girls, with their arms still linked, all tried running away in opposite directions. Finally, one of them called out "this way!" and they all disappeared into the darkness ahead. A few seconds later, I heard more screams and knew they ran into another group of hidden zombies.

Okay, this is definitely fun. For the next hour, I hid and stalked and scared everyone who dared to walk past our outpost.

Girlfriends clutched their boyfriend's hands.

An eight-year-old who had wandered away from his mom ran away in tears.

Two pre-teens hid from me in a store. I waited outside the door until I heard one of them say to the other, "Don't worry, Megan. They can't come inside!"

No one told me I couldn't come inside.

I went inside.

They backed into a corner screaming before darting past me. They were still screaming as I chased them 100 yards down the path.

The crowds thinned out as the night wore on and Karl came out to check on us.

"She scared somebody just by smiling!" Shawn exclaimed loudly, pointing at me. "She literally was like this," he said, imitating a happy smile. "Just like this and she scared somebody. TO DEATH!"

"Babe!" Heath said in shock.

"That's the job, Heath," I replied gravely. "I take this documentary very seriously."

"How did you do, Heath?" Karl asked.

"I, uh, well I don't think I made anyone cry. So not as good as Alyssa over here," he said, bumping me with his shoulder. "I think we found her calling."

Everyone laughed.

"Hey, you can always come back next Halloween," Karl invited us.

Chapter 27

Keeping with our theme of finding free places to park, one of Heath's friends from high school heard we were headed to Tennessee and offered up her house east of the city. Cirby and her two sisters sang in a country music trio called Sister C and even made it onto *The X Factor*. They bought a house in town to make it as country artists. I couldn't help but compare all of the people we met on the road. Every person we met was doing something more brave and bold than the last as they pursued their dreams. Heath said it was because we were finally doing something bold in our own lives that we started to meet people like us who were chasing after big dreams.

I quietly wondered if he was right as I navigated him through the trendy, colorful homes. East Nashville was southern charm meets hipster village. The old homes with welcoming front porches all glistened from fresh coats of brightly colored paint with hidden coffee shops and restaurants mixed in between.

After we left New York, working on the documentary was a breeze. Heath easily found jobs now that he was able to send over links to our story on CNN and Fox. The stories gave us instant credibility (if you didn't read the comments at least). Heath flipped burgers in a White Castle in New Jersey, worked as an electrician on a sprawling estate museum in Delaware, and got us the gig at Six Flags. Plus, a church in Pennsylvania let us park for free for a few days (and even let us use their laundry room!) and an old friend in Virginia let us crash in her house for a few nights.

We sailed south smoothly, other than a quick pitstop at the mechanic in West Virginia who let us know that our brake pads had "shattered." We had to replace the brake pads and the rotors, but nothing phased us when it came to things breaking on the RV now. It cost us money, sure, but the inconvenience was a small price to pay to travel.

I carefully monitored our bank account and instead of draining slowly, it was maintaining a steady balance finally. With a little luck, we might even break even in December as Heath predicted. Financially we still had to figure out plane tickets to Hawaii and if we would fly or drive to Alaska. Alaska was the biggest question mark since driving would take a couple of weeks and cost the same as flying. But the words of the RVer from the hot tub in Las Vegas bounced around my head that the drive to Alaska is on every RVers bucket list. I wondered if this RV could make the haul across the Canadian Rockies.

We pulled up to a gorgeous old home in a cute Nashville neighborhood with an Audi parked on the street next to a very narrow driveway. Cirby came out in a sweatshirt and waved.

"Hey! Welcome back to Nashville!" she greeted us with a smile. "I pulled my car out of the driveway. Think you can fit?"

The answer was no. The driveway looked barely long enough to fit our RV and was bordered by a garage and a fence. We would have trouble opening our door if we could fit at all. Plus it was on a steep incline, which we learned from St. Louis had the power to destroy refrigerators.

One thing we were starting to learn was people who didn't own an RV typically assumed you could park almost anywhere, like a regular vehicle. It was always well-intentioned, but this thought process had left us in some relatively precarious situations (like when we were told there was "definitely room to park" in downtown Seattle and Heath had to parallel park on a tiny one-way street).

But it was free and we needed to be in town for a week. We had already dumped our tanks and filled up our water tank to 100% in preparation to driveway camp for as long as possible.

"We can make it work," Heath said.

"Perfect!" Cirby said before saying the sweetest words in the English language. "I have a guest bedroom set up for you guys to stay inside while you're here."

I'd only met Cirby briefly at a trendy coffee shop on our way out of Nashville back in September, but she was officially my favorite person on planet earth at that moment. We may have prepared the RV for boondocking, but after seeing her driveway, it was way too unlevel to actually stay inside the RV. We would be sleeping at a 45° angle!

Not to mention the tiny detail of the winter storm moving in as Heath tried to park the RV. The clouds were darkening, snow was predicted, and the lows the next few nights were in the teens. We had our small space heater, but needed electric hookups to run it. We maybe had enough propane to keep the furnace running for a few days. This would be a solid 20 degrees colder than any other temperatures we'd faced in the RV. A warm bed in an insulated house had never sounded so good.

However, we still had to make this RV fit.

Heath backed up for the fourth time to attempt pulling straight into the driveway instead of turning in, which kept resulting in almost hitting the fence or almost clipping our mirror on the corner of the garage. Our RV blocked the entire road as he lined up the tires and inched forward straight up the concrete. A familiar crunching sound happened as we started to ascend the mountain of a driveway and Heath pressed harder on the gas as our bumper scraped the asphalt for the 214th time in the past six months. We had metal support wheels just under the bumper to keep it from dragging, but we broke those turning into a grocery store somewhere in Oregon.

"We're going to have to put bricks down to get back over that dip when we back out of here," Heath strategized as he shifted into park.

I climbed out of the warm RV and thanked Cirby with a hug. Broke as we were, it was the only thanks I could offer for her generosity.

"How long do you think y'all will stay?" she asked, after welcoming us into her house and giving us a brief tour.

"At least a week, if that's okay with you. We haven't found my job yet and there are a bunch of people in the city we want to hang out with while we are here," Heath replied.

"Of course! Stay as long as you want. We leave to drive to Texas for Thanksgiving tomorrow. I'll leave you the keys to my car so you can get around while you're here. Do you mind watering Celbi's plants every day?"

"We don't mind at all," I replied. A house, a car, a bathtub—was this luxurious life a dream?

"Thank you so much, Cirby. Seriously," Heath said.

"Hey, can we put some food in your fridge?" I asked.

"Sure," she replied.

There's no way I'm running a fridge in a driveway again.

I sat at the dining room table sipping my coffee and watching the snow fall gently in the backyard. The temperatures continued to drop outside, but I had heated floors to keep me warm. I smiled into my third cup of coffee.

"Kara and Nate are in for coming over tonight. What do you want to cook?" Heath said, walking into the kitchen from the living room. It was weird to be under the same roof but not actually be able to see and hear everything the other person was doing. We were always so close in the RV that any distance between us felt bizarre.

"Oh yay! I have some chicken in the freezer and a few potatoes. Maybe baked chicken, mashed potatoes, and green beans? I don't know what people normally cook for dinner parties!"

We met Kara and Nate briefly at Chris's book signing and immediately connected. They dreamed of traveling full-time and gushed about their upcoming trip. In a few weeks, they would fly over to Milan and travel Europe before making their way to Thailand.

This would be the first time Heath and I hosted anyone for

dinner since we got married. It was definitely my first time cooking for anyone other than Heath. I may have Googled "what to cook for a dinner party" and searched dinner party playlists on Spotify in preparation. As thrilled as I was to have a real kitchen and even a house with a dining room table to host our guests, I was terribly nervous. This was so *adult.*

If I had to dream up a life for myself when I was 18 of what I thought marriage would be like, it would have probably involved a house in a cute little walkable neighborhood with plenty of friends nearby who could come by to grill out on the weekends. While this was infinitely in another direction, it somehow felt even more fulfilling.

Somehow, in a moment of brash, bold craziness, we'd decided to live on the road for a year and travel to all 50 states. Further, we were even starting to build a sense of community. Not community in the traditional sense of coming over on the weekend to watch the football game, but community in the sense of "Hey! We're driving our RV back into town. Let's hang out again!" The best part about it was that this community was built on common values. We were beginning to make friends with people not because of proximity, but because our dreams aligned with theirs.

Which meant I needed to get out of my pajamas and get ready to host our new friends. I mentally kicked myself for not taking five minutes to pack a bag with clothes for the next few days before the storm hit.

I pulled on my coat and boots over my pajamas to trudge through the one inch of snow covering the ground all of 50 feet to the RV. I unlocked the door and immediately noticed that the RV was exactly the same temperature as it was outside.

Crap, I thought. We forgot to turn the furnace on low. Coming from Austin, my apartment complex would post signs on doors if the low ever dipped below 32°, urging everyone to leave their sinks dripping so the pipes wouldn't burst—a strategy that got a weird look in Massachusetts when I asked a local if they had to leave their sinks dripping all winter. Apparently, most of the country is better prepared for winter than Texans.

Google told me that instead of leaving my sinks dripping, which would require leaving the water pump running for hours and hours (when that thing already sounded like it was on its last leg every time we turned it on), we should set the furnace in the RV to 50° and open the cabinet doors where our pipes were.

When we arrived, we ran an extension cord from the garage to our RV so we could at least power the furnace fan for a few days to keep our pipes from bursting. And we completely forgot to turn on the furnace.

I walked slowly over to the sink, nervous to turn it on. I didn't see water spewing out of any broken pipes, so it seemed like our pipes were intact. Maybe we got lucky, even though the thermostat inside read 29°.

I turned the knob on the sink, heard the grunting and grinding of the water pump working, and watched as ice sludged out of the faucet. It looked like a white cherry Slurpee being dispensed into my sink. The temperatures were predicted to keep dropping as more snow and ice moved in, and it would be days before the air warmed enough to thaw the ice in our tank. I turned off the sink and cranked on the furnace to 50° praying it would be enough to keep any pipes from bursting in the extreme weather.

"Hi! Thank you guys so much for having us over!" Kara said excitedly.

"We brought some wine," Nate said in his southern drawl.

We welcomed them into Cirby's home and opened the bottle. Heath poured the wine into real wine glasses—not plastic cups like we always used in the RV—and toasted to the group.

"Cheers to making new friends," he said.

"Cheers," we all said in unison, clinking our glasses.

"So," said Kara conspiratorily. "Can we see the RV now? I was so bummed we didn't get to tour it when y'all were here last time!"

Heath and I laughed. "There isn't much to see, but come on out. You may want to put your coats back on first though. The RV is really cold right now."

We bundled up and made our way out to the RV. The temperatures in the upper teens were at war with our furnace and despite running it all afternoon, the RV was barely 40° inside.

Keeping our jackets on, we welcomed Kara and Nate inside and gave them the full tour of the RV. As usual, it took less than 30 seconds for them to see every square inch of our igloo on wheels. We boasted about how it offered us everything we needed, highlighting the full kitchen, shiny new fridge, and shower. Heath had his tour spiel down packed at this point, carefully designed to persuade everyone who entered to also start RVing so we could have friends on the road. I shared how we renovated the inside with a few fresh coats of paint to eliminate the fifty shades of brown.

"Ah, that makes sense," Kara said. "Because this doesn't look like what I pictured an RV to look like inside."

"That," I said, "is probably the highest compliment you could give us."

We all laughed.

"I think I could do it," Kara said, uttering the same words that someone from every single other couple who toured our RV had said.

"Really?" Nate said in genuine surprise, which is exactly what the spouse of the first person always said. "I feel like we need to have a conversation about this," Nate said earnestly. Based on the mischievous looks on their faces, I wouldn't have been surprised if they texted us a photo of an RV a week later.

"Oh," Heath said, "before we go inside, we need to check our water tanks."

"Ugh," I groaned. "Earlier when I came out here, a slushie came out of our sink."

"Why?" Kara asked with concern.

"Because the tank was almost completely frozen."

Heath turned the knob on the kitchen sink.

Nothing happened.

"And now it's completely frozen," I said. And the temperatures wouldn't get above freezing for the next five days.

"We can maybe bump up the furnace a few degrees or put the space heater on for a couple hours before bed?" Heath suggested. "It's only getting colder tonight."

"That's really our only option at this point," I shrugged.

We crossed our fingers and Heath turned up the heater to

keep our pipes from busting. We all climbed down the metal stairs to retreat back inside the warm house for dinner.

Okay, maybe Kara and Nate wouldn't be seduced into RV life after all.

Chapter 28

Icicles clung to the rocky cliffs when we left Nashville, and the cold temperatures permeated the RV, reminding us to hurry south. We boondocked in Black Mountain, North Carolina, parked on the beach in South Carolina, and fought the insane traffic of Atlanta, Georgia. Finally driving to the southmost point of our route, we spent five days enjoying all the amusement parks in Florida that we could.

When we first told our families that we were leaving on a honeymoon adventure and wouldn't be back until Christmas, Heath's family asked where we would be for Thanksgiving. We'll meet you there, they said. Lucky for them, the answer was Florida. Sunny, warm, Mickey Mouse-filled Florida.

The highlight of Florida should've been the pumpkin spice gelato macaron sandwich I devoured in Epcot, but Heath's 42nd job swooped in and took the cake.

He worked in a scooter shop, which initially only involved Heath learning how to change the oil on a scooter. Not incredibly exciting. But the shop owner, Collin, had a sidecar attached to his scooter and taught Heath how to ride.

"Let's go for a spin," Collin suggested after giving Heath a 60-second lesson in Vespa driving.

I climbed into Collin's sidecar and filmed Heath navigating his scooter across the parking lot with his legs hovering over the ground in case he tipped over. He quickly got the hang of things once we took to the road. My hair whipped in the wind as we zoomed around the University of Florida campus. It felt like a Hollywood production with the light filtering through the mossy green trees. I leaned over the back of the sidecar trying to keep the camera steady as I filmed Heath zipping around on his Vespa.

Is this how they film car chases in the movies? Because other than my hair blowing in front of the camera lens and messing up my shot, it felt like I was filming a chase scene from a *Bourne* movie.

After that, Heath resolved to find the most fun jobs possible to finish out the documentary. He worked as a cameraman for Wes' production studio in Alabama. He made eleven pounds of fudge as a chocolatier in Mississippi—which the chocolate shop owners generously gifted to us at the end of the day. In Louisiana, Heath worked as a vigneron, tending to the grapevines in a vineyard and tasting wine.

Hard work, I know, but someone's got to do it. Our final weeks of travel flew by as we drove west back toward Texas.

"I don't know that I've ever been so excited to be back in Texas," I said to Heath as we drove our final miles across Arkansas.

For Heath's job last night in the tiny town of El Dorado, he helped the local ranch coach their horse-drawn carriage rides around the twinkling lights of the downtown square. Carolers and hot chocolate kept us warm.

Lining up the end of the lower 48 with the holidays made the accomplishment that much more magical. Every town we drove through on our way back home was covered in Christmas decorations and sparkling lights. The celebration obviously wasn't for us. But after all of the help we received along the way—the free nights in driveways, the free meals, the advice—it felt like the whole country was coming together to celebrate this moment with us.

"200 days. 48 states. We actually did it," Heath said with a mix of excitement and relief. "I kind of don't believe it."

"Don't jinx it. Franklin will break down. We won't make it."

"What?!"

"I'm jinxing us for negative things to undo your jinx. Duh," I smiled.

"Okay, goober," Heath laughed. "We have to take a picture with the Texas sign as soon as we cross."

"Oh. Yes! I should make a list of all the states where we couldn't stop and get pictures with the state line sign, like when we crossed into New Jersey from New York and couldn't stop. It would be so cool to go back so we can have all 50. Or 49 maybe. I doubt Hawaii has a state line sign posted anywhere."

"I see it coming up," Heath said, slowly letting off the brakes.

I leaned over to see around the car in front of us. "Oh yay—oh no! There's no spot to pull over for a selfie."

"Nope. I do not accept that." Heath shook his head. "This is a big deal. We need a picture."

"Please do not stop on the interstate for a picture," I begged as he continued to slow down.

"I'm not, don't worry. Just looking for the state line rest stop. This is Texarkana. Their whole thing is being half in Texas, half in Arkansas. They have to have a big Texas sign somewhere for tourists."

He was right. You don't name yourself Texarkana and not have signs touting that you're in Texarkana, Texas, and Texarkana, Arkansas. "You're brilliant, you know that?"

"Texarkana Travel Center...I'm exiting," Heath flipped on his blinker. He navigated into the parking lots of the rest stop and there it was in front of a grassy field waiting for excited tourists like us: *Welcome to Texas. Drive Friendly – The Texas Way.*

Barefoot and too excited for something practical like shoes, we hopped out of the RV and walked over to the green sign painted with the Texas flag. Heath pulled out his phone and snapped a picture of our wide smiles. We did it.

We actually did it.

What's next?

That's the question everyone asked us at my family's Christmas Eve party.

It took 200 days from leaving Austin to crossing back over the Texas border. The obvious answer to what's next is Hawaii and Alaska. But it isn't a simple one.

While we were *finally* making enough money to break even for the first time since we quit our jobs (shout out to all the people who let us stay with them for free and stick our food in their fridges), getting all the way to Hawaii and Alaska was going to take a few grand that we didn't have yet. We would have to arrange flights and hotels in Hawaii, despite everyone always joking about how we were going to drive the RV all the way there. That would cost a couple thousand at least, not to mention a rental car and food. And Alaska was an even bigger question mark.

"I'm not going to Alaska in January. Are you kidding me?" I looked up at Heath from the clothes I was folding.

"Hey everyone thinks of Alaska as nothing but snow anyway. We can go in a couple of weeks, not see the sun all day, and for my job, I can race sled dogs!" Heath said with a goofy smile on his face.

"You're...joking...?" I said with a question in my eyes.

"I'm joking. Most of the stuff we'd like to do in Alaska would be hard to do in the winter. Plus, I really want to drive."

"Not this again," I groaned.

"You remember what that hot tub guy said in Vegas! Every RVer dreams of driving to Alaska!" Heath exclaimed.

"Every RVer," I began talking slowly as Google Maps loaded on my phone. "Wants to drive sixty-six hours to Alaska?! There's no way Franklin can make it that far. The roof is still leaking, he can't handle towing a car, and it would take at least a month to drive all the way up and all the way back. I can't even imagine how much we would spend on gas!"

I looked around the RV as we cleaned out and re-packed everything we owned. When we made it back to Texas, we had two weeks to enjoy the holidays before we needed to drive out to California. Heath's boss—err, client—wanted to up his hours and work in person so we planned to spend January and February in Santa Cruz, California.

I was excited to spend two months in one spot and get to know the tiny beach town. We always told everyone that the most beautiful state we visited was California (Maine took a close second) and we saw this as our chance to travel slowly, make some money, and spend more time in our favorite state. After feeling a little burned out from constantly driving and spending only a couple of nights in each state, a couple of months sounded like the balance we knew we needed. I loved that this tiny home on wheels could allow us to live in one of the most expensive parts of the country and actually afford it. Plus, the RV park Heath found had a hot tub. A hot tub in a beach town. You can't ask for more.

"I might have a solution for that," Heath said, not letting go of his dream to drive to Alaska.

"Uh oh."

"Not uh oh. Something good. Two good things actually."

I raised my eyebrows.

"Jon at Snagajob is working on getting us funding to make it to Hawaii and Alaska."

"Really?" I said incredulously. My eyes lit up. They initially agreed to pay us for seven months of filming and writing blogs for each state in the lower 48. Finishing off the last two was always a question mark and they had floated the idea of helping us out to finish our journey, but we didn't have anything in writing. I'd checked flights and knew the trips would cost a few thousand dollars even if we flew on budget airlines and stayed in the cheapest accommodations possible. I think the team over there was waiting to commit any funds until they were sure we'd finish the journey. Now that we'd made it back to Texas—and gotten their name across multiple national media outlets—I think they saw the value in helping us make it happen.

"And you heard me talking to my mom outside just a minute ago?"

"Yeah...?"

"They are actually planning on road tripping with my grandparents from Seattle to Alaska this summer."

"Wait, what?"

Every summer since Heath graduated high school, his parents and his mom's parents hopped into their RV and spent two weeks traveling together. This year, the plan was for Heath's grandparents to drive their rig up to Washington where they would pick up Heath's parents from the airport and make the drive up to Alaska together.

"I kind of invited us along. My grandpa's motorhome can sleep six. We would probably sleep at the dinette table. I think it's one of those that lowers and you put cushions on top so it's a makeshift bed. I haven't seen their rig in person, but that's what it sounded like. But then we could actually make the drive to Alaska, not have to drive Franklin, and split the costs of campsites and gas."

"You really just asked me to go to Alaska in January to make it sound better now that you're asking me to sleep on a table, didn't you?"

Heath's grin said yes. "So what do you think? They're probably going in June or July."

"I think if we want to drive to Alaska—"

"And we do."

"And we do...that this is the only way to make it happen.

Franklin wouldn't make it. And if Snagajob sends us anything, that will make it even better."

"So I can tell them to plan on us going with?"

Flights to Seattle would be cheaper than flying to Alaska. Plus we could stay in the RV instead of renting a car and finding hotels. And we could actually explore national parks and the coast and all the parts of Alaska we were dying to experience.

"Why not? I can sleep on a table for a couple weeks."

Chapter 29

"Would you like some punch?" The flight attendant in a purple floral dress asked with a smile.

"Absolutely," I replied with excitement.

"I just need to see your ID first."

I elbowed Heath to let him know to pull out his ID too. There's something about sipping a cocktail on a long flight that feels fancy. Even if that cocktail is free and you booked the cheapest possible flights to get to Hawaii. The drink was sweet with pineapple and rum and set the perfect vibe for our next four nights in Maui. It felt like a summer celebration in a plastic cup.

Snagajob came through with funding our travels to Hawaii and Alaska and since we were already in California, we took a direct flight from Santa Cruz to Maui at the end of February. It was off-season for tourism in Hawaii, but the internet told me it was whale migration season. The next few days would be nothing but beaches, sunshine, and wildlife sightings.

Because Heath made a two-month commitment in

California with Jia, we had an awkward break in between finishing the lower 48 and flying to Hawaii which gave us a little more time to reflect on our first year on the road.

Yep, that's what we called it now. For months, we called it our "trip" or "our honeymoon" but now that it was a fresh new year and we were making enough money to cover our expenses, we knew. 2014 was year one. Of many, hopefully.

My heart beat faster just thinking about that. Not from nerves or anything, just pure excitement that we took this honeymoon adventure and somehow swirled it around and transformed it into full-time traveling and working on the road.

After blogging all year about our travels and filming the documentary, we picked up more skills than we realized—including working surprisingly well together. (I.e. Heath carried all the heavy film equipment and I edited the videos.)

We had gotten into a good rhythm with our work projects and were full-fledged remote entrepreneurs now. With the filming of the documentary wrapping up soon, we could slow down and enjoy our travels a little more too.

But we expected Heath's job in Hawaii wouldn't really feel like work anyway: paddle board guide with whales.

This was one of the dream jobs we were always on the lookout for when making the documentary. We would be filming and interviewing workers, but we would be doing it all while paddle boarding with whales. A guided tour cost upwards of $150 per person and it was not lost on me that we would get to do it for free.

I sipped my punch and stared out the window. I could see tiny green specks growing on the horizon.

The captain interrupted my daydreaming.

"We are now beginning our final descent into Kahului Airport here on the island of Maui where it's 72° and sunny. Welcome to Hawaii."

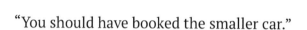

"You should have booked the smaller car."

"You're used to driving an RV every day! How is a Nissan too big?" I retorted as Heath honked the horn.

He was right, not that I was going to admit it. The normal-sized car felt way too big on the winding Road to Hana. He honked before every curve to let any oncoming traffic know we were coming. If someone honked back, we stopped and waited for them to pass before making the sharp, narrow turn with rocky cliffs on either side of us. Almost every other person was in a Jeep and we saw multiple cars abandoned on the side of the road. Many cars had been sitting there for so long that they had plants growing inside. The road was so intense and narrow that a tow truck would never be able to pull them out.

We started our first full day in Hawaii before the sun while our bodies were still on California time. After RVing for so long, it only made sense that we spend our first-day road tripping across the island and making the famed journey along the Road to Hana. I wore a swimsuit under my t-shirt ready to beach hop all day. We'd already stopped at one black sand beach and one roadside stand selling banana chocolate chip bread with macadamia nuts. Other than Heath's white knuckles as he waited for a car to pass us before crossing a one-lane bridge, the trip was idyllic. After months focused on work and growing our income, this definitely put us back into feeling like we were on our honeymoon.

"Waterfall, waterfall!" I said, dissipating the silent chill in the air created by Heath's frustration with our giant four-door car.

"I can't stop. There's no place to pull over," he pointed out in minor annoyance.

"There were people swimming in it! There has to be a place to park!" I pleaded with Heath.

Sure enough, a hundred yards up a hill and on a bend was a shoulder just wide enough to fit two cars. Heath parked, already lamenting that pulling out would be a nightmare, and "hey, be safe please" he called out as I bounced out of the car with the GoPro in hand. I skipped down the hill in the middle of the road so I could better see if any cars whipped around the mountains in front of me or behind me. Heath jogged up behind me and wrapped an arm around my waist to pull me to the side of the road closer to the rocks.

We stood on the bridge beneath the waterfall and felt the cool mist on our faces. The 30-foot waterfall poured off the black cliffs into a small lagoon where another couple was shivering in the dark green water. We may have been married for less than a year, but I knew one thing for certain: Heath wanted to get in that water.

"How do you think they got over there?" We were above the lagoon on the bridge and water streamed beneath us down the rocks toward the ocean. The slick rocks weren't ideal for climbing.

"Car," Heath said, pointing at a red Jeep slowly coming

toward us around the corner. We walked to the opposite end of the bridge and stepped over the concrete barrier to get off the road. "Hey, over here."

"What's that?" I asked, walking closer to Heath.

"Someone made a ladder." In between the concrete bridge and a large boulder was a homemade ladder made from sturdy sticks and rope. I tested it with my weight and shrugged at Heath. He held the top steady while I climbed down and held the bottom so he could follow. We scrambled over a couple of boulders before our toes hit the icy water on the edge of the lagoon. It was still early and I didn't want to take off my shirt and venture into the cold water until the sun was higher.

"Hold this for me?" Heath asked, taking off his shirt while simultaneously kicking off his shoes.

I didn't have a chance to answer before he tossed his shirt toward me and waded into the water. I watched his muscles tense as the cold water hit his skin. He sank under the surface and swam across the pool under the cascading waterfall. Through the crashing white mist, I saw his red hair pop up on the other side, duck back under, and swim back to me.

He climbed out of the water shaking his head like a dog.

"Ah, I needed that." He paused. "Towels are in the car aren't they?"

"Yep."

"I should've thought of that before I jumped in," he shivered.

"Yep."

He smiled at me. "Sorry for snapping at you about the car. This drive is way more intense than I thought it would be."

"Way more intense," I agreed. "We should've booked the smaller car. Hindsight."

"Hindsight. Ready for the next beach? Or the next waterfall? Or maybe a waterfall on a beach?"

I smiled. "Absolutely."

We spent the rest of the day hopping from beach to beach, body surfing in the waves, and drying off in the sun. A small hut near Koki Beach, which we both agreed was our favorite beach of the day, served pulled pork and Huli Huli chicken with rice and salads. I wasn't sure if it was the sun or the salt water, but we both agreed nothing had ever tasted as good. If we weren't planning to keep traveling, I'd have moved to the remote beach right then.

We ended the day at Haleakalā National Park where we used our national parks pass to get in for free and joined the throngs of tourists. The crowd was surreal after having every other beach to ourselves all day. We swam in the seven sacred pools, a series of pools connected by waterfalls cascading down the mountain slope, and hiked with ocean views before making the return trip to our hotel room.

Tomorrow we would work.

Well, "work."

We pulled up to Peg's house at 6:30 AM and the sky was still completely black. Peg owns the stand-up paddle boarding tour company and keeps the paddle boards at her house. She needed us there to help load the boards up into her truck so we could follow her to the beach where they launched.

It felt weird starting a job at a stranger's home, but Peg welcomed us in with island warmth.

"So what do you guys have?" she asked once we were in her kitchen.

"What do you mean?" Heath asked.

"You need swimsuits, sunscreen, rash guard, hats," she prattled off tapping her fingers.

"We've got our swimsuits and sunscreen, and I've got a rash guard and a hat."

"I don't have a rash guard or a hat," I said. Heath always wore a rash guard when swimming to protect as much of his fair skin as possible. He put on sunscreen any time he was going to be outside. I, on the other hand, was less prepared to spend the next three hours floating in the ocean.

Peg froze.

"We are going to get you one," she said seriously. "Go ahead and put on your sunscreen now before we head out," she instructed as she pulled out her phone to text one of her employees and get me a shirt.

It felt strange to lather on sunscreen before the sun was up, but Peg was the boss. I applied it to the tops of my legs and feet and Heath helped me cover my neck and face.

I picked up the camera to film Heath applying his sunscreen but the expensive equipment started slipping in my lotioned-up hands. "Yikes," I said, grabbing the strap before the camera crashed to the ground. *That was close.*

"I've got a rash guard for you on the way and I'm ready to head out," Peg said, looking up from her phone. "Let's go load up some boards."

I adjusted the camera settings on our big camera to shoot in the dark as Peg and Heath loaded up enough boards for the day's tours. We followed her truck toward the water as the sky began to lighten. Parking next to some hotel dumpsters, we met Heath's coworker for the day, Brittany. She and Heath carefully pulled each board off the roof rack on the truck and piled them up in the grass next to the parking lot. Carrying two boards at a time, Heath grabbed the back ends and tucked them under his arms while Brittany grabbed the front. They carefully maneuvered the ten-foot boards across the grass, past the showers, down a set of stairs, and around some black volcanic rocks to the sandy beach before walking all the way back to the parking lot to grab the next set of boards. Peg watched over the growing pile of boards on the beach while tourists walked in the sand with cups of coffee in hand.

By the time everything was unloaded and set up, the sky was light blue and painted with pink wispy clouds.

"You've paddle boarded before?" Brittany asked us.

"Yep," Heath said while I handed him the chest harness with the GoPro attached. "But in Austin where you're on a very still lake. Never in the waves."

"No worries. Let's grab a board and I'll show you how to pull the board into the waves and get up. Then when our customers get here soon, you'll be able to teach them, yeah?"

"Sounds great," Heath agreed, eager to get in. 49 jobs in and it still astounded me how willing people were to let Heath jump in and do their jobs without any training.

"Wait," I said, walking up to Heath before he picked up a board. I fiddled with the GoPro mounted on his chest and made sure it was on the video setting. I pressed record and the tiny screen started counting the seconds letting me know it was recording.

Heath and Brittany splashed into the water with a board

while I took advantage of our time on land with a higher-powered camera. I walked along the shore with water lapping at my toes getting shots of the boards, the sunrise, and Heath in the water. Knee deep, a one-foot wave knocked Heath onto his butt.

"Never turn your back on the ocean," Peg admonished, joining them in the water. "You never turn your back to a wave. You need to see what's coming."

"Right. Okay. Sorry," he said as they moved into deeper water. The waves were small, but I filmed as he battled the moving water to climb onto the board. After timing it between waves, he mounted the board and sat on his knees.

"Yep, just like that," Brittany said. "And we usually tell people to wait to stand up until they are past the waves just because this is the easiest spot to fall off and no one wants to start their day falling off the board."

"Okay. I think I got it," Heath said, dipping his paddle into the water.

"Perfect because people should be showing up any minute."

There were only a handful of people on the morning tour and Heath taught them all how to get on their boards while Brittany supervised. She led the tourists off toward the deep blue waters. We didn't want to encroach on anyone's holiday by filming them, so we paddled slowly with Peg to hear more about her business and why she loved paddle boarding. Unsurprisingly, she shared how this was a job that never felt like work. She would be on the water every day no matter what. Might as well get paid to come out here.

Her story was interrupted by a loud noise coming from the rest of the group.

"Whoa," they all said from 100 yards away as a whale crested the top of the water near them.

"Oh, there they are," Peg said as if recognizing a friend in a crowd. "Let's paddle closer so you can get a shot." Before getting in the water, she reminded us to always keep our distance between ourselves and the whales if possible. I had asked what she meant by if possible. "Well, you never know when one could breach right next to you. Whales are curious creatures and they see the shadow of your board and want to come to see what it is," she explained.

Heath and I were transfixed by the humpback whales swimming 200 feet away from us.

"Do you hear that?" Pam asked.

I listened and heard the water knocking against our boards.

"Wait, hold on a second," she paused. "*That.*"

A low bellow rang out through the water. Our eyes widened.

"That," she continued, "is the sound of whales communicating. Or singing, really."

"It's so loud!" I exclaimed.

"They are just talking to one another."

"Turn on the GoPro and hopefully it can pick up the sound. It sounds exactly like *Finding Nemo,*" I said to Heath.

He fussed with the GoPro mounted to his chest before handing the whole harness to me when he couldn't get the camera to work. I knelt down on my board and put the harness on to start recording Heath narrating what was happening all around us. I had already tried filming and holding the camera in my hands while standing on my paddle board in the ocean but the rocking water threatened to tip me over. Swimming with Humpback whales bigger than my RV was not on the to-do list for the day. I awkwardly turned my chest to point the camera at Heath and then at the whales splashing 100 feet away.

"Dang it," I said. "I barely missed him before he went back underwater!"

"He'll come back up in a few minutes," Peg said. She leaned forward on her toes and peered into the water beneath us. "He's right under you!"

I took a deep breath and leaned over slightly to look underneath my board. It rocked at the movement and I shot straight back up. Nope. I'm going to trust Peg and not try looking down. I prayed the whale didn't decide to breach with me above him.

The song of the whale was crystal clear as he made his way under my board. I quickly unhooked the harness and held the camera out over the water to try to capture the magnificent creature swimming deep below.

We stayed on the water for a couple of hours, paddling, taking pictures, and talking to Peg. As far as jobs went, this one felt the least like work. If the goal of Heath's travels was to find work that didn't feel like work, this was definitely it.

"You know what I almost forgot?" Heath said as we paddled back to shore.

"What?" I asked.

"Technically, this is still our honeymoon."

I laughed. "I guess technically you're right. We're on our honeymoon until after Alaska."

"I like that plan. We'll leave for Alaska at our one-year anniversary and, hopefully, the Al-Can Highway will be thawed by then."

Chapter 30

"Hey, you need to get back in your RV. Hey! You're too close!"

But the man didn't speak English.

We were on the side of the road in the middle-of-nowhere British Columbia making our way toward Fairbanks. It was hard to drive for very long without stopping for wildlife. So far, we'd seen a handful of bears, moose, and elk and we just slowed to join another RV parked on the side of the road. Down a slight embankment stood a powerful herd of bison and their babies. After making our way across the country, we'd seen enough pamphlets on wildlife safety to know how to be respectful of the dangerous animals. Every national park out west hands you one when you enter the gate along with a stern look that says "don't be an idiot." Keeping our distance as we drove the rugged highway, we usually took photos of the massive creatures through the open windows of the RV or from the doorway.

But the Frenchman walking toward the herd of bison didn't get the memo to stay 25 yards away. Or he just didn't care as he closed the gap between the road and the beasts. And with his eyes trained on his camera, he didn't notice the momma bison dragging her hooves on the ground as if readying to charge. He wasn't too close yet, but he was walking straight toward her calves and she wanted none of that.

We warned him to get back in his RV, but he looked at us with a face that clearly said he didn't understand what we were saying. We motioned for him to come back up toward the road, but he turned his attention back to his camera, probably muttering something about the stupid, loud Americans ruining his vacation.

He took another step down the embankment toward the herd and the momma bison had enough. She broke into motion, sprinting toward him to defend her children. The man scrambled back up the hill, catching himself with his hands as he almost fell. Luckily, as he turned and retreated, the momma bison halted and gave her most scathing look at the man who was now hiding on the other side of his RV.

"Well that got my blood pumping," said Heath's dad from the driver's seat after the ordeal was over.

The six of us—Heath and I, his parents, and his grandparents—were all pressed up against the windows watching the encounter. Thank God the bison stopped when the man retreated because we were hundreds of miles from any town and I had no idea how to treat a man for being impaled by a bison.

The wild road stretched on for miles as we made our way north from Seattle across British Columbia. It would take us days to make our way to Fairbanks, but with the summer solstice a couple of weeks away, the sun kept the sky lit so we could drive until 10:00 PM and still watch the sunset from our campsite. Heath hadn't found his job yet in Alaska and with no cell phone service in the remote reaches of Canada, we had nothing to do but stare out the windows and soak up the sights.

I sat in the dinette booth facing forward and staring out the window as the mountains flew past. I couldn't believe we were almost there. Well, we still had over a thousand miles to drive, but there were many more moments on this trip when I wasn't sure if we'd even get this close. Now the border was only a few days away. (And hot tub guy was right. Driving the Al-Can is definitely the way to go.)

After forty-nine states and tens of thousands of miles driven, a small part of me felt like we had seen it all. We traversed mountains and coastlines and deserts. Seen wolves and moose and bison and bears in national parks.

But Canada was beyond anything else we'd experienced. It felt truly untamed. We passed grizzlies ambling along the road. We drove down unpaved roads for miles and bounced up and down on frost heaves. We used the annual Milepost book to let us know where gas stations and grocery stores would be along our route so we didn't end up stranded in the wilderness. Okay, we also used it to find Tim Horton's. If you're taking any route to Alaska, Milepost gives you directions and landmarks for every mile along the way. Why not take advantage of the donut options they listed?

We filled up at every single gas station we passed after reading horror stories online of RVers getting stranded hundreds of miles from the nearest services. The handy guidebook would let us know how many miles we would be traveling between towns and give us landmarks to look out for, like a secluded hot spring just south of the Yukon.

Liard Hot Springs was truly in the middle of nowhere. We camped at Muncho Lake last night after driving through the remote Canadian wilderness for hours on end and woke up to head straight to the hot springs. With no chance of internet or cell signal, we used the Milepost guidebook to find the hidden gem. We pulled into the parking lot, paid our fee to the attendant, and were told to watch for moose. The guidebook specifically warned us that bear sightings were common here too. In our travels, we often heard about hot springs, but hadn't visited any natural hot springs. From the photos, Liard Hot Springs looked like a small aquamarine pond surrounded by a forest. We even had to take a short hike to get to the waters.

Heath and I changed into our swimsuits and hopped out of the RV with the rest of Heath's family who were less enthused with the idea of hiking to hot springs with bears and moose.

"Where is the pool?" I asked, looking around the parking lot.

"There's a platform trail over here," said Heath's dad. We followed him to a raised platform pathway similar to the one we hiked back in Glacier. Beneath the platform were the marshy grasses moose are known to love. Our little group made our way toward the pools talking loudly to ward off any dangerous wildlife.

"Look," I said to Heath pointing at the grasses just ahead. The grasses rose tall all around us, but here they were matted down in small clusters, like a family of moose or elk had made their bed there recently. We hurried along the path just in case the animals were hidden in the trees nearby.

We came upon a small wooden open-air building. We walked through the opening to reveal a spacious deck leading down to the natural hot springs. Only a handful of other people were in the water so early and one of the friendly swimmers called out to us.

"The water is coming up over here," she said pointing to our right, "and it gets cooler as you go that way."

"Thanks," Heath called out. "How hot is it?" He asked as we shed our clothes.

The woman laughed. "Pretty hot."

I pulled off the clothes I had over my swimsuit and stepped into the water. Slightly warmer than a good bathtub, the water was the perfect temperature for this cool morning. The blue skies stretched overhead mirroring the sparkling blue water. I could see every pebble underneath my feet through the clear water as I soaked deeper into the pool. The pool was created in a flowing river and with the swimmers relaxing, all you could hear was running water and birds chirping in the trees.

"Okay," I told Heath. "We don't even have to make it to Alaska. This is perfect." I sank down into the water letting the warmth relax all my muscles. "I'll just stay here."

"Want to go see where the hot springs bubble up?" Heath challenged.

"Absolutely I do," I replied. We did that awkward walk-swimming that you do in shallow waters, squatting down low so our shoulders were submerged in the warming water as we moved. Steam plumed into the air where little bubbles came up signaling the source of the hot spring. I felt my body begin to sweat despite the chill hanging in the air. "This is getting really hot," I told Heath once we were 10 feet away from the bubbles. I felt little pinpricks on my skin as the heat turned my pale skin bright red.

"Chicken," he teased slowly making his way forward while I bailed to float downstream. Without thermometers, we didn't know the exact temperature, but it was hot enough that I swam over to the opposite end of the pool and sat under a small waterfall to cool off.

I closed my eyes and let the falling water drown out Heath's family chatting on the deck. As excited as we were to save money and make the drive to Alaska, Heath and I were regretting our decision to jump into a 33-foot motorhome with four other adults. It isn't that we don't love Heath's family. But if you spend a few nights in a row "sleeping" on a dinette table in the summer where the sun never sets and someone is snoring five feet away from you, you start to be annoyed at everyone out of pure exhaustion. This is still technically my honeymoon, in-laws and grandparents-in-law and all. I wondered if everyone else was equally as annoyed or if parents have a higher tolerance.

Even with the challenges, I was just grateful to still be on this adventure. I thought back to where we were before I asked Heath if we could visit all 50 states for our honeymoon. I thought that was the mission for our honeymoon. It was clear-cut, easy to share with strangers, and every American got it because they pretty much all want to visit every state too.

But visiting each state wasn't really my mission. It wasn't to film a documentary either.

Back in New Orleans, my dream was just to live a life. To

stop letting life pass me by without taking action toward my dreams. Visiting all 50 states was my first dream to take action on and it led us to the RV, to full-time travel, to starting our own little business that makes just enough each month to let us keep traveling indefinitely.

I never knew a life like this was possible before. Where you didn't need to set an alarm in the morning. Where you often forgot where you were when you woke up because the scenery out the window was rapidly changing. Where I could spend a Tuesday morning lounging under a hot waterfall. I didn't even know there were hot waterfalls. I leaned my head back and let the water relieve the tension in my back from sleeping on a dinette table. RV life wasn't perfect, but it brought me here, where the water temperature is perfect.

Heath swam up next to me.

"*This* is what I thought Canada and Alaska would be like," he said, leaning his head back and floating in the water.

"This, plus all of the wild animals we've seen," I added.

"We've seen so many it's kind of crazy. We saw more animals yesterday than we did during our whole trip across the country."

I laughed. "You're definitely right. Canada has exceeded expectations. And you know what is blowing my mind?" I said not waiting for an answer. "We are about to cross into the Yukon. If you had asked me what's the furthest north you could travel, Yukon is farther north than that. And we're still a couple of days away from Fairbanks."

"There's a lot of road left. Not a lot of sleep left," he grumbled. "Whoa, what's on your finger?"

I looked down quickly, expecting to find some mutant leech

that can withstand 100° temperatures latched to my hand, but instead saw a circle of black around my middle finger.

"Oh shoot. I read in the guidebook to remove any silver jewelry before getting in and completely forgot." The sulfur in the water turned sterling silver completely black. I pulled the no longer shiny ring off my finger and spun it around. "Kind of looks cool all black. It'll go back to normal with some soap and water. Hopefully."

After soaking for a little while longer we used the changing rooms to slip out of our swimsuits and back into regular clothes. As we continued north, we saw a rental RV pulled over on the side of the road and I'll give you one guess as to who was standing outside fifteen feet away from a grizzly bear.

Oy vey.

Chapter 31

"What are Sorels?" I interrupted Heath.

"Literally no idea. But she said she has sleeping bags and Sorels and gloves for us and she will store our bags while we're gone. She'll pick us up tomorrow morning early and drive us to the national park office where we will chopper out!"

"Ever think you would say those words?" I said with a smile.

"No!" Heath glowed with excitement.

When it came to ending our fifty-state journey and our documentary, Heath wanted to find an epic job as a grand finale. Kind of a tall order when your last job involved paddling with humpback whales in an island paradise. Since cell signal was sparse—and we were distracted by exploring the natural beauty of Canada and Alaska—Heath skipped cold calling businesses and casually posted on Facebook saying he was looking for his last job, which led to a friend connecting him with a friend who knew someone who runs a mountaineering company out of Denali National Park.

Heath of course wasn't qualified to lead expeditions that involved crossing crevasses at 20,000 feet. I guess we finally found the limit of what people would allow Heath to do. There was no way it would be safe for us to join in with her employees climbing the tallest peak in North America. But the friendly owner, Sara, knew everyone in the National Park Service in the small town of Talkeetna and hooked us up with our final gig: The next day they were doing a supply run to base camp on the mountain and agreed to let us ride along. Excuse me, fly along.

The plan was to chopper us up to the base camp at 7,200 feet. Heath would work as a national park ranger at base camp and we would fly off with a crew of national park volunteers disembarking the mountain. But it wasn't a true park ranger experience if we didn't actually sleep on the glacier, so they had a tent for us to stay the night. When it came to finding a job in Alaska after RVing across the country, working for the national park service on a glacier was the icing on a perfectly baked cake.

When we had crossed the border into Alaska, we expected to go through border patrol like we did when we crossed into Canada. Instead, we drove straight into the US and parked in a small rest area. There was no border patrol station or anyone to check our passports, but there were plenty of "Welcome to Alaska" signs and benches and markers noting where you could simultaneously sit in two countries at once. We snapped a hundred pictures to commemorate that we made it to our fiftieth state, but decided we hadn't officially completed our goal until we finished the documentary too.

We had less than 10 days to explore all of Alaska once we crossed the border. We spent a couple of days driving to

Fairbanks and Chena Hot Springs before we found a campsite in Denali National Park for three nights. We hiked and crossed white water rafting off Heath's bucket list before passing through Anchorage and driving winding roads bordered by the Chugach mountains on one side and the bay on the other. We were planning to head further south to Kenai Fjords National Park as our last stop before flying back to our RV in Texas when the call came to drive back up to Denali National Park for Heath's last job.

The whole experience came about so quickly, we had to buy bus tickets to rush from the southern coast of Alaska back north to the national park. We said goodbye to Heath's family and found a small guest house in the tiny town of Talkeetna to stay the night before our early morning helicopter ride into the mountains.

"I've always wanted to ride in a helicopter," I gushed. "Do we need to pack anything? Wait, will there even be a bathroom up there? It's *on* a glacier?"

"I know about as much as you do. But it sounded like we should charge up every battery we own and bring the camera bag and that's it. You can't add much weight to the helicopter."

"Okay, that makes sense. I'll just layer up my clothes for warmth. I can't believe this is happening. I looked into us doing a flight tour over the national park and it was over $300 per person. And now we are choppering up and flying down? And staying the night? I can't believe after all of the national parks we fell in love with during this trip, now we get to end like this!"

"This is a flame retardant flight suit," the pilot said, tossing us army green suits. "Pull it on over your clothes."

In the office, we signed release forms and were given official National Park Service beanies to begin Heath's last job. Usually, we were the ones asking people to sign release forms to be included in the film, but with a job in the government, there had to be a little paperwork. We headed outside where a bright red helicopter waited on us. The pilot was giving us instructions on how to get in and out of the helicopter.

"Those blades dip down a little as they slow. So when we land, you'll climb out and squat down right next to the landing skids. Keep your head down. Do not stand up," he continued firmly, "until I fly away. You do not want to get hit in the head with these blades. Got it?"

We nodded furiously. He left us to continue his check of the aircraft while I filmed Heath pulling on his flight suit. Heath looked very *Top Gun* as he slipped on his sunglasses and adjusted the mic on his helmet. He stepped into the Sorels that Sara brought us—thick, rubber-soled boots that could handle the snow and ice ahead. I quickly pulled the flight suit on over my clothes and we climbed into the chopper. We buckled ourselves into the harnesses and plugged our helmets in so we could talk through our mics to the ranger and pilot in the chopper with us.

I was slightly disappointed that the pilot didn't start up the engine until we were already all safely inside, so we didn't get to do the dramatic squatting down run toward the chopper like they do in the movies. Noise crackled in my ear as the blades above began to whir loudly. This would be our first time ever flying in a helicopter and my heart raced nervously as the pilot flipped switches in the seat in front of me.

I kept my camera continuously running, racking focus from Heath next to me to the pilot, to the landscape growing smaller below us as we took off. The Susitna River stretched out beneath us as the chopper turned north toward the national park. The tiny town of Talkeetna disappeared in an instant as we soared toward the towering snow-covered peak of Mount McKinley.

The ranger, David, talked in our ears, pointing to something out the right side window that I couldn't see. I could barely make out every other word over the static in my helmet and the thunderous whipping blades. I messed with the plug hanging from the ceiling to make sure it was plugged into my helmet correctly so I could hear the crew better, but I could only make out static as they talked.

Heath elbowed me gently. I turned in his direction and he nodded out the front window. McKinley stood tall in front of us, towering over the surrounding mountains with thick white clouds clinging below the summit. I leaned to the right and pointed my camera out the front window. In every direction, you could only see mountain peaks and snow. We rounded a mountain and started our descent toward a long river of ice. Small dots came into focus as we lowered—a camp with a dozen soft tents clustered together. The glacier doubled as a safe base camp and an airstrip for planes.

I felt my heart thumping in my chest. Crossing into Alaska was exciting. But officially ending our journey like this was astonishing. The views took my breath away as we flew over the pristine wilderness. We were really about to finish job fifty.

The pilot lowered to the ground next to the waving orange flags that designated the safe landing zone. We waited as the pilot and ranger quickly unloaded the gear and supplies in the baskets attached to the outside of the helicopter. I kept the camera rolling as we climbed out of the chopper and squatted down next to the door as we were instructed. I looked up to see our reflection in the glass door, looking so official in our flight suits, helmets, and boots.

The pilot climbed back in, closed the door, and took off again.

"That was crazy," Heath said as the helicopter grew quieter in the distance.

"I know! Hands down, the most unspoiled, gorgeous thing I've ever seen," I said, referencing the mountain range and glaciers.

"What? No. Did you not hear what happened? A medical call came in while we were flying. They have to go rescue someone at 17,000 feet."

"What?! What happened?" I asked. How did I miss that?

"You guys can take your bags and start making your way toward the bright orange tent. The guy's name down there is Cory. Introduce yourself," David, the ranger, interrupted.

We stood up from our places in the snow and Heath grabbed two duffel bags of supplies and a couple of sets of ski poles while I tossed our camera bag over my shoulder. Here at job 50, it still amazed me how willing people were to let us just jump in and work. "Yeah, you're fine to walk across this glacier by yourself. Sure, you can wire this electrical system. Yes, I trust you to go terrify some children." You'd think you need a pass or some "level" to have been reached but sometimes all you need to do is ask.

"Wow," Heath said, once we took a moment to appreciate where we were.

Ice stretched out in every direction. With the sun beaming overhead and the mountains towering all around us, it was hard to tell just how far the ice went. 100 yards? A mile? It sparkled so brightly that I squinted behind my sunglasses.

Our boots crunched at least six inches deep into the snow as we made our way slowly toward the bright orange tent David had pointed out. We met Cory and Mike, who looked exactly as rugged and adventurous as you would expect men who had been living in the harsh conditions of the snowy mountains for the past month to look.

Mike was friendly and welcoming and gave us a quick lay of the land. Here's the kitchen. Here's the "refrigerator" which was really just a shaded cavity of snow with surprisingly normal things like apples and a box of spinach. So this is what we needed when our fridge broke in the RV. The mountain of snow kept everything at the perfect temperature. Next to the kitchen was a bank of snow peppered with colored flags, the kind you might see on a construction site to note sewer lines.

Upon arrival, he explained, climbers bury supplies in the snow to have for when they get back to base camp. Most climbers spend a couple of days at base camp before and after a climb, so they keep food and extra clothes at the camp. Campers have to pack in all their own food and they leave a little behind at camp for their descent back to Talkeetna.

He pointed at a cluster of yellow and gray tents on the other side of the kitchen.

"Those are all empty. We've got a crew of volunteers skiing down from the camp at 14,000 feet right now who will be staying in them. Pick one and go ahead and drop off your gear," Mike said, pointing to our camera bag and sleeping bags.

After choosing a tent, far away from the bathroom, but not too far from the kitchen, we came back to the kitchen area so Heath could get to work.

"Are you guys good to go?" David asked.

"All set," Heath replied.

We stripped off our flight suits and I internally lamented losing a layer of warmth despite the warm sun on my back. David collected our flight suits and helmets, said a quick goodbye, and made his way back to the landing area to return to town.

The helicopter flew over the kitchen tent a few seconds later returning from the rescue on the mountain. David climbed aboard and the helicopter sat for a few minutes while we speculated about what might have happened. A man dressed in a bright red jacket hopped off and the helicopter continued down toward Talkeetna.

"They're taking him back down," the man said to Cory when he made it to the tent.

"Bummer. He'll be okay?"

"It's just HAPE. He'll be fine," the doctor said, pulling off his balaclava to reveal skin chapped by days of exposure to cold and wind. "Got me out of skiing down the mountain too."

Mike laughed. "This is Heath and Alyssa," he said, bringing us into the conversation. "They're filming a documentary and showing what it's like to be up here."

The doctor introduced himself as Derek from Ohio. He won

the lottery to be the volunteer doctor up at the 14,000-foot base camp and had spent the last month helping the climbers as they made their ascent up to 20,000 feet. Because Denali is one of the most popular national parks, you put your name in a lottery to become a volunteer on the mountain. Only a few people are accepted each season. Derek took over a month off of work at his hospital back in Ohio to be on the mountain, something that he did in countries around the world as often as he could.

"It's usually just high altitude stuff," Derek said, explaining the most common injuries he treats after I asked. Since the town of Talkeetna was at sea level, climbers were highly susceptible to altitude sickness because of the rapid gain in elevation. They spent time at each base camp to acclimate as much as possible, but the steep rise in elevation still affected many climbers. "Like that guy earlier, we picked him up at 17,000, took him to 14,000, and then brought him down to 7,200 feet here to see if he would get better because all you need is to get down in elevation. But he wasn't improving, so they will take him back to town and he'll be instantly better," Derek said with the nonchalance of a man who saves people's lives regularly.

The roar of a crash echoed. My eyes widened as I saw an avalanche flying down the side of the mountain behind Derek.

"You get used to it," he said without looking up. "There are a hundred avalanches a day out here. You'll see them all around." He pointed at the mountains surrounding us. "They can't reach us where we are on the glacier."

My brain hurt as it processed everything we'd already learned and experienced after only ten minutes at camp.

"You ready to work?" Cory asked Heath.

"Bring it on," Heath replied.

"Let's go," he said and tossed Heath a shovel.

Heath," I whispered.

He grunted in response, half asleep.

"I have to pee."

"Go pee," he grumbled with his head buried in his sleeping bag.

"It's midnight! I don't want to go by myself."

Heath popped his head up and gave me a pointed look. "Seriously, babe." He looked up at our bright orange tent. "It's still light outside. You will be fine."

He wasn't wrong. When I climbed out of the tent, I pulled out my phone and snapped a picture of the sunset. The entire sky glowed pink as streaks of golden orange lit up the clouds. I trudged across the hard snow with my arms wrapped around my waist for warmth. The bathroom looked open, I thought as I awkwardly peeked around the snowy wall that gave semi-privacy. Although calling it a bathroom was generous. It was really just a semicircle of piled up snow that was shorter than me with a black bucket sitting in the middle. During orientation earlier that day, we were given instructions on how to go to the bathroom: pee in the snow and use the bucket for #2. All toilet paper went in the bucket.

The outdoor bathroom didn't smell as bad as you'd think, but because we were camping on a massive block of ice that stretched for what felt like a mile in each direction, privacy was scarce. I desperately hoped everyone else in the camp was asleep. I quickly squatted and peed in the snow and watched an avalanche cascade beautifully off a cliff in the distance. I shivered as I pulled up my damp double-layer of pants. Don't worry—it wasn't from the pee.

Sara gave us sleeping bags for our tent, but a sleeping bag on top of the thin layer of the tent on top of a thousand feet of pure ice was more than uncomfortable. The snow melted from my body heat and soaked through the tent, through my sleeping bag, and through my clothes. The outdoor temperatures were in the upper 20s and it didn't really feel too cold outside. But I couldn't feel my hip from curling up in a ball on the cold, hard ice and after hours of laying down, I wasn't sure I'd actually gotten any sleep.

I crawled into the tent and sat on top of my sleeping bag. Heath tossed in his next to me.

"Babe," I whispered.

"What?" Heath asked, sounding much more awake.

"I can't sleep. It's too cold. And wet."

He sighed. "My butt is wet too. I can't feel it anymore. What do we do?"

I felt justified in my previous assumption that tent camping is indeed an extreme outdoor adventure. My butt is literally freezing.

"I have an idea. But it might be impossible," I said, weighing our options. Heath raised his eyebrows. "We lay down one sleeping bag as a sort of pad and then put the other one on top and then we both sleep in the same sleeping bag."

"There's no way we can both fit in here," said Heath, gesturing at his sleeping bag. The subzero-rated sleeping bags were cozy partially because of how skinny they were. They enveloped us perfectly. And fitting in two people would be a stretch that could easily pop a zipper. Maybe we wouldn't be able to zip it up at all. But that would be better than laying down on wet ice.

I convinced Heath to at least try. Not even climbing out of his sleeping bag, he scooched his butt on top of my sleeping bag and unzipped the side to let me wiggle in. I was wearing a long sleeve shirt, a fleece pullover, and an oversized sweatshirt along with my double-layered leggings. Heath also wore multiple layers since we had packed for weather in the 50s and 60s, not below freezing mountaintops. Between our poofy layers and a sleeping bag meant for one, we couldn't zip the zipper past our hips even when we both lay on our sides snuggling close. Heath wrapped his arms around me, more out of space-saving necessity than actual cuddling.

"This is better. Warmer," Heath clarified.

"Much warmer...my hip kinda hurts on this hard ice though."

"Yeah, I can't really feel my shoulder anymore with you on it."

We wiggled and adjusted and eventually cobbled together sleep in one-hour bursts before it was finally time to wake up. Heath wandered into the kitchen tent in search of coffee leaving me with the now incredibly spacious sleeping bag all to myself. I curled up and got a little extra sleep until he returned with hot cups of coffee.

"So," he said, sticking his head and a cup of coffee through the zippered entrance of the tent, "apparently there are little blow-up mats you're supposed to put under your sleeping bag. Cory told me that this morning when I went into the kitchen tent. And they had extras in there."

"Ah, a mat. That would've been way easier." I yawned and rolled my neck in circles to relieve the kinks. "We should've followed your idea to go sleep in the kitchen at 4:00 AM."

"I don't think I got any sleep. I can't believe we never thought of using a mat."

"Hindsight."

"We should've had hindsight. Anyway, there's oatmeal for breakfast if you want some food."

I pulled on my heavy-duty Sorels, grateful that I had something warmer than tennis shoes to tromp through the snow.

"How'd you sleep?" The doctor asked me with a silly grin when I walked up to the kitchen.

"Fine," I said, sharing the socially acceptable response when someone you barely know asks how you are.

He laughed. "Heath told us. I can't believe y'all didn't use mats!"

"We didn't know!" I said.

"Sleeping directly on the ice. You guys are terrible at this," he teased.

"Plane will be here soon," Cory announced. "Everyone pack up, clean up."

I ate a quick bowl of oatmeal and we sat down with Mike, our last person to interview before saying that's a wrap on our documentary. We spent the whole afternoon the day before grabbing b-roll shots of the scenery and filming Heath's final job. Mike, Cory, and Heath spent the afternoon shoveling around a giant bag of fuel for the planes. If they don't rotate the bag every couple of days, the fuel at the bottom of the bag would start to freeze from the ice. Heath had shed multiple layers sweating from the hard work.

After his work for the day was done, we hung out with the group of volunteers who had skied down from 14,000 feet all day, hearing their stories about life on the mountain and listening to their easy camaraderie after a month together. They all had red faces, chapped from the wind, cold, and intense sun, and one girl very casually tossed out that she had frostbite. We sat there for hours, soaking up their stories until we couldn't keep our eyes open any longer, even though the sky was still bright.

Heath and I ducked back into our tent to roll up our wet sleeping bags and pack up the camera before the plane arrived.

"We did it," Heath said. "Has that sunk in yet?"

"It didn't when we crossed the border. It started to while we were driving around exploring Alaska. But yesterday I was sitting in one of those camping chairs outside the kitchen watching avalanche after avalanche and seeing all the climbers pitching tents and packing up just thinking about how truly bizarre it is that I—me, *me* of all people!—could camp at base camp for the tallest mountain in the country to polish off state 50.

"It was only a little over a year ago that I was working in New Orleans, sneaking out of work a little early so I could beat traffic and catch *Castle* reruns on TBS. That was like, the best day of the week when that happened. And look at where we are now." I gestured around the tent. "If we hadn't quit our jobs. If I hadn't suggested going to all 50 states. If you hadn't actually taken me seriously and said yes..." I trailed off marveling at it all.

My comfort zone back in New Orleans was tiny. Like not going to try a new recipe or even a new type of wine tiny. The boldest thing I did was run a 5K and that was only because my friend signed me up.

As we planned our fifty-state tour, bought the RV, renovated the RV, and moved in, my comfort zone inched a little wider. With every passing state, it grew until we ended up here, at a mountaintop—a fitting parallel to the peak of our journey.

We took each risk one at a time. Quitting. Dreaming big. Buying the RV. Parking at a sketchy RV park. Taking the longest hike I'd ever attempted. Sprinting through a lightning storm to shelter. Living without a fridge. Making our way slowly to this moment. If we'd set out from the get-go to RV full-time and visit all fifty states and film a documentary, I don't think it would've happened. If Heath even floated the idea, I would've said he was crazy. We didn't know how to do any of those things. But by building up this adventure one block at a time, we expanded what was possible. For some people, their wedding day is the most exciting moment of their lives for years to come, but ours was just a blip compared to everything we accomplished together in our first year.

There were times when it felt too daunting to complete our goal to visit all fifty states. We hit wall after wall as every little thing on the RV fell apart. Our bank account hit zero. A legal team told us to stop, or else. We broke down, ran out of water, clogged our black tank, killed our batteries, flooded the floor.

And we watched the sun slowly dip below the Pacific Ocean with a glass of $3 wine from Walmart.

We woke up to deer walking past our window while the sunrise turned the Rockies pink.

We walked the red carpet in New York City, even if it was only to escort actual famous people.

We made new friends all over the country who we couldn't wait to see again.

Perhaps most of all, we learned what it meant to be partners and how to encourage each other—through thick and thin. I looked over at Heath in the tent next to me, grateful to have found someone who agreed so easily to adventure.

For the first time since we were kids, it felt like anything was possible. Our biggest most out-there dreams, like Heath running his own company and us traveling the world together, suddenly didn't seem so far-fetched.

And instead of returning to the "real world" after Alaska, we would fly home to our RV and keep traveling. Our parents wondered why, after going everywhere, we still wanted to travel. But I think that annoyingly cheesy quote is right: *Travel is rarely about the destination. It's the journey.* Travel for us meant stretching our comfort zone, experiencing something new, and overcoming challenges to get there. If it was easy—and Franklin made sure it was never easy—it wouldn't have been as meaningful.

"This was an awesome honeymoon. And an awesome start to our lives," Heath said to the camera. "And now we'll fly home, back to our home on wheels, and we'll see where it all goes from here."

We heard the hum of a plane breaking the natural silence and climbed out of our tent to leave this chapter of our adventure behind. Heath carried our sleeping bags over to the pile of gear to be loaded onto the ten-seater plane. I filmed until it was time to go, trying to capture every detail of the beauty surrounding us until the last second my feet were on the ice.

When it was time, Heath climbed up into the plane and outstretched his hand to pull me up through the tiny doorway. Our things were loaded up, the volunteer crew was already onboard and buckling in, and it was time to go. The glacier became a runway as the tiny red plane rumbled forward picking up speed down the ice until we kicked off the ground and climbed higher than the staggering peaks surrounding us.

Sitting on the bush plane, I looked out the window at the peaks with the camera bouncing up and down in my hands as I tried to get a stable shot. My hand throbbed from all of the filming I'd done in the past 24 hours. It took me back to sitting in that tiny office a little over a year earlier when my hand ached from removing staples for hours and hours.

My new office views weren't bad. Not bad at all.

Afterword

I pivoted on my toes, pacing back and forth in the tiny backstage area to get my blood flowing. An eight-foot wall of black curtains separated me from the packed room while Heath stood on stage.

It felt weird that he was on stage introducing me to our attendees, considering we hosted this conference together every year, and everyone here had already seen me on stage a dozen times throughout the weekend. This was our fifth RV Entrepreneur Summit—the business conference for RVers that we started when we realized we weren't the only crazy people who wanted to travel full-time and run their own business.

During our second year on the road, we grew our video production company and found clients all over North America who we traveled to film. We figured out how to turn our little travel blog into a business that year too. Then we started The RV Entrepreneur with a podcast, school, and events. Then a software company. Then a campground.

Five—that's how many businesses we've started while traveling together. (We've sold three of those businesses, but that's a story for a different time.)

If you would've told me back in Missouri that I would not only find a way to replace my fridge, but also continue RVing the country and build not one business, but five while still traveling, I would've said you were crazy.

But I also told Heath that his idea to work a job in all 50 states was crazy and look how that turned out.

"Welcome back to the stage, my wife," Heath said. The crowd clapped.

I grabbed the black railing and slowly made my way up the stairs, gripping my microphone and my clicker in one hand.

"Do you want a chair?" Heath asked, grabbing my elbow to help me up the last step.

"Nah, I'm fine," I replied, even though I was out of breath.

To end the day, I was giving a keynote presentation with 15 tips on how to work on the road. Or maybe how *not* to work on the road, considering my first story involved toilet deodorant and the important lesson to always plan ahead when you have a meeting on the calendar, lest you squeal on two wheels into a Walmart parking lot.

It's not lost on me that the person who couldn't even figure out how to shower in her RV now teaches people about life on the road.

I launched into my story, not making it very far before I paused.

"Babe?" I said into the microphone, breathing heavily. "Can you actually bring me that chair?"

Heath grabbed the folding chair he had ready for me and jumped on stage. I clutched his hand as I tried to lower my eight-month pregnant body into the chair.

Two years ago, I said on stage that I was never going to host a conference pregnant again after waddling around seven months pregnant with my daughter. But here I was weeks away from my son's due date, collapsed in a chair to deliver my talk.

For years, we heard people say that it was good for us to

get traveling out of our system before we had kids. But Ellie took her first road trip at four weeks old and, in her first two years, she visited 14 states and three countries. Our daughter may actually love traveling more than we do. I hoped the little guy kicking me while I tried to focus on my presentation would be the same way because once he arrived, we planned to keep traveling—two babies in tow.

Heath was right when he said there's no perfect time to travel. There's always something seemingly in the way.

We could have waited until our savings had more padding or until we had more life experience or marketable skills or business plans before we first started RVing, but waiting would have been a never-ending game.

Sometimes we have a tendency to put things off for an "optimal future date" when maybe today is good enough.

Perfect?

Far from it.

But sometimes good enough is all it takes to get started.

Today, as I finish typing this book, I'm balancing writing during nap time while also packing for our first international trip as a family of four. Our conference took place last fall, and now our son is six months old and we are all ready to spend a few months in Europe.

As I pour through my packing list of diapers, car seats, bibs, onesies, and other items that seem to go on forever, it's hard not to ask the same question as I did back in 2014:

"Are we crazy for doing this?"

Probably.

However, I feel similar to how I felt sitting in my office in New Orleans—yearning for an adventure. Nobody would have argued had we taken the conventional path. Jobs. 401K. One-week honeymoon.

Nobody would blame us for packing away our suitcases and passports.

But if we took anything away from our first year on the road, it's that we want to continue to be the types of people who chase after their dreams—even when it's hard.

Reflecting on our first year on the road, we encountered so many challenges that might've convinced us that full-time travel was an unattainable goal. So many times during that first trip, it felt like the universe was working against us to prevent us from traveling, from hitting all 50 states, from starting a business. Looking back, those were the moments we remember most because they forced us to choose what we were willing to suffer for.

Not that traveling full-time is suffering.

It's awesome.

Except for living without a fridge...*that* was suffering a little bit.

We chose, again and again, to pursue a life of adventure.

If you are still reading this, I hope when the chance for adventure presents itself in your life, you say yes.

And perhaps, most importantly, know that if two kids who made mistake after mistake could somehow stumble along and eventually figure it out, you can too.

Thank You

If you made it this far, thank you so much for reading about our crazy honeymoon.

Also, if you enjoyed the book and feel compelled, a review on Amazon would mean the world to me! It helps other people sneaking chocolate in their desk drawers break out and find adventure.

For more of the behind-the-scenes, how-to information on full-time RVing, check out my first book, *A Beginner's Guide to Living in an RV.*

A Beginner's Guide to Living in an RV

After years of full-timing, we've learned the ins and outs of RVing America. In *A Beginner's Guide to Living in an RV*, I answer all of the most common questions we have received about RV living, from how to choose the right RV to how we get mail on the road, to how to find free camping.

This guide is for anyone exploring the RV lifestyle and looking for RVing books to help make the transition easier.

A few topics I cover in the guide:

- How to find great internet on the road
- The costs of full-time RVing
- Whether or not to tow a car behind your RV
- What we do for health insurance while traveling
- The best RVing clubs and memberships
- Our favorite apps for RVers

Transitioning to living on the road was the best decision my husband and I could have ever made. This book isn't about our story or why you should travel. It's a useful tool to reference as you find yourself asking a million different questions about what RV life is really like. Available exclusively on Amazon.

Acknowledgements

You can't write a good story if you don't live a good story and thanks to you, Heath, we've lived a very crazy story. Thank you for being the person who always pushes me to accomplish big dreams, like finally getting this book published seven years after I started it. And thank you for reading this book sooooo many times as I wrestled with which stories to tell and which ones to delete. This book would not be possible without you.

To my editor, Brooke Baum, a MILLION thank yous for keeping me accountable to my deadlines and editing this book for me. Without your advice, this book would've been 30,000 words longer and had zero commas. You helped me refine a crazy story into one book.

Kelsey, you've been there for me in a thousand ways since we met. (Also a big thank you to your mom, Christy, for sending you my blog and saying that we needed to be friends. We did need to be friends.) You've given me endless encouragement as I've written this book and used your Amazon expertise to help me elevate this book. You're a genius and I'm so grateful to have you in my life!

The book cover you see on this book is because of the amazing talents of Lee Taylor. Lee, you came through for me at five o'clock on Friday when everything fell apart and I thought needed to push back my publishing date. And then you sent me this gorgeous custom cover and made this book possible.

Saying thank you doesn't even begin to cover how grateful I am for you!

Mom and Dad, thank you for not buying us a fridge. You told us years later how hard it was for you to not swoop in and help us financially that first year, but if you had, we might not have had to work so hard to make this lifestyle a reality.

Reading books gave me the ideas and the confidence to embark on this untraditional life. Thank you to Ally Fallon for your book *Packing Light* that made me realize you can travel to all 50 states in your 20s. Jia, your book *Rejection Proof* and your wild idea to work a job in all fifty states greatly changed the course of my life. Chris Guillebeau, your conference for unconventional thinkers is where Heath and I met so many of our favorite friends. Your blog, books, and travel stories continue to inspire us. Thank you for being a huge encourager to us over the years.

To the amazing friends we met that first year on the road who we still love:

Wes & Tera, you two continue to show Heath and I how to balance running a business together as a couple (and how to somehow manage it all with kids in tow!). We love you both so much and are forever in your debt for the support you've shown us.

Jedd & Michelle, I still love that we met on a street corner in downtown Portland. I cannot wait to continue traveling the world with you guys!

Kara & Nate, you two are the most genuine, kind souls. Every time we talk to you or travel with you, Heath and I walk away feeling like better people. You continue to inspire us (and the world) to be the best versions of ourselves.

This trip wouldn't have been possible without some high-intensity penny-pinching. Thank you to all the people who let us park for free in your driveways and parking lots and sometimes even sleep on your couch:

Mike & Dana (TX), Granny (TX), Sandoval's Tire and Repair Shop (AZ), Jace (CA), Stacie (OR), Cherene and Jerry (WA), Erin and Concordia University (OR), Alan and Debby (CO), Steve and Abby (MN), Hinchley's Dairy Farm (WI), Frank and Mary Anne (IL), Mom & Dad (TX), Dave (OK), Jim and Cathy (MO), Chris (TN), Andy (IN), Phyllis (MI), Rachel (MI), Shelburne Orchards (VT), Steve and Mary Ellen (MA), Roxborough Presbyterian Church and Mike (PA), Robin (DE), Victoria (VA), Camp Rockmont (NC), Daniel and Becca (GA), Tim and Bea (AL), Wes and Tera (AL), Bar J Ranch (AR), the National Park Service (AK).

Without you, this journey truly would not have been possible.

Lastly, thank you to everyone who has followed HeathandAlyssa.com over the past eight years. Because of you, we get to travel and write books.

About Alyssa Padgett

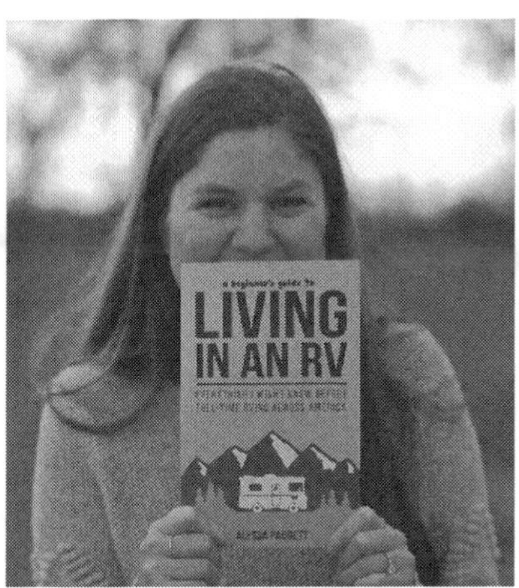

In 2014, Alyssa Padgett convinced her husband Heath to take her to all 50 states for their honeymoon. Somehow he tricked her into doing it all in an RV. They've lived and traveled in an RV ever since.

Alyssa directed and produced *Hourly America*, a documentary film about their 50-state honeymoon, that was featured on CBS, CNN, Fox, People, Yahoo, Huffington Post, and more.

A Beginner's Guide to Living in an RV, an Amazon bestseller, was her first self-published book.

Alyssa and Heath continue to travel with their two children and have big plans to RV all over the world.

Follow Alyssa at HeathandAlyssa.com.

Made in the USA
Monee, IL
02 December 2022

19339280R00194